Chocolate Lover's Cookbook

FOR

DUMMIES®

Chocolate Lover's Cookbook
FOR
DUMMIES®

by Carole Bloom

Wiley Publishing, Inc.

Chocolate Lover's Cookbook For Dummies®

Published by
Wiley Publishing, Inc.
909 Third Avenue
New York, NY 10022
www.wiley.com

Copyright © 2002 by Wiley Publishing, Inc., Indianapolis, Indiana

Published simultaneously in Canada

For general information on our other products and services or to obtain technical support, please contact our Customer Care Department within the U.S. at 800-762-2974, outside the U.S. at 317-572-3993, or fax 317-572-4002.

Wiley also publishes its books in a variety of electronic formats. Some content that appears in print may not be available in electronic books.

Library of Congress Cataloging-in-Publication Data:

Library of Congress Control Number: 2002110301

ISBN: 0-7645-5466-2

Manufactured in the United States of America

10 9 8 7 6 5 4 3 2 1

1B/RT/QZ/QS/IN

Ⓦ Wiley Publishing, Inc. is a trademark of Wiley Publishing, Inc.

About the Author

Carole Bloom, CCP, is a European-trained pastry chef and confectioner, cookbook author, food writer, media chef, cooking instructor, and spokesperson. In addition to having professional experience in world-class hotels and restaurants in Europe and the United States, Carole has taught her art for over 20 years at cooking schools throughout the United States. She has also worked as a consultant for both new and established culinary enterprises.

Carole is the author of six cookbooks. Her most recent is *Cookies For Dummies* (Wiley). Carole's other books include *All About Chocolate: The Ultimate Resource for the World's Favorite Food,* winner of Best Chocolate Book 1999 at Eurochocolate; *Truffles, Candies, and Confections; The International Dictionary of Desserts, Pastries, and Confections; The Candy Cookbook;* and *Sugar and Spice.* She also contributed to the candy chapter for the newly revised edition of the American culinary classic *Joy of Cooking.* Carole's food articles appear regularly in national magazines, including *Bon Appétit, Fine Cooking, Food & Wine,* and *Gourmet.* She is often on television for cooking demonstrations and interviews, with appearances on the *Today Show, ABC World News This Morning,* CNN, and Better Homes & Gardens Television. Carole was the Chairperson for the 24th annual conference of the International Association of Culinary Professionals, held in San Diego, California, in April 2002. She speaks frequently at national and international conferences and is one of the chefs who make annual appearances at the Chef's Holidays in Yosemite, California. She has also been the National Spokesperson for the American Boxed Chocolate Manufacturers Group.

Dedication

Dedicated with love to my two favorite chocolate lovers, my husband, Jerry Olivas, and my mother, Florence Bloom, both of whom make my life sweet.

Author's Acknowledgments

Thanks to Senior Editor Linda Ingroia for opening the door for this book. And thanks to Pam Mourouzis for stepping in so expertly when Linda had to take on other assignments. My appreciation to my Project Editor, Elizabeth Kuball, for guiding this book through the publishing maze. Thanks, also, to Patty Santelli, Technical Editor and Nutrition Analyst, and to everyone at Wiley who worked to make this book a success. I appreciate all the chocolate manufacturers who supplied me with their wonderful chocolate to use in recipe testing: Robert Steinberg of Scharffen Berger Chocolate Maker, Gary Guittard of E. Guittard Chocolate, Bernard Duclos of Valrhona, and Alessio Tesseri of Amedei Chocolate. Thanks to Stacey Glick and Jane Dystel for so ably representing me.

My ice-skating friends were always happy to eat my recipe tests and gave me great feedback. Thanks to all my friends and colleagues who gave me moral support while I wrote this book and planned an international culinary conference at the same time. Many thanks to my husband, Jerry Olivas, who tasted every single recipe in this book (after all, someone had to do it!), washed many dishes, kept my computer running, ran numerous errands so I would have the time to write, planned a much-needed vacation, and gave me lots of moral support. My "boys," felines Tiger and Casanova, were also helpful in keeping me entertained with their antics and sleeping on my desk while I worked.

Publisher's Acknowledgments

We're proud of this book; please send us your comments through our Dummies online registration form located at www.dummies.com/register/.

Some of the people who helped bring this book to market include the following:

Acquisitions, Editorial, and Media Development

Project Editor: Elizabeth Kuball

Acquisitions Editor: Pamela Mourouzis

Acquisitions Coordinator: Holly Gastineau-Grimes

Technical Editor: Patty Santelli

Recipe Tester: Emily Nolan

Nutrition Analyst: Patty Santelli

Editorial Supervisor: Michelle Hacker

Editorial Assistant: Carol Strickland

Cover and Color Insert Photos: David Bishop, photographer; Brett Kurzweil, food stylist; Randi Barrett, prop stylist

Cartoons: Rich Tennant, www.the5thwave.com

Production

Project Coordinator: Maridee Ennis

Layout and Graphics: Joyce Haughey, Barry Offringa, Jacque Schneider, Julie Trippetti, Erin Zeltner

Proofreaders: John Greenough, Andy Hollandbeck, Carl W. Pierce, TECHBOOKS Production Services

Indexer: TECHBOOKS Production Services

Illustrator: Elizabeth Kurtzman

Publishing and Editorial for Consumer Dummies

Diane Graves Steele, Vice President and Publisher, Consumer Dummies

Joyce Pepple, Acquisitions Director, Consumer Dummies

Kristin A. Cocks, Product Development Director, Consumer Dummies

Michael Spring, Vice President and Publisher, Travel

Brice Gosnell, Publishing Director, Travel

Suzanne Jannetta, Editorial Director, Travel

Publishing for Technology Dummies

Andy Cummings, Vice President and Publisher, Dummies Technology/General User

Composition Services

Gerry Fahey, Executive Director of Production Services

Debbie Stailey, Director of Composition Services

Contents at a Glance

Recipes at a Glance

International Desserts

Milk-Chocolate Desserts

Molded Candies

Mousses

Muffins and Scones

Nut Desserts

Pies

Puddings

Quick Breads

Table of Contents

Part II: Foolproof Methods 61

Chapter 4: Techniques for Great Chocolate Desserts Every Time ... 63

Foreword

I met Carole in Berkeley in the early 1970s, heady times in the very vortex of an American culinary revolution. I was the owner of Cocolat, a brand-new kind of dessert and chocolate shop, and Carole was making desserts at a very popular local restaurant. Recognizing the passion and drive in a fellow chocolate and dessert lover, I promptly offered Carol a job at Cocolat. But Carole had bigger plans. She was off to Europe to work and study pastry and chocolate. When I turned around just a few years later, Carole had published her first book, *Truffles, Candies, & Confections,* which I have always admired for its clarity and simplicity, in addition to its excellent recipes.

How pleased I was when Carole asked me to write this foreword! Carol has taught and written about chocolate for many years now. She has been the national spokesperson for the American Boxed Chocolate Manufacturers Group, and she received the award for Best Chocolate Book for her book *All About Chocolate* at Eurochocolate in 1999. Today, when the discussion turns to chocolate, Carole's name always comes up. Once not so long ago, I was exploring a tiny Parisian chocolate shop, quite off the well trodden trail of tourists. As I chatted with the proprietress and tasted her favorites from the tempting array, she asked me if I knew that American author and chocolate expert Carole Bloom! I was pleased to say that I did.

Carole has the special gift of being able to simplify dessert making so that even a novice cook can be successful. I can't imagine anyone else writing this book. Carole provides a solid foundation for making chocolate desserts, and her recipes couldn't be easier to follow. Chock full of tips and great information on techniques, *Chocolate Lover's Cookbook For Dummies* is a gift to all chocolate lovers whether they are experienced or brand new to the pleasures of working with chocolate.

Alice Medrich
Author of *Cocolat: Extraordinary Chocolate Desserts* and *A Year in Chocolate*

Introduction

●●●

Mention the word *chocolate,* and a smile will spread across most people's faces. Why? Because they're thinking about the great experiences they've had eating it. Some people have a preference for milk chocolate, while others prefer dark chocolate. Some people die for chocolate cakes and pies, while others go gaga for candies and ice creams. Some like their chocolate with nuts, and others prefer it straight up, with nothing else competing for their attention. Finally, there are those who are passionate about *all* chocolate. These people are called *chocolate lovers,* and I'm proud to say that I'm one of them.

Chocolate, I believe, is the best flavor in the world. Yes, it's thought of as sweet, but chocolate is much more than that. Describing the flavor of chocolate is next to impossible because there's nothing else like it. Chocolate, quite simply, makes you feel good — and there is even some scientific evidence to back this up. Chocolate has been found to release endorphins in the body, which generate a feeling of euphoria.

When you want chocolate, you're not alone if you rely on what you can buy in the store or what you get in a restaurant or coffee bar. Getting your chocolate this way is fine, but the best chocolate desserts are the ones that are homemade. And making great chocolate desserts at home is much easier than you may think. The ingredients are readily available, and you probably already have most of what you need in the way of utensils and equipment.

If you're not sure what to serve for dessert or give as a gift, chocolate is your best bet. You may have a hard time deciding which chocolate dessert to serve, because there are so many great ones. But I can assure you that all chocolate will be greatly appreciated — and the more, the better!

About This Book

The overriding purpose of this book is to show you how fun it is to work with chocolate by helping you to make great chocolate desserts with ease. This book gets you ready to make chocolate desserts and provides you with numerous techniques for working with chocolate. It does this in a manner that is very easy to understand, walking you through every aspect of the chocolate dessert–making experience.

I've chosen to include in this book what I consider to be the best chocolate desserts in the world. These include chocolate dessert recipes for baked goods like cakes and cookies; chocolate desserts that require minimal baking like custards, mousses, and ice creams; and fancier chocolate desserts, including some European specialties. I've written all of these recipes in a step-by-step manner that's very easy to follow.

This book also provides all kinds of great chocolate information, including ways to serve chocolate and sources for buying chocolate and equipment. Good support is provided throughout the book in the form of tips and illustrations.

Conventions Used in This Book

As you read the recipes in this book, you'll want to keep a few things in mind:

- All eggs are large and should be at room temperature, unless otherwise stated.
- All butter is unsalted.
- All flour is all-purpose, unless otherwise stated.
- All vanilla extract is pure vanilla extract (not synthetic, which tastes like chemicals).
- All white chocolate should be the variety that contains cocoa butter.
- All oven temperatures are Fahrenheit.
- When a recipe calls for nutmeg, freshly grated is preferable because it's more flavorful, but pre-ground is also acceptable. (The amount used is the same.)

Make sure the spices you use are fresh. Check the dates on the containers, and replace any spices those that are more than 6 months old.

When a recipe calls for butter, don't substitute margarine. The taste won't be the same.

Be sure to use the correct measuring cups for the ingredient at hand — use liquid measuring cups for liquids, and dry measuring cups for dry ingredients. And when you measure brown sugar, be sure it's firmly packed in the cup to get an accurate measure.

Finally, use the best quality ingredients you can afford. Your recipes will taste better for it.

Foolish Assumptions

This book doesn't require you to have any previous knowledge of baking or dessert making. Even if you barely know your way around the kitchen, with a little practice you'll be able to make all the chocolate dessert recipes in this book with great success. However, if you *have* done some baking, and maybe even worked a little with chocolate, this book can take you even further. In other words, no matter what your background or skill level, this book has something to offer.

A host of great basic kitchen "how to" information is given throughout the book that will support and guide you every step of the way. I also make sure to provide you with plenty of illustrations, so you can see exactly what I'm talking about, and I sprinkle helpful tips throughout the book so it's almost like I'm right there in your kitchen with you, offering help when you need it.

Of course, the more you make the recipes, the better you'll get at it. But I can assure you that it won't be long before you'll consider yourself a chocolate-making expert. I've heard people say that they can cook "regular food," but they can't make desserts, especially chocolate desserts. You'll soon see that this book totally dispels that myth.

How This Book Is Organized

This book is divided into parts. The first two parts guide you through the basics of chocolate dessert making, and the last three parts have all the recipes. If you aren't already motivated about making chocolate desserts, the first two parts will definitely get you fired up. They're also good confidence builders, because they tell you what you need to know to get started and they cover some important chocolate dessert–making techniques. This is where you'll find out which ingredients you should have on hand, see how to care for chocolate, and get many other helpful tidbits regarding working with chocolate. The illustrations and tips in these sections provide a great foundation for easily and successfully making all your chocolate desserts.

Part 1: Getting Started

This part is a good starting place for the novice cook. I let you know exactly how you can get your kitchen ready for chocolate dessert making, so you're not left empty-handed along the way. You'll find information on utensils and equipment that you will want to have on hand. The fun begins in this part.

Part II: Foolproof Methods

Knowing just the right method to do anything is your ticket to quick and successful results. This part provides you with all the necessary methods for ensuring that your chocolate dessert making goes smoothly and efficiently. You'll discover methods for handling and caring for your chocolate along with how to read a thermometer and use a pastry bag. Here you'll also find out how to temper, dip, and decorate with chocolate. This part is filled with a lot of great tips that will make you a pro in no time.

Part III: Baked Chocolate Goodies

This is where you get to taste the fruits of your labor. Actually, you'll find that all the yummy chocolate desserts in this part don't require much labor at all. Chocolate cookies and fudgy and chewy brownies start off this part with a bang. You'll also find quick breads, muffins, and scones. Several chocolate cake, pie, and tart recipes are included, with something for everyone. You'll also find chocolate layer cakes to die for. I can guarantee you that this will be a much-visited part, so let the mixing and baking begin!

Part IV: Chocolate Treats with Minimal Baking

If you like to use a spoon to eat your chocolate, or you like to drink it instead, this part is for you. Chocolate mousses and puddings are the mainstay of many chocolate lovers. Here you'll find out how to make these treats in a jiffy. You'll also get your hands on various candy recipes, including the famous chocolate truffle. If you like chocolate ice cream — and who doesn't? — you'll find several recipes here, along with other delicious cold chocolate desserts. And if you like to consume your chocolate in liquid form, or use chocolate sauces, you'll find some great quick-and-easy recipes that go down smoothly and provide a tasty accent.

Part V: Chocolate Desserts to Dazzle and Impress Your Friends

If you want to make a big splash with your chocolate desserts, this part is the place to be. Here you'll find some rather creative chocolate dessert recipes as well as some old favorites, such as Chocolate Soufflé. Also, this is where those fabulous world-class chocolate desserts — like Chocolate and Hazelnut Dacquoise — are lurking. These are the ones you've been wanting to make but probably thought were too difficult. You can put those thoughts aside, because you'll soon see how quickly and easily you can prepare these masterpieces. My very favorite chocolate desserts are in this part.

Part VI: The Part of Tens

This part is full of short chapters that provide the most oomph in the least space. Like a small square of chocolate can sometimes satisfy your craving when you don't have time to make a whole cake, the chapters in this part will give you a quick dose of chocolate desert–making information when you're on the run and don't have time to snuggle up with one of the longer chapters in the book.

In this part, you'll find suggestions for giving your chocolate away. Creative and fun ways to package your chocolate gifts are in these pages as well. I also steer you toward stores where you can find all the supplies you'll need to make chocolate desserts with ease.

Appendix

Should the need arise, this appendix is where you'll find an easy-to-use table to help you convert Fahrenheit to Celsius and metric to other measurements.

Icons Used in This Book

Icons are those little pictures in the margins throughout this book, and they're there to draw your attention to certain kinds of information. Here's what each icon means:

This icon points you to extra advice and hints to make chocolate dessert making hassle free and easy.

I use this icon to repeat information you don't want to forget. The information here will keep your chocolate dessert making on a smooth track.

This icon tells you to pay close attention. I'm giving you a caution about what to avoid or what to do so you don't make mistakes along the way.

This icon provides some factual information that may be more than you need to make chocolate desserts successfully, but is still of interest. This is information you can skip if you want to — but you may want to come back to this information at a later time.

Where to Go from Here

If you're new to cooking, you probably want to begin by reading through the information in Parts I and II. This will give you all the information you need to start making the recipes. Don't get bogged down in this information or feel like you have to memorize it — you can easily flip back to it for help at any time.

If you already have a little experience, you may want to skim through the first two parts so you know what's there in case you want to reference them later. You may also want to have a look at the Part of Tens at the end of the book to get some ideas on eating, serving, and giving away your chocolate desserts and sources for ordering chocolate supplies and equipment.

Next, thumb through the book to see which yummy chocolate recipes you want to try. You don't need to follow any order when it comes to the recipes in this book. If you see a cake, or pudding, or candy, just jump right in, and in no time at all you'll be eating a wonderful chocolate dessert.

Because the recipes in Part V require a little more time and effort, you may want to hold off on making these until after you've made some of the other recipes in the book, especially if you're a chocolate dessert–making beginner.

As you begin to make these delicious recipes, you'll see how very easy it is to make fabulous chocolate desserts. I'm certain you'll have a great time along the way. Personally, I can't think of a better way to have fun than to make and eat chocolate desserts. Enjoy the pleasures of chocolate!

Part I
Getting Started

The 5th Wave   By Rich Tennant

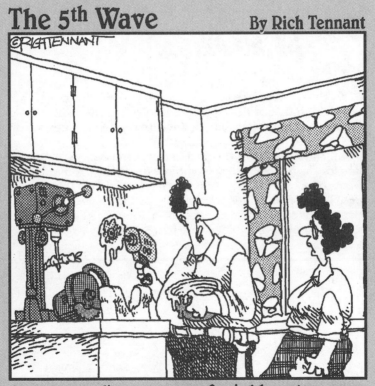

"...because I'm more comfortable using my own tools. Now-how much longer do you want me to sand the cake batter?"

In this part . . .

Motivation is no problem when it comes to chocolate. But before you get started making chocolate desserts, you need to be prepared. Selecting the right recipe and organizing your kitchen are good first steps. Next, you want to have the correct utensils and equipment. Following this, you need to select the type of chocolate for the recipe, with an emphasis on quality. You also want to pay special attention to other ingredients that you use. This part provides you with all the information to begin your chocolate dessert–making journey — a journey that will provide much pleasure from beginning to end.

Chapter 1

Taking Your First Steps toward Chocolate Nirvana

• •

In This Chapter

▶ Understanding why you love chocolate

▶ Getting the satisfaction of making your own chocolate desserts

▶ Preparing yourself for great rewards

▶ Gaining expertise as you go

▶ Finding quick ways to satisfy your chocolate desires

• •

Chocolate is the one food loved by almost everyone. Why? Because it has wonderful flavor, texture, and aroma. You're not alone if you think of chocolate as a feel-good food — eating it really does make you feel good. Even thinking about having some chocolate can be enough to bring a smile to your face.

Being lured by chocolate is very easy. For one thing, it's just about everywhere. Most restaurants offer at least a few chocolate desserts, and the supermarket is packed with chocolate in every form — from chocolate cookies to chocolate milk to the chocolate candy bars in the checkout lane. All of this makes chocolate very hard to resist.

But despite the popularity of chocolate, many people are afraid to make their own chocolate desserts. They think working with chocolate requires an expert's touch. Nothing could be farther from the truth. Dessert making does require a bit more exactness than general cooking, and you do need to measure ingredients precisely and follow the steps of each recipe. But that's all that's required. If you read the recipe and follow the steps, you'll wind up with a great chocolate dessert every time. And when you become adept at making chocolate desserts, you'll gain the confidence to experiment a little with some different flavor combinations and variations.

Where chocolate comes from

Chocolate comes from cacao beans, which grow on cacao trees. However, you can't eat chocolate straight from the cacao tree. Several steps are involved in transforming the raw beans into the chocolate you know and love. The beans grow in pods that are about the size of a football when they reach their full growth.

Cacao trees are very finicky and must have just the right environment in order to thrive. The trees grow only within 20 degrees of the equator and require a lot of rain, shaded sunlight, very little wind, and loose soil. In the wild, cacao trees can grow as tall as 60 feet, but on plantations they are usually kept to around 20 feet in height, making them much easier to harvest.

When the large pods are ripe, they are cut from the trees. This usually happens twice a year. The way to tell if a pod is ripe is generally by its orange or red color. The pods are cut open to reveal their inner treasure of about 40 almond-shaped, ivory-colored beans enclosed in a milky white membrane. The beans look a bit unappetizing at this point. The membrane and beans are scraped out of the pods and spread out on leaves or in baskets. They are left to ferment in the sun for a period ranging from a few days to a week. The beans are turned or stirred a few times while they dry. During this process, the milky white membrane evaporates and the beans darken. After this process, the beans are shipped to chocolate factories around the world to begin their journey into chocolate.

At the factory the beans are roasted to bring out their flavor. If the beans are to become part of a blend, they are mixed together at this point. The next step is a process called *winnowing,* which removes the outer shell of the beans, leaving the inner nib. The nibs are crushed and then heated in order to melt the cocoa butter part of them. Then they are ground to a thick paste between large steel or granite rollers. From this point, the process goes in different directions, depending on whether the thick paste will become cocoa powder or chocolate.

For cocoa powder, the mass is pressed to remove the cocoa butter, which leaves behind a dry cake called *presscake.* This is ground and sifted further to make a fine powder. More of the cocoa butter may also be removed to make lowfat cocoa powder. If it is to be Dutch-processed cocoa powder, alkali is added. This darkens the color and softens the flavor of the cocoa.

To make chocolate, the cocoa mass is mixed with varying amounts of sugar, depending on the type of chocolate it will become (unsweetened, extra bittersweet, bittersweet, or semisweet). Some cocoa butter is added in also to help make the mixture smoother. If milk powder or solids are added, the chocolate will become milk chocolate. To make white chocolate, only cocoa butter, sugar, and milk powder or solids are mixed together. All chocolate has a bit of vanilla and a little lecithin, which helps to make a silky smooth texture. The next step is a process called *conching,* in which the mixture is stirred continuously for many hours. Named after the shell shape of the original machine (*conch* in Spanish), invented by Swiss chocolatier Rudolphe Lindt, conching rids the mixture of any residual grittiness and produces a velvety smooth texture. In the last step in its journey, chocolate is tempered and then shaped into its final form, usually bars.

What makes brands of chocolates different from each other is the quality and types of beans that go into them. The roasting time and temperature can also make a difference, as can the proportion of the ingredients and how long the final mixture is conched. Each manufacturer closely guards its recipe for chocolate. After all, it is what sets them apart from the rest.

Making Chocolate a Part of Your Life

Nothing quite beats eating a chocolate dessert freshly made in your own home kitchen. Homemade chocolate desserts have a special ingredient that can't be found in a store-bought or restaurant-made dessert: the love and care that you put into them.

When asked what type of dessert they would like, most people eagerly reply, "Chocolate!" Watch people when asked if they would like anything made out of chocolate. Their eyes usually start to glow and a smile forms on their faces. Chocolate has that kind of effect on people.

But not too long ago, chocolate eaters felt that they had to hide their consumption of chocolate. But they don't have to hide anymore. Chocolate is actually good for you! No, this isn't something made up by a clever marketing group to promote sales of chocolate. It's true. All the bad myths about chocolate have been dispelled. Here's the good news:

- ✔ **Chocolate contains antioxidants.** And antioxidants help counteract some of the bad things in our systems by keeping oxygen from combining with fat and other substances, actually blocking their negative effects.

- ✔ **Chocolate doesn't raise your cholesterol level.** Although chocolate does contain fat, in the form of cocoa butter, it comes from a plant source. This means that chocolate doesn't contain cholesterol the way animal products (such as butter) do.

- ✔ **Chocolate makes you feel good.** Eating chocolate causes the brain to release two feel-good chemicals called serotonin and endorphins. These chemicals bring on a sense of well-being when they're released. Serotonin is a neurotransmitter that helps stabilize your mood. Endorphins send a feeling of euphoria to your brain and even act as painkillers. Chocolate also contains phenylethylamine, a substance that acts like an antidepressant. So there's a reason why you eat chocolate when you're feeling a bit down-in-the-dumps.

- ✔ **Chocolate boosts energy.** It contains fat, carbohydrates, and sugar, all of which your body uses for fuel. Chocolate also contains a very small amount of caffeine (less than the amount of caffeine in a cup of decaf coffee).

- ✔ **Chocolate doesn't cause tooth decay.** In fact, chocolate helps to coat the teeth and protect them from other sugary foods that *do* cause decay.

- ✔ **Chocolate doesn't make your skin break out.** In fact, food doesn't contribute to skin problems.

Some people just can't get enough chocolate — and I'm one of them. But I've come to realize that there are ways to consume chocolate that, believe it or not, can make it even better. Choosing my chocolate desserts wisely and eating a variety is my approach to getting the most from my chocolate-eating experiences. I also try to eat my chocolate in small portions and savor every bite.

Always eat the best quality chocolate and you will easily satisfy your chocolate cravings.

Chocolate through the ages

Chocolate is made from the cacao plant. Archaeological findings suggest that cacao originated in the Amazon basin in South America over 1,000 years ago. As early as A.D. 600, the Maya tended cacao trees in Mexico and used cacao beans as a form of money. When the Aztecs were in power in the 13th century, they demanded payment of tributes, kind of like bribes, from other tribes in cacao beans.

In the 16th century, Christopher Columbus was the first European to encounter a drink made from cacao beans that the natives loved so much. Although he wasn't impressed — finding the drink to be bitter — Columbus did bring some cacao beans back with him to Spain, as a novelty. Not too many years later, Hernan Cortés conquered the Aztecs and recognized how valuable cacao was to them. He established a cacao plantation in Mexico in the name of Spain and brought cacao back with him to Spain. When the Spanish added sugar and various other ingredients to cacao, they found it quite tasty and began to enjoy drinking it in earnest. They tried their best to keep chocolate to themselves and succeeded for close to 100 years, but their secret got out. The French began to enjoy it, too. The English also indulged in chocolate, and the rest of Europe wasn't far behind.

The natives in South and Central America enjoyed chocolate as a beverage, and at first the Europeans did as well. After chocolate began making its way into the mainstream of Europe, several clever people developed technological innovations that led to making chocolate edible. We can thank Coenraad Van Houten, a Dutch chocolate maker, for inventing the screw press in the early 19th century. The screw press removed most of the fat from chocolate, which led to the development of cocoa powder.

Chocolate bars were the first type of eating chocolate, but they were a far cry from the velvety smooth chocolate bars we eat today. It wasn't long before chocolate candies and bonbons were available. The Swiss were very active in developing many techniques and methods for working with chocolate that led to great leaps forward in chocolate history. They found a way to take the gritty texture out of chocolate and make it a smooth blend. In the late 19th century, a man named Daniel Peter invented milk chocolate.

The Italians, too, lent their expertise to chocolate, creating *gianduia,* a blend of hazelnut and chocolate that is enjoyed to this day by chocolate connoisseurs. John Baker opened the first chocolate factory in America in 1765. In the late 19th century, Milton Hershey created an American style of chocolate and made it affordable for the average person.

Throughout the 20th century, chocolate history was marked by many notable events. Several candy companies were born both in Europe and the United States. The rise of specialty chocolates was notable along with the return to small, handmade chocolate making. In the 21st century, there continues to be a steady increase in the availability of a wide variety of chocolates from around the world. As a result, the consumption of chocolate continues to rise.

Preparing for Your Chocolate Experience

One of the keys to enjoying the experience of making your chocolate dessert is being prepared. Preparation involves a few steps.

Start by setting aside time so you can enjoy yourself in the kitchen without feeling rushed.

Choosing and reading your recipe

This book contains numerous chocolate recipes. When you're trying to decide which one you want to make, think about when and where you will serve it. Are you making dessert for an elegant dinner party, for a picnic, a casual potluck dinner, an afternoon tea, as a gift, or for everyday? In most cases, the occasion will dictate the type of dessert you choose. You probably don't want to make an elegant chocolate layer cake for a picnic, but that layer cake would be just right as the dessert for a posh dinner party.

If you're a novice or an inexperienced dessert maker, start with the easiest recipes in the book. When you've have had success with these, you'll be confident and will easily be able to tackle the more complex recipes (although none of the recipes in this book are beyond the abilities of a beginner in the kitchen).

When you've decided which dessert you want to make, read through the recipe once before you do anything else. Make sure you understand the ingredients called for. If you haven't made the recipe before, be sure that it sounds appetizing to you. Also, check that the recipe makes enough servings for the amount of people you intend to serve. (You don't want to make a great dessert and not have enough to go around.)

Be sure that none of the ingredients poses any problems. For example, if you're allergic to peanuts or you think someone who will be eating your dessert is, you don't want to choose a recipe that uses them.

Gathering and preparing the ingredients

Check your pantry and refrigerator, and assemble the ingredients you need before you start making the dessert. If you notice that you're missing an ingredient, now is a good time to go to the store to buy it, or see if there's an acceptable substitute you can use. You don't want to get midway into making the recipe only to discover that you're missing a key ingredient.

Mix it up!

Eating a variety of different types of chocolate is lots of fun. Dark chocolate (and its variety of levels of intensity — see Chapter 3 for more information), milk chocolate, white chocolate, and *gianduia* (hazelnut chocolate) all have their own special qualities and contribute to whatever dessert they are in. I love to use milk chocolate or white chocolate to decorate a dark chocolate dessert and vice versa. The contrast of colors makes a visual feast, and the different tastes also add variety. I don't think it's possible to get bored eating chocolate, but eating a variety is a good way to prevent this tragedy from ever occurring.

Keep your eyes open for specials on ingredients that you use often, like flour and sugar. You may have to buy a little more than normal, but in the long run, you'll not only have it on hand, but you'll save oodles of money.

After you have your ingredients out, do whatever preparation is called for to get them ready to use. For example, if it's called for, soften the butter, measure the dry ingredients, chop the chocolate into small pieces, toast the nuts, and bring the eggs to room temperature. Having the ingredients prepared will make your mixing and baking time go quickly. It also allows you to concentrate on each step as you go, which means you won't have to think about getting something else ready while you're in the middle of a step.

Assessing the equipment

Just as you did with the ingredients, assemble the equipment called for in the recipe. If the recipe requires a piece of equipment that you don't have, you can borrow it from a friend or buy your own if you think you'll use it often. (Or you can choose to make a different recipe.)

If you're low on any items, like waxed paper or aluminum foil, make a list so you can pick them up the next time you're at the grocery store.

Make sure the equipment and utensils are clean and in good working order. Put all the equipment on the countertop within easy reach. This will save steps and time while you're preparing the dessert. You don't want to be digging around in a drawer or cabinet looking for something when you need it.

If you're baking, preheat the oven. Be sure your oven temperature is accurate. It's a real disappointment to spend time preparing a great dessert only to overbake it.

If you have the time, you can schedule an appointment for the gas and electric company to come to your home to check your oven for accuracy. But a quick way to check whether your oven is accurate is to use an oven thermometer. Be sure to check it often so you're familiar with your oven's temperature. If the oven thermometer reads a different temperature than the dial setting on your oven, adjust the dial up or down as necessary.

Working with the space you have

Not everyone has the kitchen of their dreams. Far from it. Most kitchens are adequate and can handle more tasks than they are given credit for. I have a friend in New York City who has a kitchen that is no bigger than a small closet, but he manages to turn out some pretty incredible food in this tiny space. I thought it was magic at first, but it's all in how he works with the space he has.

Organizing your kitchen equipment

When you're in the kitchen making desserts, being organized really helps. Get rid of excess items that are merely taking up space. If you find that you have pots and pans or any other kitchen items that you don't use, stack them up (in another place) and plan to give them to a friend or donate them to your favorite charity. You'll be delighted to have more space in your own kitchen, and I bet you won't miss any of the things you let go.

Set up one area of the kitchen for baking and dessert making. If you have a stand mixer, keep it on the counter so it's easy to reach and is always ready to be used. Do the same for your food processor.

Keep your dry measuring cups and measuring spoons in a drawer. Use separate drawers or drawer separators for other utensils, like rubber spatulas, bowl scrapers, and pastry bags and tips. When you keep items separate, you'll never have to go digging around in the back of drawers looking for an item that you think you have.

Put baking pans, mixing bowls, cookie sheets, and cooling racks in the cabinets directly under the counter where you store your mixer. If you don't have enough room, try stacking some items. Place the cooling racks on top of the cookie sheets. Stack bowls together in order of their size. You'll be amazed at how much extra space you can create by using a few simple organizing tricks.

Keep your knives in a knife block or a knife rack so they can't be damaged by other utensils. In a drawer next to the oven, keep pot holders, timers, toothpicks, and cake testers. Having these items right where you need them makes your time in the kitchen a lot more fun. If you have to run halfway across the kitchen to find a potholder when you want to check the cake baking in the oven, you may not bother to look at all. You don't want to tempt any disasters, like burned hands.

If you have room for a hanging pot rack, this is a great way to create extra storage space. Just make sure you won't bump your head into it while you're working in the kitchen.

After you're finished using an item or after it's been washed and dried, put it back where it belongs. Next time you want to bake or make desserts it will be right where you expect it to be.

Keep cleanup items nearby, too. A broom and dustpan, towels, aprons, and sponges need to be within easy reach. You don't want to have to waste time looking for these things when you need them. Under the sink, keep a small plastic basket that holds extra sponges and scrubbing pads.

If your kitchen needs to be completely reorganized, don't despair! Think of it as a chance to start fresh. Draw out your plan on paper, and label each cabinet and drawer with what will go into them. This will make shifting things around a lot easier and a lot more fun!

Finding a place to put all your food

Keep the pantry neat and organized so you can easily find the ingredients you need for whichever recipe you're in the mood to make. I like to keep dry ingredients, like flour, sugar, and salt, near each other. I put flour and sugar into large, clear, wide-mouth containers. This way I can easily see what's in each container and easily scoop it out. If you don't use these ingredients very often, it's a good idea to keep track of when you bought them. You can do this in a snap with masking tape and a marker.

Do the same with items in the refrigerator. When you buy nuts, transfer them to a plastic container with a tight-fitting lid. Then label and date the container. This way you know exactly what's in each container and how long it's been there. If you have two containers of the same ingredient, always make sure to use the one with the oldest date first. Also, try to keep similar ingredients near each other. Butter and cream cheese can share a storage compartment. Milk and cream fit on a shelf on the door.

Considering environmental factors

Any time is a good time to make chocolate desserts. But you should be aware of a few environmental conditions. The first thing you need to watch for is temperature. Chocolate likes a cool temperature, between 65 and 70 degrees. You definitely don't want to work with chocolate when it's too warm because it has a tendency to melt. This may not be a problem for many chocolate desserts, but if you're making candy or dipping anything in chocolate, it is a concern. You don't want to have chocolate soup on your hands. If your environment is on the cool side, this is usually not a problem, except if you're making delicate decorations that may set up too quickly.

Quality counts

Being moderate about chocolate consumption isn't hard at all if you're eating top-quality chocolate. Great chocolate is so satisfying that a few bites or one small serving will take care of your chocolate craving for the day. There's nothing as good as eating a chocolate dessert made from the best-quality ingredients. Sure, there are times when you'll be in the mood for more than a small serving, and it's okay to indulge from time to time, especially when it comes to chocolate. I can't stress enough how important it is to eat top-quality chocolate. When you do, you won't be tempted to eat poor-quality chocolate ever again.

When working with your chocolate desserts, be careful not to set them under warm lights or next to the oven or stovetop. These areas can be much warmer than the rest of the kitchen.

High humidity is dangerous for serious chocolate chefs. The dampness from the air mixes with the chocolate and changes its consistency, which makes it do strange things.

Also, don't be fooled by high humidity outside. If it's raining, it doesn't mean you can't work with chocolate in your kitchen. You may be able to control the humidity inside your house by using a dehumidifier or an air conditioner.

Improving Your Skills

Like so many other things, the more you work with chocolate, the better you'll get at it. The old adage "Practice makes perfect" is an adage for a reason. In order to accelerate your chocolate dessert–making ability, you should make a lot of chocolate desserts.

Make notes while you're working on a recipe. You may devise a variation for the recipe that you want to try next time. Or you may come up with a good idea for how you want to serve the dessert. You may even encounter a problem with something and jot down how you corrected the problem. Any and all notes are a help.

After you've made something several times, you begin to gain confidence. You won't even notice it, but you'll begin to be more efficient when you make chocolate desserts. You'll also make them faster. Greater confidence leads to more creativity. It's a great feeling when you can very easily make chocolate desserts without even thinking about it. After a while, you'll be making chocolate desserts in your sleep and eating them when you're awake.

Seeking Instant Gratification

Are you in a hurry to satisfy your chocolate cravings? There are many quick and very easy ways to put together a chocolate dessert that will hit the spot. The supermarket is chock-full of products that can be assembled into dynamite chocolate desserts. Here are several ways you can satisfy your craving in less time than it would take you turn the page (or almost!):

- **Hot fudge sundae:** Drizzle your favorite flavor of store-bought ice cream with hot fudge sauce out of a jar.

- **Chocolate-drizzled angel food or pound cake:** Buy a cake at the bakery or grocery store, and drizzle it with chocolate sauce.

- **Quick chocolate pie:** Buy a chocolate or regular graham cracker crust, fill it with chocolate pudding, and top it with whipped cream.

- **Ladyfinger ice cream sandwiches:** Sandwich chocolate ice cream between store-bought ladyfingers.

- **Chocolate wafer sandwiches:** Take chocolate wafer cookies and make a sandwich with peanut butter, jam, ice cream, or chilled fudge sauce.

- **Chocolate hazelnut pie:** Buy a chocolate or regular graham cracker crust, fill it with chocolate hazelnut spread, and top it with whipped cream.

- **Chocolate hazelnut bread:** Buy a loaf of French or Italian bread, slice it, toast it, and spread it with chocolate hazelnut spread.

Chapter 2

Chocolate Paraphernalia

· ·

In This Chapter

▶ Choosing tools and utensils

▶ Selecting pots and baking pans

▶ Deciding which machines to buy

▶ Understanding ovens

· ·

*H*aving the right tool makes the job easy. This is true for any type of work or hobby. But you don't have to own every piece of baking and dessert-making equipment to make great chocolate desserts.

Walking into a cookware shop or the cookware section of a department store can be overwhelming if you're just starting out in your chocolate dessert–making endeavors. So start with the basics that you need to make a dessert or two. If you enjoy the experience, you can buy more equipment as you go.

I always recommend buying the best quality equipment you can afford. It will pay for itself over and over throughout the many years you'll own it. Conversely, poor-quality equipment will wind up costing you more over time because you'll have to replace it. Try not to get sidetracked or pulled in by a "special deal." If this happens, most likely you'll wind up buying something you don't really need or want.

In this chapter, I describe the equipment for chocolate dessert making, starting with the basics and moving on to all the extras it's nice to have. Refer to this information before you go shopping so you know what you want to look for.

Keep your eyes peeled for sales at cookware shops, in cookware sections of department stores, and through catalog and online sources. Often you'll find a just what you're looking for at a reduced price.

Instruments of Measurement

Dessert making requires a fair amount of precision in measurement. Recipes are formulas that have been developed over time with a good deal of trial and error. If you start to throw in a pinch of this and a dash of that, pretty soon the formula is out of balance and it's no guarantee that the dessert will come out the way you expect. Following dessert recipes closely is important — and this means measuring ingredients to be sure you have exact amounts. To do this, you need to have the correct tools and pay attention to what you're doing.

Measuring cups

Measuring cups are at the top of my list for accurate measuring of ingredients. There are two types of measuring cups, those that measure dry ingredients and those that measure liquids.

- ✔ **Dry measuring cups:** These are available in nesting sets of graduated sizes that range from ¼ cup to 2 cups. They can be found in various materials such as plastic, aluminum, and stainless steel. Dry measuring cups are used for ingredients such as flour and sugar and solid fats. The ingredient fills these cups to the top so you can easily see exactly what the amount is.

- ✔ **Liquid measuring cups:** As their name implies, these are used to measure liquids. This type of measuring cup has a pour spout on one side and a handle on the other. They come in a variety of sizes ranging from 1– to 4-cup capacity and in different materials, such as glass, plastic, and metal. Lines on the sides of these cups mark off the quantity of the ingredient. These measuring cups have room at the top for the liquid to move around and not spill out. I like to use glass or plastic liquid measuring cups because seeing the quantity is easy.

Having on hand more than one set of each type of measuring cup is helpful.

Measuring spoons

Like measuring cups, measuring spoons come in a set of graduated sizes ranging from ¼ teaspoon to 1 tablespoon. Some sets also include ⅛ and ¹⁄₁₆ teaspoon measurements. Measuring spoons are used for measuring small amounts of both liquid and dry ingredients. They're available in plastic and metal.

I like to take apart the graduated sets of measuring spoons and store the same sizes together in small glass jars on my kitchen counter. This makes seeing the different sizes easy. It also makes using the measuring spoons more efficient than working with the entire set.

Chocolate thermometer

This specially designed long glass mercury thermometer (see Figure 2-1) has clear markings and reads in 1-degree gradations in the range of 40 to 130 degrees. It's mainly used for tempering chocolate, when extreme accuracy is necessary. This thermometer should be hand-washed and –dried and stored where it won't be jostled by other utensils.

Figure 2-1:
Chocolate
ther-
mometer.

Candy thermometer

This thermometer is designed for registering the temperature of cooked sugar and candy mixtures. It reads in the range of 100 to 400 degrees and is marked for the various stages of cooking sugar. Try to find a candy thermometer marked in 2-degree gradations so you'll identify small changes in the temperature of sugar.

Candy thermometers made with mercury are the most accurate because mercury is a consistently reliable material for registering heat. Choose a candy thermometer with a base that sits on the bottom of the pan and suspends the bulb of the thermometer into the mixture. If the bulb of the thermometer hits the bottom of the pan, it will register that temperature, which is likely to be several degrees hotter than the mixture itself.

Oven thermometer

All dessert recipes that need to be baked specify an oven temperature. Home ovens have a bad reputation for being somewhat inaccurate. So I like to keep an oven thermometer (shown in Figure 2-2) in my oven — and I check it often. An oven thermometer is a great tool for knowing if my oven is running hot or cold, and I can easily adjust the temperature dial in either direction accordingly. Baking at the wrong temperature can cause problems with either under– or overbaking and with the final texture of desserts.

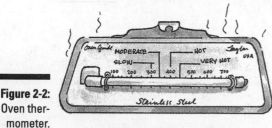

Figure 2-2: Oven thermometer.

OVEN THERMOMETER

Scales

Scales come in very handy for weighing ingredients, especially chocolate and butter, if you buy it in bulk and need to chop or cut it for each recipe. There are three types of scales: spring, balance, and electronic. A spring scale is the easiest to use. It can be set to 0 for each new ingredient that's weighed, even when other ingredients are in the bowl. Spring scales measure up to 4½ pounds. Some of them are marked in metric measurements also, which is nice if you're trying to convert measurements. Balance scales work on the principle of balancing ingredients on one side against weights on the other side. Electronic scales show a digital readout of the weight of the ingredient. This type of scale is the most accurate, but it is heavy and can weigh up to 10 pounds.

Timer

Keep a timer on hand so you know when your baked desserts need to come out of the oven. Always set a timer for the minimum amount of time specified in a recipe. You can easily add more time if it's needed, but you can't take it away if the dessert is overbaked. Many types of timers are available in cookware departments and shops and through online and catalog sources. When you're choosing a timer, just make sure it's loud enough that you can hear it and that you can read its face clearly.

Essential Utensils

When making chocolate desserts, you often need to perform a variety of steps. The following utensils make short work of these chores.

Knives

A good-quality sharp chef's knife makes cutting, chopping, and slicing chores a breeze. Choose a knife by how it feels in your hand. You want the weight of the knife to do the work instead of having to put all your weight behind it. An 8-inch blade is a good multi-use size. If you can afford more than one chef's knife, get both an 8-inch and a 10-inch.

A serrated knife is great for slicing cakes and other desserts. I use one with a long blade for slicing cake layers horizontally into pieces.

Store knives in a knife block that sits on the countertop or in one that fits in a drawer. This keeps them from becoming damaged by other equipment. Be sure to keep your knives razor sharp. They're much easier to use when sharp, and a dull knife can actually be more dangerous than a sharp one.

Don't wash knives in the dishwasher. It will dull the blade and ruin the handle.

Pastry brushes

Pastry brushes come in handy for several chores in the chocolate kitchen. I use them to brush excess flour, cocoa powder, and confectioners' sugar off of dough. You can also use them to apply glazes, brush down the sides of the pan of a cooked sugar mixture, and butter the insides of baking pans. Keep the brushes that you use for sugar separate from those you use for butter — this way, the two don't contaminate the different mixtures. Be sure to wash pastry brushes in warm, soapy water and dry them well. Buy pastry brushes with natural bristles because nylon bristles tend to tear dough, and they can catch on fire easily if exposed to too much heat.

Use a 2-inch-wide pastry brush to brush excess flour, cocoa powder, and confectioners' sugar off of dough. Use 1-inch wide pastry brushes for most other chores.

Rolling pin

A rolling pin is essential to rolling out dough smoothly and evenly. My favorite rolling pin is a long, solid hardwood cylinder without handles. I don't have to worry about making handle marks in my dough and I can place my hands anywhere on the cylinder while working with it. Use a heavyweight rolling pin so it does the work for you. Wipe the rolling pin off or wash it after each use, then dry, and store.

Don't wash a rolling pin in the dishwasher, because it will become warped.

Rubber spatulas

Rubber doesn't hold on to other flavors like wooden spoons do, which makes rubber spatulas essential for stirring chocolate as it melts and for blending and mixing ingredients together. It would be impossible for me to work in the kitchen without a variety of rubber spatulas. I prefer the short-handled ones for stirring chocolate, and I like the long-handled ones for most other uses. The heat-resistant rubber spatulas come in a variety of different colors. These withstand very high temperatures so there's no worry about them melting.

I like to use rubber spatulas that are one solid piece of plastic. There's no chance the handle will break away from the head and they can be washed in the dishwasher easily.

Strainer

Strainers come in handy for sifting small amounts of ingredients like cocoa powder, confectioners' sugar, and flour. They're also great for dusting these ingredients on the top of finished desserts. I prefer to use strainers made of plastic because they can be washed in the dishwasher. Have a variety of sizes of strainers on hand for different tasks.

Cooling racks

This utensil is made of closely spaced parallel metal wires that rest on ½-inch-high feet. Cooling racks allow air to circulate around baked desserts while they cool, which prevents steam from building up and making the bottoms soggy. Cooling racks come in a variety of sizes and shapes, such as square, rectangle, and round. Keep several on hand so you always have one when you need it.

Look for cooling racks that are made of sturdy metal with the wires spaced closely together. This makes them strong and prevents small items from slipping through the wires.

Specialty Utensils

This group of utensils isn't essential, but they bring fun to your dessert-making experiences because they make many tasks very easy to accomplish. These are the utensils to add to your collection as you go along — don't think you have to buy them all at once.

Cake-decorating turntable

This turntable (shown in Figure 2-3), which looks like a lazy Susan, is used to assemble and decorate cakes. The turntable elevates the cake above the counter height and brings it closer to eye level, making your work more accurate. A sturdy, footed, 4-inch-high cast-iron base holds a thin flat metal plate. Round plates are available in 12–,14–, and 16-inch diameters. There's a screw in the base that can be adjusted to regulate the speed at which the plate can be rotated. Rotating the turntable slowly makes it easy to apply icing or frosting to cake layers and to decorate cakes when assembled. Turntables can be bought at many cookware shops and through online and catalog sources.

Never submerge a turntable in water. It will cause the metal to rust and make turning difficult.

Figure 2-3: Cake decorating turntable.

I don't recommend plastic turntables because they're not very sturdy.

Pastry bags and tips

You use pastry bags to shape batter and dough and to decorate finished desserts. The bags are cone shaped, and the pointed end is fitted with a tip made of either metal or plastic. Pastry bags are made of nylon, polyester, canvas, plastic-lined cloth, and disposable plastic. I prefer the nylon or polyester bags that can be washed and reused over and over. The best sizes to have are 12– and 14-inch because they're large enough to hold sufficient batter without overfilling. These sizes are easy to use and you don't have to keep refilling them.

Pastry tips come in many sizes and openings that form different shapes. I prefer to use the large (2-inch-tall) pastry cones. Basic ones to have on hand include a plain round tip with a ½-inch opening and an open star tip. You can wash pastry tips in the dishwasher.

Pastry scraper

A pastry scraper is a thin, flat, flexible piece of plastic or nylon shaped like a half-moon that fits in the palm of the hand. You use it for tempering chocolate, scraping out bowls, cutting dough into pieces, and cleaning work surfaces. You can wash pastry scrapers in the dishwasher for easy cleanup.

Truffle and chocolate dippers

Truffle and chocolate dippers (shown in Figure 2-4) are, as the name implies, designed to hold truffles and candies for dipping into chocolate. They come in several shapes and sizes — round, oval, spiral, and long-tined fork — each of which is used for a particular shape of candy. Dippers are made of thin stainless steel with 3½-inch long wooden handles. Some dippers are made of a solid piece of plastic. The tools are available singly and in sets, ranging from six to ten pieces.

Chocolate molds

There are two types of chocolate molds: shallow molds used for solid molding, and two-part molds used for hollow molding, solid molding, and filled chocolates (both shown in Figure 2-5). The flat shallow molds are generally made of plastic and are very flexible. Each mold is for a particular shape or design with 6, 12, 18, or 24 cavities per mold, depending on its size. A wide variety of designs is available. The two-part molds are made of either metal or sturdy plastic and are also available in many shapes and sizes.

Handle chocolate molds carefully. If they are scratched, the chocolate won't release from them.

CHOCOLATE DIPPERS

Figure 2-4:
Truffle and
chocolate
dippers.

CHOCOLATE MOLDS

2 SIDED

Figure 2-5:
Chocolate
molds.

Flexible-blade spatula

In this spatula, a long, narrow stainless steel blade with a rounded end and straight sides is set into a wooden handle. The blade is flexible, but not wobbly. Flexible-blade spatulas come in a variety of sizes ranging from a 3-inch-long blade to a 14-inch-long blade. These spatulas have many uses including icing cakes and pastries, spreading frostings and batters, and releasing desserts from molds. Keep a few sizes on hand.

Offset spatula

This tool (shown in Figure 2-6) has a flexible stainless steel blade that is stepped down about 1 inch from the wooden handle, forming a Z-like shape. This spatula has many uses in the chocolate dessert kitchen, like tempering chocolate, transporting cake layers and cookies, and spreading batter in jelly roll pans. Offset spatulas come in a variety of sizes ranging from 3 to 12 inches. I like to keep a small one on hand for decorative work and a large one for tempering chocolate and other uses.

Figure 2-6: Offset spatula.

OFFSET SPATULA

Marble board

A marble board is the ideal surface for tempering chocolate. Marble is a hard natural material that maintains a consistently cool temperature because it dissipates heat faster than other surfaces. Marble also stays dry because it doesn't hold moisture. I like to use a marble board that measure 18 x 24 inches and is ¾ inch high. This size is fairly easy to move around yet large enough for my chocolate uses.

Don't use your marble board as a cutting board. It will dull your knives and any grooves in it will hinder chocolate work.

Marble stains if it comes in contact with citrus juice and other acid materials, so be sure to keep those away from your board.

Dredger

A dredger looks like a large salt shaker. It's about 3½ inches tall and 2½ inches round with a handle on one side. The top has either an arched mesh screen or is flat metal with holes, depending on the material it's made of. You use a dredger to sift a small amount of cocoa powder or confectioners' sugar on top of desserts. It's also useful for dusting a small amount of flour on the work surface when rolling out dough.

Pastry comb

This utensil is also called a cake comb or icing comb. It's made of either metal or plastic and has serrated edges, similar to saw teeth. Pastry combs come in two shapes: triangle and rectangle. The triangle shape has different size teeth on all three sides. The rectangle shape has teeth along one side that graduate in size periodically. You use a pastry comb to make patterns in the icing or frosting around the sides and tops of cakes and other desserts.

Pie weights

These are round ceramic or flat aluminum pellets. They're used to weight down a pie crust or tart shell that is baked without a filling. The pie weights keep the sides of the crust or shell from collapsing and the bottom from puffing up. They also conduct heat to the top and sides of the shell as it bakes. The weights should fill the shell almost full. Pie weights are available in most stores that sell kitchen equipment.

Always place the weights on top of a piece of aluminum foil so they don't bake into the crust.

Countertop Equipment

This category includes the workhorses of the kitchen: food processors and electric mixers. Making chocolate desserts without them is possible, but these machines sure make life in the kitchen easy. They should last close to a lifetime, so shop around for the very best quality you can afford. Keep them on the countertop so you don't have to go digging in the back of a cabinet when you're in the mood to make chocolate desserts.

Food processor

A food processor can cut preparation time by more than half. It easily chops nuts; mixes cookie, pie, and tart doughs; purees fruit; and slices fruit, to name just a few of the chores it accomplishes. I don't think I could live without my food processor. You can buy extra bowls and cutting blades so you can do several chores in succession without having to stop and wash the bowl each time. Shop for a good quality food processor that's heavy enough to stay in place and doesn't move around the countertop when it's in use.

Mixers

An electric mixer may be the most important piece of equipment in your dessert kitchen. Among other things, it mixes batters and doughs, whips cream and egg whites, and blends ingredients. I prefer to use a heavy-duty stand mixer so my hands are free for other tasks.

Stand mixer

Stand mixers are the most versatile type of mixer. They have a solid base that sits on the countertop. A heavy-duty motor is important so the mixer won't burn out when working. It's also nice to have several adjustable speeds so the mixer can work on many different types of tasks. Most stand mixers come with a variety of attachments. A wire whisk is great for whipping air into mixtures and a flat beater is the perfect tool for mixing ingredients together.

Buy an extra bowl, wire whip, and flat beater for your mixer. Having two sets allows you to accomplish several tasks without having to stop and wash the bowl and attachments before each.

Handheld mixer

A handheld mixer is portable and easy to use. This type of mixer has two removable beaters set into a housing that holds a motor. It usually has a few speeds. Some models come with different attachments. A handheld mixer is good to use for smaller quantities, because handheld mixers often take longer than a stand mixer to mix the same ingredients.

Mixing bowls

Keeping a variety of mixing bowls on hand is helpful. You'll want several different sizes and materials, such as stainless steel, glass, and ceramic. Look for bowls with a flat bottom so they sit securely on the countertop while you're mixing. Many mixing bowls come in graduated sizes that nest together, which makes it easy to store them.

Leave enough room in the mixing bowl for stirring ingredients so they won't splash over the sides. An use a mixing bowl that's large enough to hold ingredients that increase greatly in volume when whipped, like egg whites and cream.

Chocolate tempering machine

If you're going to temper lots of chocolate, a chocolate tempering machine (like the one shown in Figure 2-7) is a nice extra to have. It melts and tempers chocolate, and holds it at the correct temperature for dipping and molding truffles and candies. Tempering machines come in a few sizes that work with different capacities of chocolate. There is a panel on the top or front of the machine with various buttons to control the melting and tempering according to the type of chocolate in use. A stainless steel bowl sits in a cavity on top of the machine and is divided in half horizontally by a large plastic scraper, which holds a probe and often a chocolate thermometer. Finely chopped chocolate is placed behind the scraper. The bowl rotates and, as the chocolate melts, it flows through to the front of the bowl. A tempering machine is very easy to use. You simply turn on the machine, put in the finely chopped chocolate, and set the mode. Within an hour, the batch of chocolate is perfectly tempered. Extra bowls and scrapers are available, which makes it easy to switch from one type of chocolate to another without having to take the time to wash and dry them on the spot.

CHOCOLATE TEMPERING MACHINE

Figure 2-7:
Chocolate
tempering
machine.

Pots and Pans

You don't have to have a lot of pots and baking pans, but there are several that are useful. As with other equipment, buy good quality. Heavy-duty pots will last many, many years.

Double boiler

A double boiler insulates and provides a consistent source of heat for melting delicate ingredients such as chocolate and butter. It keeps these from burning because it cushions them from direct heat. A double boiler consists of two pots that fit snugly together or a bowl that fits snugly over a pan (see Figure 2-8). A small amount of water sits in the bottom pan. It's the heat from the water that transfers to the top pan, which holds the ingredient.

Double boilers come in a variety of materials, but I prefer glass because I can see the water in the bottom. If it starts to bubble I can remove it from the heat so it won't become too hot and burn the ingredient in the top pan.

Figure 2-8:
Double
boiler.

double boiler

It's important that the top bowl fit the bottom pan snugly so no water or steam can escape and mix with the ingredient in the bowl, especially if it's chocolate (because chocolate and water don't mix well). If the bowl doesn't fit snugly, there's a risk that it may float around in the water in the pan.

Saucepans

You'll want to have a few sizes of saucepans handy. I use 1–, 2–, and 3-quart saucepans most often. They're good for heating cream, scalding milk, and cooking custards and sauces. Use good-quality, heavy-duty saucepans so you don't burn your ingredients. I've used enameled cast-iron pans for many years with great success.

Making your own double boiler

You can easily make your own double boiler with a heatproof bowl that fits snugly over a bottom pan. Stainless steel and glass are the best choices for bowls because they both conduct heat efficiently.

Baking pans

Many different baking pans are used for different desserts, and you certainly don't need to own them all — unless you want to. But it's good to know about them so you can add to your collection when you want. Choose good-quality baking pans of durable material. I prefer to use heavy-gauge aluminum because it conducts heat evenly and consistently.

Glass baking pans conduct heat more rapidly than other materials. If you use them, turn the oven temperature down by 25 degrees and start checking for doneness 5 to 10 minutes earlier than the recipe calls for.

Square

The two most popular sizes of square baking pans are 8 x 8 x 2 and 9 x 9 x 2 inches. These are used for making brownies and bar cookies and for some candies.

Rectangle

Rectangular baking pans come in a few different sizes. These are useful for brownies, bar cookies, and other desserts. Make sure the sizes you buy will fit in your oven.

Measure the inside of your oven to make sure your baking pans fit. Allow at least 2 inches around all sides of the pans so air can circulate.

Round cake pans

These are used for baking cakes and cake layers. Have two pans in the sizes you use often. I prefer to bake most cakes in 9-x-9-x-2-inch pans, but 8 x 8 x 2 is also a good size to have. Heavy aluminum pans are the best type to use. I don't like nonstick pans because it can be difficult for the cake batter to hold the sides of the pan while it rises.

Always buy cake pans that are at least 1½ inches tall with straight sides so they will hold the cake batter and allow room for it to expand when baking.

Springform pan

A springform pan (shown in Figure 2-9) is used for baking cheesecakes and some other delicate chocolate cakes and for molding some desserts. A springform pan is a deep round pan with straight sides secured by a clamp to a bottom rim. When the clamp is opened, the sides of the pan expand and release the bottom. This feature makes it very easy to remove a cake from the pan because you don't need to turn the pan upside down. Springform pans come in a variety of sizes ranging from 4 to 12 inches in diameter. They are 2½ to 3 inches deep.

It's a good idea to place your springform pan on a jelly roll pan before it goes into the oven. The lower pan will catch any drips that may escape through the seam, and it makes transporting the springform pan easy.

Figure 2-9:
Springform
pan.

Tube pans

Tube pans (see Figure 2-10) are also called angel food pans because they are used for baking angel food cakes. The pan has 4½-inch-high straight sides that allow the airy batter to climb up them as it rises. There's a tube in the center of the pan that conducts heat and helps to bake the center of the cake. Often, these pans have metal protrusions above the rim of the pan, called *feet*. After the cake is baked, the pan is turned upside down onto the feet or is hung over the neck of a bottle. This allows the cake to cool without compacting. A 10-inch diameter pan is the most common size.

Figure 2-10:
Tube, or
angel food,
pans.

Another type of tube pan is called a *Bundt pan*. This pan has sculptural grooves and designs molded into the sides, which transfer to the cake it holds. Many different designs are available.

Loaf pans

This pan is designed to bake rectangular cakes and quick breads. The standard size is 9 x 5 x 3 inches, but many sizes and types are available. Loaf pans are made from a variety of materials including glass, aluminum, tinned steel, black steel, or ceramic.

Pie pans

Pie pans or plates have sloped sides and most are 1½ inches deep. The most popular diameter sizes are 8 and 9 inches. Pie pans are made of glass, tinned steel, aluminum, and ceramic. Glass is a good choice because it conducts heat evenly and will brown the crust, but you need to lower the oven temperature by 25 degrees or the pie may become too dark. Aluminum is also a popular choice and browns the crust evenly. Pies baked in ceramic pie pans may need to bake slightly longer to bake evenly.

Tart pans

The classic pan for baking tarts is round and shallow with fluted, slightly sloping sides and a removable bottom (see Figure 2-11). The fluted edges give the tart shell an attractive design. Tart pans are available in other shapes, such as square and rectangle, and in a wide variety of sizes from mini, measuring 1½ inches, up to large, measuring 16 inches in diameter. They vary in depth from ¾ inch to 1¼ inches. The typical material is tinned steel. Black steel is also available, but it bakes quicker because it conducts heat faster, so adjust the oven temperature accordingly. A straight-sided flan ring or mold is also used for baking tarts. This is placed on a lined baking sheet, making the baking sheet the bottom of the ring.

Figure 2-11: Tart pans.

Muffin pans

A muffin pan is a rectangular baking pan with 6 or 12 cup-shaped cavities that's used for baking muffins, cupcakes, and small cakes. Some muffin pans have nonstick surfaces. Otherwise, the pans are often lined with paper bake cups or greased and floured to make removing the muffins and cakes easy. The standard size cavity is 3 inches wide and 1¼ to 1½ inches deep. Mini muffin pans are also available with cavities that measure about 1½ inches wide. Giant muffin pans measure 3½ to 4 inches in diameter. Muffin pans are made of heavy aluminum and tinned steel. There are also mini-Bundt pans (see "Tube pans" earlier in this chapter), with a variety of designs molded into them, that shape small cakes.

Be sure to choose a muffin pan made of sturdy material so it won't warp when baked.

Special pans and containers

The following items are nice extras and it's really helpful to them when making the particular desserts they hold.

Soufflé dish

A soufflé dish (shown in Figure 2-12) is a deep, round, straight-sided porcelain dish used for baking soufflés and holding other desserts, such as custards and mousses. The dish is typically smooth on the inside with a fluted exterior. Soufflé dishes are available in various sizes from 4 to 9 inches in diameter and 2¾ to 4 inches tall. The sizes used most often are 1½ and 2 quart.

Figure 2-12:
A soufflé dish.

Custard cup

A custard cup (shown in Figure 2-13) is a deep, flat-bottomed individual-size cup with slightly flared sides measuring about 2 inches deep and 3 inches wide at the top. Custard cups have no handles. They are smooth on the inside and often ribbed on the outside. Generally they are made of porcelain or glazed earthenware. A pôt de crème cup is similar, but it's usually rounder with a lid and small loop handles on each side.

Figure 2-13:
A custard
cup.

Crème brûlée dish

A crème brûlée dish (shown in Figure 2-14) is a shallow porcelain dish with a smooth interior and fluted edges. It creates a wide surface for caramelizing the top of the custard. Crème brûlée can also be baked in individual soufflé or custard cups.

Figure 2-14:
A crème
brûlée dish.

Cookie sheets

These thin, flat sheets of metal are hard to live without. They are used for baking cookies and other tasks, such as holding springform pans and acting as the bottom for flan rings or tart molds (see "Tart pans" earlier in this chapter). Sturdy aluminum is the best material for cookie sheets because it conducts heat most efficiently and consistently. Cookie sheets have a rim on one side. Jelly roll pans, also called baking sheets, have a 1-inch rim on all four sides. They're used for baking cookies and low cakes.

If the bottoms of your cookies are baking too quickly use an insulated baking sheet that sandwiches a layer of air between two sheets of metal. You can also create your own by stacking two cookie sheets together.

Nonstick cookie sheets don't have to be greased or floured, but some cookie batters will spread too much when baked on the non-stick surface. Dark cookie sheets bake cookies too quickly and may overbake them, making them dry.

Line cookie sheets with parchment paper and you won't have to grease and flour them. Cleanup is a breeze, because you simply toss the parchment paper when done. If there are no spills, you can reuse the parchment paper.

Have at least two, and preferably four, cookie sheets. That way you won't have to wait for each batch to cool before baking the next.

Don't buy thin cookie sheets. They'll warp in the oven and result in unevenly baked cookies.

Measure the inside of your oven to be sure the cookie sheets you buy will fit. There should be at least 2 inches of space around them so air can circulate well during baking.

Ovens

The oven is one of the most important pieces of equipment in your kitchen. You can't bake anything without an oven. If you're considering buying a new oven, keep in mind that looking into the oven at eye level is much easier than having to constantly bend over. Other features to look for are a glass door and an internal light. This makes it easy to see how your baked goods are doing without having to open the door, which can disrupt baking, lower the oven temperature, and even cause a cake to fall.

No matter what type of oven you use, be sure to keep an oven thermometer in it so you can monitor the temperature.

What's the best type of oven?

Both gas and electric ovens keep a consistent source of heat and do a fine job of baking. Electric ovens provide heat from both the bottom and top, which is great if you need to caramelize the top of a custard. Gas ovens provide heat only from the bottom and the heat may come on and off to maintain the temperature at a constant point. Personally, I like using an electric oven because it bakes very evenly.

Microwave ovens aren't a good choice for baking because the source of heat is so much different. They're fine for softening butter and frozen dough, and for melting chocolate.

In convection ovens, a fan circulates hot air, which shortens the baking time by as much as 25 percent. It's a nice feature, but you have to remember to shorten the baking time and lower the baking temperature or you'll wind up over-baking. Some ovens have a convection feature that can be turned on whenever you choose.

Supplies to Keep Ingredients and Desserts Fresh

A variety of kitchen supplies help keep both ingredients and finished chocolate desserts fresh and tasty. Keep your pantry stocked with the items listed here and you'll be ready for anything.

Aluminum foil

This kitchen staple performs a variety of tasks. Foil is invaluable for covering baked goods for storage, both at room temperature and in the refrigerator. It creates an almost airtight seal and helps prolong freshness. It's also great for lining cookie sheets, especially for meringues. Foil is also good for lining baking pans for bar cookies and brownies. This makes it easy to lift them out of the pan so they can be cut on a board instead of in the pan. And foil is excellent for lining containers for storing cookies and other desserts.

Wax paper

I don't think I could live without wax paper in my kitchen, because it has numerous uses. I use wax paper to hold small amounts of dry ingredients as they're sifted. It's easy to lift up and move from one place to another and to add the ingredients into a mixture in the mixing bowl while the mixer is going. I always place a piece of wax paper on the countertop next to my mixer when it's in use, so I have a place to set the rubber spatula I use to scrape down the sides of the bowl. That way I keep the countertop clean. I also use wax paper to line the baking pans that hold dipped truffles and candies and dough that need to chill before baking. Wax paper comes in handy for shaping cookie dough into rolls and for lining containers for storing cookies, candies, and other desserts.

Plastic wrap

This is another valuable kitchen staple with lots of uses. It covers ingredients that are pre-measured so they don't dry out or lose flavor from long exposure to the air. It covers dough that needs to chill or warm up to room temperature. Cake layers that are cooled need to be covered so they don't get crusty before they're assembled and many finished chocolate desserts are covered with plastic wrap to keep them fresh before they're served. In my kitchen, I keep a large roll of plastic wrap that I buy at a warehouse-type store. It's the same kind they use in restaurant kitchens.

Use good-quality plastic wrap that clings strongly. The wimpy stuff isn't worth the cost because you wind up crunching it up into a ball and throwing it out in frustration.

Parchment paper and nonstick pan liner

Nonstick parchment paper is one of the best inventions ever developed for dessert makers. It's ideal for lining cookie and baking sheets so baked goods won't stick. This eliminates the need to grease and flour the pans. If there are no spills on the baking sheet then there's no need to wash it, which saves time. Parchment paper is also used to make pastry cones for decorating and piping out batters. It comes in sheets, rolls, and triangles.

A nonstick silicone pan liner works the same way as parchment paper, but its reusable. Liners come in several sizes to fit different size baking pans.

Be sure to buy the size of silicone pan liner that fits your pans because they can't be cut to fit.

Cardboard cake rounds, squares, and rectangles

These corrugated cardboard pieces are placed underneath cakes to stabilize and hold them for assembling, decorating, and serving. They're also used under baked tarts for serving and transporting. These pieces come in a variety of precut shapes and sizes. Circles range from 6 to 20 inches in diameter and rectangles are available in 9 x 13 inches, 11 x 15 inches, 13 x 18 inches, 14 x 20 inches, and 18 x 26 inches. Any of these can be cut into squares or other sizes.

Make an attractive serving plate by covering a cardboard cake circle, rectangle, or square with colorful foil, then top it with a paper doily. This really comes in handy when you're taking a dessert on the road because you don't have to worry about forgetting to bring your plate home.

You can always make your own corrugated cake support by tracing the size you need onto a piece of cardboard and cutting it out. Just make sure the cardboard is sturdy enough to hold your dessert.

Foil and paper candy cups

These cups are designed to hold finished truffles and candies. They make the candies look attractive and protect them from fingerprints as they're transported from one place to another. Foil candy cups are made of sturdy colored foil. They're 1 inch wide and ⅝ inch high with fluted edges. They're available in boxes of 40 or 60 in gold, silver, green, and red. Fluted-edge paper candy cups are slightly wider than the foil ones, 1½ inches in diameter. Glassine is the best kind to use because it doesn't absorb oil from the candies, which dries them out. These cups are available in a variety of seasonal patterns and designs and in dark brown. Both types of candy cups are found in cookware and cake-decorating supply shops, catalogs, and online sources.

Candy boxes

Specially designed boxes to hold chocolate truffles and candies come in a variety of shapes, sizes, and colors. White is the most common color, but I like to use ½-pound gold boxes. All I have to do is tie a colored ribbon around the box and it's ready to go. Some candy boxes have a cellophane window on top so you can see what's inside. Candy boxes are available in cake decorating supply stores, catalogs, and online sources.

Storage Tools

Taking good care of your ingredients and finished chocolate desserts is as important as how good the desserts look and taste. And how ingredients and desserts are stored makes a big difference in how they taste.

Plastic containers

I keep a large variety of plastic containers stacked in a cabinet in my kitchen. This makes it easy to find a container when I need it. For small amounts of plain chocolate, whether in a chunk or chopped, I like to store it in a plastic container that seals tightly. It's protected from the air and the tight seal keeps any moisture from building up. I store the container in my pantry and make sure to label and date it so I know what it is without having to open the container every time.

Ganache and truffle cream also store well in airtight plastic containers in the refrigerator or freezer. Shallow airtight plastic containers are the perfect storage container for finished truffles and other chocolate candies. These are best stored with layers of wax paper between them and no more than three layers deep so they don't get crushed.

Chocolate cookies and other chocolate desserts, such as brownies, also keep very well in plastic containers that seal well. These can be kept for several days at room temperature protected from air and moisture. Keep them in a pantry or cabinet so they're also away from light and heat.

Glass containers

I love glass jars of all shapes and sizes and often store ingredients in them. Plain chocolate, truffle creams, chocolate sauces, and ganache all store well in glass jars with tight-sealing lids. Be sure the jars are clean and dry and don't smell like olives or any other strong-flavored foods that they once contained.

Plastic and glass containers can be washed in the dishwasher. It's a good idea to do so to remove any lingering flavors before storing any chocolate in them.

Chapter 3

Choosing Your Chocolate and Other Ingredients Wisely

- -

In This Chapter

▶ Understanding the role ingredients play in chocolate desserts

▶ Having a well stocked pantry

▶ Storing ingredients in optimal conditions

▶ Choosing substitutions in a pinch

- -

My very first attempt at baking was chocolate chip cookies when I was 5 years old. I fell in love with chocolate and baking, and I haven't looked back since. I marched forward into the delectable world of chocolate desserts with full abandon. I've learned a tremendous amount since I was 5 — and I'm still learning.

One of the most important lessons I've learned about chocolate desserts is this: If you start with the best ingredients available, you will end up with the best tasting chocolate dessert, bar none. Honest, true, pure flavors speak for themselves every time. Even a novice can venture into the kitchen and turn out a gourmet-quality dessert if she starts with great ingredients.

Many people are scared off when it comes to making chocolate desserts because they think it's too complicated. Nothing is farther from the truth. However, it is important that you measure accurately when making desserts. Unlike general cooking, dessert recipes are well-balanced formulas. If you start to throw in a bit of this and some of that, you'll soon have an unbalanced formula, and you won't get the results you desire. This means that you need to pay a little closer attention. Also, the more you work with ingredients used in desserts, the better you'll get at making them. Before you know it, you'll be a pro.

This chapter gives you the knowledge you need to understand ingredients, which will enable you to create fantastic chocolate desserts every time you set foot in the kitchen.

Chocolate and Cocoa

Chocolate was given the botanical name *Theobroma Cacao,* which means "food of the gods." Anyone who's a chocolate lover knows how well this name fits. Chocolate is definitely divine.

Types of chocolate

The way in which chocolate is processed and the other ingredients that are mixed with it determine the type of chocolate it will be when it's finished. Chocolate comes in a wide variety of types:

- **Unsweetened chocolate:** This is pure chocolate liquor (nonalcoholic), also called *chocolate mass,* because it is pressed from the roasted cocoa bean. Sometimes cocoa butter is added to the chocolate liquor, but it contains no sugar or other ingredients. The resulting taste is extremely bitter. Unsweetened chocolate is also known as *baking chocolate.*

- **Bittersweet chocolate:** A small amount of sugar is added to chocolate liquor along with vanilla to produce an intensely flavored chocolate known as bittersweet chocolate. Many brands list the amount of cocoa components on the package (56 percent, 62 percent, 70 percent, and so on). The higher the percentage of cocoa components, the more intense the chocolate flavor is, because the rest of the mixture is sugar, cocoa butter, and vanilla. In the United States, the minimum percentage of cocoa components chocolate must contain to be considered bittersweet is 35 percent. Some chocolate manufacturers call their dark, intense chocolates extra-bittersweet.

- **Semisweet chocolate:** This has more sugar than bittersweet and is often used as eating chocolate as well as in desserts and baking. The flavor is slightly milder than bittersweet but also rich and satisfying.

  If you hear someone refer to bittersweet or semisweet chocolate as *dark chocolate,* don't be surprised. *Dark* is the new terminology in the chocolate industry that refers to those chocolates that don't contain milk products, such as unsweetened, bittersweet, and semisweet chocolates. These chocolates are often referred to by their percentage of cocoa components (chocolate liquor and cocoa butter), which is listed on the label.

- **Milk chocolate:** Sugar, milk solids or powder, and cocoa butter are added to chocolate liquor to make milk chocolate. Milk chocolate has much less chocolate liquor than the dark chocolates and as a result, it has less prominent chocolate flavor. In the United States, only 10 percent cocoa solids are required for milk chocolate.

✔ **Dark milk chocolate:** This is a new term that some chocolate manufacturers are using to describe their milk chocolate. It is milk chocolate that has more chocolate liquor, giving it a deeper, more pronounced chocolate flavor with less sweetness than milk chocolate. Also, different types of cocoa beans with more robust flavors are used to produce this type of chocolate.

✔ **White chocolate:** This chocolate contains no chocolate liquor and, as a result, it is an ivory color. White chocolate is a confection made from cocoa butter, sugar, milk solids or powder, and vanilla. It does have a mild chocolate taste because of the cocoa butter.

Watch out for imitation white chocolate that contains no cocoa butter, but another type of fat instead. It won't taste anything like real white chocolate. These imitations are known as *summer coating* or *compound coating.* They're easier to handle than white chocolate because they don't contain cocoa butter, and, therefore, don't need to be tempered, but their taste is generally chalky and dull and their texture is gummy and waxy. Read the label and be sure the white chocolate you buy contains cocoa butter.

✔ **Couverture:** Pronounced koo-vehy-TYOOR, this is chocolate that has a high percentage of added cocoa butter, which gives it a velvety-smooth texture. Any of the types of chocolate can be a couverture. It is used by professionals for thin coatings on truffles and candies and for glazes. It can also be used as baking chocolate.

✔ **Gianduia:** Pronounced john-DO-ya, this is a specialty chocolate that is a blend of dark or milk chocolate with hazelnuts or almonds. It is much softer in texture than plain chocolate. Gianduia is used as a flavor on its own and can be used in the same way as any other chocolate.

Substituting one type of chocolate for another isn't a good idea, because the proportions of a recipe will be thrown out of balance. Milk chocolate and white chocolate have much less body than dark chocolate, so they can't be substituted one for one for dark chocolate, or for each other. However, you can interchange bittersweet and semisweet chocolate for each other without changing the balance of other ingredients in a recipe.

All of the types of chocolate are available in many cookware and specialty shops and through several online and mail-order sources (see Chapter 19 for information on sources).

Which chocolate should you use?

Don't let the huge variety of types of chocolate overwhelm you. When a recipe calls for dark chocolate, you can choose either bittersweet or semisweet, depending on your flavor preference. It also depends on the role of chocolate in the recipe. Will the chocolate be the prominent flavor or will it be a supporting player? What other flavors will be in the dessert with the chocolate? If the chocolate will be the main flavor, then you want to be sure to use a chocolate that has deep, intense flavor. But if the chocolate is one of many flavors, use one that has a subtle flavor.

No chocolate is perfect for each and every dessert. Here are some general guidelines for which type of chocolate to use for different desserts. Taste different chocolates and use those that appeal to you. If it's chocolate, you can't go wrong!

✔ **Unsweetened chocolate** is best for brownies, cookies, and other items that are very sweet. It also blends well with bittersweet and semisweet chocolate to add an extra undertone of depth to the overall chocolate flavor.

✔ **Bittersweet chocolate** is wonderful in desserts with prominent, deep chocolate flavor, such as mousses, ice creams, truffles and

candies, some chocolate cakes, and chocolate tarts. This is where you want the complex flavor of the chocolate to shine through. Many of the single-origin and varietal types of chocolate are best showcased in these desserts.

✔ **Semisweet chocolate** is a good overall choice when you want the pure taste of chocolate to be noticeable. Many chocolate desserts, such as ice cream, cookies, mousses, and custards and sauces are best with this type of chocolate.

✔ **Milk chocolate** has its own particular flavor and blends well with many other flavors, most notably peanut.

✔ **Dark milk chocolate** is a more intense version of milk chocolate and can stand alone in desserts. Try it with various cakes, ice creams, and custards, and in sauces.

✔ **White chocolate** is the sweetest of all the types of chocolate. It has a delicate and subtle chocolate flavor. It's wonderful with fresh fruits and summer berries, especially raspberries. Use it for desserts when you want a delicate, but definitely chocolate flavor, such as mousses, ice creams, and hot chocolate.

Specialty chocolate ingredients

A few special ingredients are available, and you may want to add them to your chocolate dessert pantry:

✔ **Cocoa nibs** are tiny pieces of roasted, cracked cocoa beans that have not yet been ground into chocolate liquor. They have no sugar added, so they are pure, unadulterated chocolate. They may look a little like chocolate chips, but they taste nothing like them. Instead, cocoa nibs taste like unsweetened chocolate. They are on the bitter side with a dry, crunchy texture. Cocoa nibs can be added to a variety of chocolate desserts for extra texture and an extra layer of flavor. Try them in cookies, ice cream, custards, and cakes.

✓ **Pistoles** are flat wafers or disks of chocolate. Some chocolate manufacturers are making their chocolate available in this form. It saves you from having to chop large bars or chunks of chocolate into small pieces, so you can get to your chocolate dessert making quicker. Pistoles can be melted easily, just like chopped chocolate in a double boiler or a microwave oven. They're also handy for nibbling. Use pistoles just as you would any type of chocolate.

✓ **Chocolate extract** looks like vanilla extract except it has a decidedly chocolate flavor. I like to use it when I want to add an extra layer of chocolate flavor to a dessert. Use it in addition to vanilla extract or to replace up to half the amount of vanilla extract called for in chocolate dessert recipes.

✓ **Chocolate chips** are probably the first chocolate ingredient you encountered. Chocolate chips are sweet little morsels of chocolate that were created originally for cookies but have gone on to be included in just about every type of chocolate dessert you can imagine. Chocolate chips are formulated to keep their shape in the intense heat of the oven and, as a result, they won't melt down as completely as chocolate because they have much less cocoa butter. They become muddy and grainy with too much heat. Don't attempt to use chocolate chips in place of pure chocolate. Chocolate chips are available in a variety of sizes and flavors, such as dark, milk, white, and butterscotch. They are found in the baking isle of most grocery stores. Store them in a cool, dry, dark place in a tightly covered container and they will last indefinitely.

Types of cocoa

Cocoa is the other main ingredient (other than chocolate) to come from the cocoa bean. About halfway through the processing of cocoa beans, chocolate and cocoa part ways (see Chapter 1 for more information on cocoa processing). Cocoa powder is unsweetened and pulverized chocolate liquor with most of the fat (cocoa butter) removed. There are two main types of cocoa powder:

✓ **Natural cocoa powder** has a pronounced, slightly bitter chocolate flavor and is light in color. Natural cocoa powder is acidic and is used in baked desserts in combination with baking soda, which neutralizes its acid. Because natural cocoa powder is strongly flavored, bitter, and acidic, it is best used in baked desserts.

> ✔ **Dutch-processed, Dutched, alkalized, or European-style cocoa powder**
> has had alkali added to it during processing to reduce its natural acidity.
> This darkens the color, softens the flavor, and makes the cocoa easier to
> disburse in liquid. Dutch-processed cocoa is a better choice for decorat-
> ing, candies, sauces, creams, ice creams, icings, and other desserts that
> don't require cooking.

Don't confuse natural and Dutch-processed cocoa powder with sweetened
cocoa powder mixes that have sugar, milk powder, and other added flavorings. Sweetened cocoa powder is what you use when you want to make a cup
of hot chocolate for drinking.

Store cocoa powder in a tightly sealed container in a cool, dark, dry place.
Stored properly, cocoa powder will last indefinitely.

Other Dry Ingredients

Dry ingredients have no fat or liquid. Many staples of the baking pantry are
included in this group, including leavening agents, such as baking powder,
baking soda, and cream of tartar, and flour, sugar, and salt.

Baking powder

Baking powder is the leavening agent used most often in desserts. It is sold in
a round, strong container with a tight-fitting plastic lid. It is composed of two
parts of a baking acid, usually cream of tartar, and one part baking soda. A
small amount of cornstarch is also added to keep the mixture from caking.
Double-acting baking powder is the most common type available. It reacts
first when it's mixed with liquid ingredients and again when it's heated. Store
baking powder in a cool, dark, dry place. It's perishable, so be sure to check
the date on the bottom of the can.

If you're out of baking powder, you can come reasonably close to creating
your own. Here are three methods for creating leavening agents that approximate the rising power of baking powder:

> ✔ Mix together two parts cream of tartar and one part baking soda. This
> doesn't store well, so be sure to use it immediately.

> ✔ Combine ½ teaspoon cream of tartar and ¼ teaspoon baking soda.

> ✔ Blend 2 tablespoons cream of tartar, 1 tablespoon baking soda, and 1½
> tablespoons cornstarch.

To check whether your baking powder is still good, mix 1 teaspoon baking powder with ½ cup hot water. If it bubbles vigorously, the baking powder will still be effective.

Baking soda

Baking soda is also called bicarbonate of soda. Like baking powder, it is used frequently as a leavening agent in desserts. Baking soda reacts instantly when mixed with liquid, so be sure to mix it with dry ingredients first. After it is activated, it starts to make carbon dioxide bubbles, which start the rising process. Because of this, any batter mixed with baking soda should be baked immediately.

Baking soda is used in batters that contain an acid ingredient, such as chocolate, buttermilk, molasses, and sour cream. It releases more carbon dioxide when it comes in contact with the acid. This creates more bubbles, which neutralizes the acid, and produces a more tender mixture. The standard amount of baking soda per cup of flour is ¼ teaspoon. Store baking powder in a cool place. It lasts up to a year, so be sure to check the date on the box.

 To test if baking soda is still potent, mix 1 teaspoon of baking soda with 1 teaspoon of vinegar. If it's still good, it should bubble energetically.

Cream of tartar

Cream of tartar is the crystallized sediment left in wine barrels after fermentation. It is refined and becomes a white powder that is sold in small jars in the spice section of supermarkets and specialty food shops. Cream of tartar is used to stabilize egg whites while whipping so they reach maximum volume. It's also used to keep sugar syrups from crystallizing as they cook. Cream of tartar is occasionally used as a leavening agent, and it's one of the main ingredients in baking powder. Store it in a cool, dry place.

Flour

Flour is one of the main ingredients in many dessert recipes. It provides structure and texture and serves to bind ingredients together. Flour is made from a variety of grains, but the most common type of flour is made from wheat. Knowing which flour to choose when you go to the grocery store can be confusing, because there is a very large variety to choose from. All-purpose flour and cake flour are used for the recipes in this book. The main difference between these two types of flour is the amount of protein, or *gluten,* they contain. The more protein that flour contains, the stronger the flour is, and the stronger the flour is, the less tender the baked goods will be. That's why bread flour isn't a good choice for making desserts. It has the most amount of protein of any flour, which is great for bread, but not for dessert.

All-purpose flour is a blend of both hard and soft wheat. This produces a medium texture with the right balance for most desserts. All-purpose flour has a gluten content of approximately 12 percent. You can substitute bleached and unbleached all-purpose flour for each other without any noticeable difference. Bleached flour has had all the nutrients bleached out of it to produce flour that is white. Unbleached flour is an off-white color. All-purpose flour is readily available in grocery stores in 2–, 5–, and 10-pound bags.

Cake flour is made from soft wheat. It has a low gluten content of about 9 percent. Cake flour is used when a delicate texture is desired in desserts. It is available in 2-pound boxes in many grocery stores. Don't buy self-rising flour, because it contains a rising agent. All the recipes in this book state the amount of leavening to use, if it's called for. If you add leavening to self-rising flour it will cause the dessert to rise too much, which will make it fall before it finishes baking — not a desired result!

If a recipe calls for cake flour, but you don't have any on hand, here's an easy way to approximate it: Use 1 cup of all-purpose flour minus 2 tablespoons for every cup of cake flour called for. To use cake flour in place of all-purpose flour, substitute 1 cup plus 2 tablespoons cake flour for every cup of all-purpose flour called for. This gives the cake flour the approximate amount of gluten as in all-purpose flour, so your recipe will have the same approximate finished texture.

Store flour at room temperature in a tightly sealed container for no more than 6 months. However, if you don't use your flour in that amount of time, store it in the refrigerator or freeze it for up to 2 years. Just be sure to label it and date it so you'll know what's in the container. Be sure to use up the old flour before adding a fresh batch to the container.

It's not really necessary to sift flour before using it, because it's been sifted many times during processing. But sifting does aerate flour and give it more volume. Pay attention to the instructions in each recipe. If a recipe calls for "flour, sifted," then sift the flour after measuring. If a recipe calls for "sifted flour," sift the flour first and then measure it.

Nuts

Nuts add unique flavor and texture to chocolate desserts, pastries, and confections. The flavor of most nuts works very well with chocolate to enhance both ingredients. Some combinations of nuts and chocolate are sublime, like gianduia, which is usually made with hazelnuts. Nuts are also used as decoration for many desserts, pastries, and confections. All nuts have a high natural oil content. Because of this, they should be stored in the freezer for no longer than a year, whatever their form. Label and date each container of nuts so you know how long they've been in the freezer and can use up the older ones first. Nuts that are especially good with chocolate are almonds, cashews, hazelnuts, macadamia nuts, peanuts, pecans, pine nuts, pistachio nuts, and walnuts.

Rotate your stock of nuts frequently. Be sure to label and date any new nuts you buy so you'll know what you have and how long it's been around. Use the ones that you've had the longest first.

Be sure to buy unsalted nuts for making desserts. Too much added salt in a recipe will make it unpalatable.

Any nut can be ground into a thick paste similar in consistency to peanut butter. These nut pastes are an intriguing way to include nuts in recipes because their consistency is thick and smooth, a cross between liquid and solid ingredients. This adds both flavor and unusual texture to a recipe.

Salt

Salt's main function is to enhance other flavors and add depth to the flavor of the overall dessert. Don't leave salt out of a recipe, because it won't taste the same without it, and don't use more than what the recipe calls for, because too much salt will be noticeable (and not in a good way).

Three types of salt are used in making desserts and they can be used interchangeably. Iodized table salt is fine grained and flows freely because it has additives that prevent it from clumping. This is the most common form of salt. Kosher salt is coarser than table salt, but it's actually less salty. It has no additives. Sea salt is available in crystals that vary from very fine to coarse. It's not as salty as table salt and is very flavorful. It is often used in a salt grinder. Sea salt has no additives so it should be stored airtight to prevent clumping.

Salt has an indefinite shelf life if stored in a cool, dry place. It is readily available in supermarkets, health food stores, and specialty food shops.

In humid weather, salt has a tendency to stick together. To prevent this, place a few grains of rice in your salt shaker.

Sugar

Sugar is one of the main ingredients in most chocolate desserts. It has several roles: Sugar provides sweetness, flavor, tenderness, texture, stability, moisture, and color due to caramelization, to many desserts, pastries, candies, and confections.

Stock your pantry with the following types of sugar so you'll be ready to make chocolate desserts whenever the mood strikes you:

- **Granulated sugar** is the most common form of sugar used in baking, and it's readily available in grocery stores. Granulated sugar is highly refined into tiny white grains from either sugar cane or sugar beets. It's virtually impossible to tell the difference between the two in taste and texture. Granulated sugar is available in boxes and bags and also comes in cubes. For dessert making, it's best not to use cubes, unless you want to crush them into fine particles.

- **Superfine sugar** is a more finely granulated form of sugar. It dissolves very easily and leaves no trace of grittiness. For this reason, it is often used with fresh fruit, frostings, and in liquids. Superfine and granulated sugar can be interchanged for each other.

    If you don't have superfine sugar on hand, you can easily make your own. Place regular granulated sugar in the work bowl of a food processor fitted with a steel blade or in a blender, and process for 30 seconds to 1 minute.

- **Confectioners' sugar** is also called *powdered sugar*. This is granulated sugar that is pulverized to a fine powder and mixed with a small amount of cornstarch so it won't cake during storage. Confectioners' sugar always needs to be sifted before use. It dissolves easily and is used in icings, frostings, and for decorating.

- **Brown sugar** is white sugar with molasses added. This gives the sugar its distinct flavor and a soft, moist texture. Dark brown sugar has more molasses than light brown sugar and as a result, a more assertive, deep flavor. Light brown sugar is used more often, but dark brown sugar can be used in its place. Brown sugar easily becomes hard when exposed to air. For an accurate measure, pack brown sugar tightly to eliminate the air.

    If you're out of light brown sugar, you can easily make a substitute. For each cup of light brown sugar that the recipe calls for, mix ½ cup dark brown sugar and ½ cup granulated sugar. Another substitute is to mix 1 cup granulated sugar with 3 tablespoons of molasses, which gives you the equivalent of 1 cup of light brown sugar.

    If your brown sugar has hardened, you can soften it in a microwave oven on low power for 15-second intervals.

All of these varieties of sugar are readily available at supermarkets. Store sugar in an airtight container at room temperature in a cool, dry place and it will last indefinitely. If you store sugar in its original container you may be inviting unwelcome critters to visit.

Don't try to use sugar substitutes in making chocolate desserts. They are several times sweeter than sugar and have a completely different texture. Sugar substitutes don't react well when heated. If you attempt to use a sugar substitute you will most likely have a disaster on your hands. And who needs that?

Dairy

Dairy products provide moisture, flavor, and tenderness to desserts. They are highly perishable and must be stored in the refrigerator. Check the date on the carton or wrapper and don't use them beyond this date.

Milk

Two milk products — fresh milk and buttermilk — are used most often in making chocolate desserts. *Fresh milk* refers to cow's milk. You can use whole milk, 2 percent, or 1 percent with success in any of the recipes in this book. Don't use skim milk, however — it's too thin and won't provide the correct consistency.

If you don't use fresh milk regularly but still want to have some on hand for making chocolate desserts, check out the baking section of your local grocery store for boxed milk. It can be stored in the pantry for several months without spoiling. After it's opened, it needs to be stored in the refrigerator.

Buttermilk was once made from the liquid left over after churning butter. Today, buttermilk is fermented by adding special bacterial cultures to skim milk. Buttermilk has a tangy flavor and slightly thicker texture than milk.

If you don't want to keep fresh buttermilk around you can buy packages of dried buttermilk to keep in the pantry. Just add water and voilá! You have buttermilk whenever you need it. In a pinch you can also make a decent substitute for buttermilk by adding a tablespoon of lemon juice to 1 cup of milk and letting it sit for 3 minutes before using it.

Cream

Cream is the fat part of milk that rises to the top. There are a variety of types of cream defined by the amount of butterfat they contain. All cream is highly perishable and must be kept refrigerated. Be sure to check the date on the carton and don't use it past then. Also, give cream the sniff test to see if it smells fresh.

Most cream available in grocery stores has been ultra-pasteurized, which is a process of heating it to 300 degrees to kill any bacteria that will cause the cream to sour. Sometimes this process interferes with the cream's ability to whip to full volume. Check the dairy section of health-food stores for cream that has not undergone this process.

- ✔ **Whipping cream**, also called light whipping cream, is between 30 and 36 percent butterfat. This is widely available in the dairy section of grocery stores.

- ✔ **Heavy cream**, also called heavy whipping cream, contains at least 35 percent butterfat. In some brands, the butterfat is as high as 40 percent. In most cases, I prefer using heavy cream because of its richness.

- ✔ **Light whipping cream**, also called table cream, is between 18 and 30 percent butterfat. This is used for some sauces but doesn't have enough body to whip and hold its shape. It can be substituted for whole milk and for half-and-half.

- ✔ **Half-and-half** is a blend of half cream and half milk that has been homogenized so it won't separate. It contains about 10 percent butterfat. Half-and-half doesn't whip because it doesn't have enough body, but it is useful in making custards and ice creams.

Butter

Butter adds flavor, richness, texture, and moisture to chocolate desserts. There is no substitute for butter because nothing tastes quite the same. Any dessert made with butter tastes better than one made with another fat. Different brands of butter contain varying amounts of water and salt. The softer butter is when chilled, the more water it contains.

Always use unsalted butter for chocolate desserts. It has a fresher and more delicate flavor than salted butter. Plus, by using unsalted butter, you can determine the amount of salt that goes into your recipes.

Butter is available in ¼-pound sticks and in 1-pound solid bars. Use whichever you prefer. If you buy butter in 1-pound solid bars, you will need to use a kitchen scale to measure the amount you need for each recipe.

Don't use whipped butter for making chocolate desserts. It has a lot of air beaten into it and won't give the same results as pure butter.

Butter easily picks up other flavors, so be careful where you store it in the refrigerator and make sure to wrap it tightly in plastic wrap and aluminum foil. Keeping it in the butter compartment of the refrigerator is a great way to go. Butter also freezes very well and can be stored in the freezer for up to a year. Be sure to label and date it and use the butter first that has been in the freezer longest.

If butter is very cold, let it stand at room temperature to soften or soften it in a microwave oven on low power for 15-second intervals until it reaches the consistency you need. Softened butter should be pliable but still hold its shape. If it's oily and liquid, it's too soft.

Butter can go rancid easily. If you detect any off odor or taste in butter, don't use it.

Cream cheese

Cream cheese has a mildly acidic flavor and a smooth, spreadable texture. It adds tenderness to dough. In some cases, it's mixed with butter to create a delicate dough. Full-fat cream cheese is the type most recipes call for, but lowfat cream cheese can generally be used with good results. Cream cheese is found in the dairy case of supermarkets and specialty food shops. It comes in 3-ounce and 8-ounce packages. Store it tightly covered in the refrigerator and use it by the date on the carton. Soften it to room temperature before using.

If a recipe calls for cream cheese, don't use whipped cream cheese because it has air whipped into it and will change the consistency of the dessert you use it in.

Sour cream

Thick and fluffy sour cream is made by adding an acidifier to cream and letting it stand for several hours until the cream curdles. This is what gives sour cream its characteristic tangy flavor. Sour cream provides tenderness to dough. It is available in the dairy section of supermarkets and food shops. It has a relatively short shelf life so be sure to check the date on the carton and use it by that date. You can use reduced-fat sour cream in place of full fat, but I don't advise using the nonfat type because it doesn't have the same texture as regular sour cream and will alter the consistency of the dessert you use it in.

Oils

Like butter, oils add fat, flavor, tenderness, and moisture to chocolate desserts, pastries, and confections. The oils used are derived from vegetables, seeds, and fruits. Using oils that don't have pronounced flavor is best; that way, the other ingredients in the recipe won't be overpowered. The oils used most often in making chocolate desserts are canola, peanut, and safflower. Store all oil that's unopened at room temperature for several months. After it's opened, store oil tightly capped in the refrigerator. The oil may become cloudy during refrigeration but will become clear when it reaches room temperature.

Don't try to substitute oil for butter in a recipe unless you're looking for trouble. Because oil is liquid, it acts differently than butter, which is a solid. The result will be much different than you expect.

Oil can go rancid if stored improperly. Oil that smells musty or has a stale taste should be discarded.

Eggs

Eggs are one of the most important ingredients in making desserts. They add flavor, tenderness, richness, and color; they thicken, help leaven, and bind ingredients together. That's a lot for such a small package! Eggs are used both whole and separated into egg yolks and egg whites for making chocolate desserts.

Whole eggs

Buy eggs as fresh as possible and use them by the date on the carton. Check each egg to make sure it's not cracked or dirty. Store eggs in their carton with the pointed ends down in the refrigerator, not on the refrigerator door, which is too warm and will cause them to deteriorate quickly.

To test if eggs are fresh, float one in a bowl of cool water. If the egg is fresh, it will sink to the bottom. If it's old, it will float to the top because the air pocket inside the eggshell increases as eggs age. If your eggs are old, discard them and buy fresh eggs.

Eggs come in different sizes, determined by their weight, such as jumbo, extra-large, large, medium, and small. All the recipes in this book use large eggs. It's not a good idea to swap the size of eggs in a recipe because the proportion of other ingredients will be changed. Always use the size eggs specified in a recipe. For eggs to blend well with other ingredients and to reach their full volume when whipped they need to be at room temperature. Plan ahead when making desserts and take them out of the refrigerator so they have enough time to warm up.

TIP

You can't freeze whole eggs in their shell, but they can be frozen if lightly beaten with a pinch of either salt or sugar for each egg. You can also freeze egg yolks with this same method.

CAUTION!

Don't use egg substitutes for making any desserts. They are composed of about 80 percent egg whites and don't contain any egg yolks. They may contain other ingredients as well, such as tofu, nonfat milk, and vegetable oil. As a result, this product won't react the same way as whole eggs in baking or dessert making.

Egg whites

Some recipes call for egg whites or for extra egg whites. Besides fresh eggs there are a couple of other ways you can find egg whites.

Liquid fresh egg whites

Liquid fresh egg whites are 100-percent-pure, fresh liquid eggs that have been pasteurized and checked for salmonella. They have no preservatives, colorings, or gums, and they will last up to 4 months in the refrigerator. They can also be frozen. You can find these in the refrigerator section of many supermarkets and health-food stores. The only drawback to this product is that, because the egg whites have been pasteurized, their ability to hold air changes and they can't be whipped. However, if you search around you may be able to find a new product of pasteurized egg whites that can be whipped.

Dried egg whites

If you feel that keeping egg whites in the freezer is a lot of trouble, you can use dried egg whites. This product comes in powder form and can be found in a sealed can in the baking aisle of many supermarkets. Using dried egg whites is easy. You just mix them with water, following the instructions on the can, to make the equivalent of an egg white. Dried egg whites have an unlimited shelf life if stored tightly sealed in a cool, dry place.

Egg whites freeze very well and are as good as fresh when defrosted and brought to room temperature. Freeze egg whites in ice cube trays. Each cube is one egg white. After they're frozen you can transfer them to another container, then defrost as many as you need at a time. This makes it easy to know how many egg whites you have in the freezer. Another way to determine the number of egg whites is to measure them in a liquid measuring cup. One-half cup is equal to three large egg whites.

After egg whites have been defrosted, they can't be frozen again. That's too inviting to bacteria.

Flavorings

Flavorings add extra depth to chocolate desserts. Often it's that little something extra that creates unique flavor in a chocolate dessert. Extracts, spices, and instant espresso powder are great to have on hand in the pantry so you can be creative when making chocolate desserts.

Extracts

Extracts are highly concentrated flavorings obtained by a process of either distillation or infusion from various foods such as fruits, flowers, and herbs. These solutions are then diluted with alcohol. Vanilla is the most popular extract and the one most commonly used to make desserts. Almond, orange, and lemon are also used in desserts. Be sure to use pure extracts, not synthetic, for a pure flavor. Because extracts are so concentrated, only a small amount is needed. Extracts enhance and round out other flavors. Store them tightly capped to prevent alcohol evaporation, in a cool, dark, dry place. If stored properly they have an indefinite shelf life.

Vanilla beans

Vanilla beans are the pod of a climbing orchid plant that is native to southern Mexico. Vanilla is grown in tropical regions around the world. Where it is grown has a big influence on the taste of the vanilla pod. The other important factors that contribute to vanilla's taste are the type of vanilla it is and how it's processed. After the pods are harvested, they go through an intense drying and curing process that brings out their flavor. Tiny white crystals form on the outside of the pods and the seeds inside become very black. It is these tiny seeds that hold the essence of vanilla flavor. The pods are split open and the seeds are removed when making desserts. The seeds are steeped in alcohol to make vanilla extract.

These are the types of vanilla beans grown:

- **Bourbon vanilla** is the largest variety grown, available, and used. Madagascar and the island of Reunion, off the African coast, are the world's biggest producers of Bourbon vanilla beans. This vanilla is the slimmest type of bean grown. It imparts a rich, smooth, deep flavor.

- **Tahitian vanilla** is grown only in Tahiti. It is intensely floral in both aroma and flavor, but more delicate overall than the other types of vanilla. The beans are shorter and plumper than Bourbon vanilla beans.

- **Indonesian vanilla** is grown only in one location. It has a smoky, earthy quality because of the way it is cured. Indonesian vanilla is the second most available type.

- **Mexican vanilla** is the most robustly flavored of all the types of vanilla. It is also the most difficult type of vanilla to find because it is grown in very limited quantities. Most of this type of vanilla never makes it out of Mexico.

Vanilla beans should be plump, slightly greasy or oily, and flexible. If the beans are dry, they won't have much flavor. Store vanilla beans tightly sealed in plastic wrap or in a glass jar. If exposed to the air, they will dry out and lose their flavor.

After using a vanilla bean, let it dry, then store it in a canister of sugar where it will continue to lend its particular scent to the sugar. Use this sugar for dessert making to add an extra layer of vanilla flavor.

Vanilla blends beautifully with and enhances the flavor of chocolate in the same way salt is used in general cooking. Most chocolate recipes contain vanilla.

Spices

Spices come from a variety of plants grown in tropical regions around the world. They are the fruit, seeds, berries, bark, buds, or the dried roots of these plants. Each spice has a particular flavor and aroma that it imparts to desserts. Ground spices have a short shelf life because when they are ground their oils begin to evaporate. It's these oils that give the spices their flavor. Either grind your spices fresh for each use or buy very small quantities of ground spices that you will use quickly. Discard any ground spices that are over 6 months old. Spices are best stored in tightly sealed glass containers in a cool, dry place, away from the heat of the stove. Label and date your spices so you know how long you've had them. Grind whole spices in a spice grinder or a clean coffee grinder, or use a mortar and pestle to crush them. For whole nutmegs use either a nutmeg grinder or grater.

To remove the aroma of spices from a coffee grinder, grind up some fresh bread. This will absorb any lingering aromas.

Instant espresso powder

Using instant espresso powder is a great way to add deep coffee flavor and color to desserts without adding much extra liquid. Dissolve 1 teaspoon instant espresso powder in 1 teaspoon warm water and add to the other ingredients. Instant espresso powder is available in the coffee section of many supermarkets. Store it in a cool, dry place to prevent caking.

Part II
Foolproof Methods

The 5th Wave   By Rich Tennant

"We're making hand-formed cookies, why?"

In this part . . .

Making chocolate desserts easily and efficiently means using the right methods. Measuring ingredients, using thermometers, and knowing different mixing techniques are core methods that every chocolate dessert maker needs to know. Handling and working with ingredients like eggs, nuts, and chocolate are tasks that you'll need to be familiar with as you make the recipes in this book, so I fill you in on everything you need to know. Storing, melting, and tempering chocolate, as well as dipping, molding, and decorating are all covered in this part as well. Perfecting a technique can take a little time, but when your guests say, "It's the best I've ever eaten," I can assure you they will mean it.

Chapter 4

Techniques for Great Chocolate Desserts Every Time

In This Chapter

▶ Measuring ingredients for accuracy

▶ Using pastry bags

▶ Working with eggs

▶ Handling nuts

▶ Mastering mixing

You've probably heard the saying, "It's all in the technique." When it comes to making chocolate desserts, these words hold true. The good news: Most of the techniques used to make chocolate desserts are very easy. And you may have already had some experience with some of them. Flip back to this chapter as often as you need to as you work through the recipes in this book.

Measuring

Correct measuring will go a long way toward making your chocolate desserts great. Desserts are carefully developed formulas. If you get creative with what you add to the mix, the formula quickly becomes unbalanced and you may wind up with a disappointment on your hands instead of what you expected. The best way to prevent this from happening is to pay attention to the quantities called for in a recipe, use correct measuring techniques, and follow the instructions carefully.

Sifting flour and other dry ingredients

If a recipe calls for *sifted flour,* sift the flour and then measure. If it calls for *flour, sifted,* measure the flour first and then sift it. Be sure to follow the instructions in each recipe. Sifting flour adds air to it, so it will measure more after it's sifted. This may sound like semantics, but there will be a difference in the quantity — and that will affect the way the recipe turns out.

You can sift flour with a traditional hand-cranked sifter or you can push it through a drum sieve. If you don't have a sifter, use a fine-mesh strainer. This is the method I prefer because it's quick and easy. Place a piece of waxed paper under the strainer to catch the sifted ingredients.

How to Sift Flour If You Don't Have a Sifter

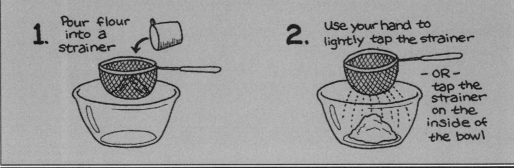

1. Pour flour into a strainer

2. Use your hand to lightly tap the strainer
   — OR — tap the strainer on the inside of the bowl

Dry ingredients

Flour, sugar, confectioners' sugar, and other dry ingredients need to be measured in cups designed for this purpose that can be filled to the top (see Chapter 2). There are two main methods for measuring dry ingredients: the scoop-and-sweep method and the spoon-and-sweep method.

The scoop-and-sweep method of measuring involves scooping the measuring cup into the dry ingredient and then sweeping off the excess amount with a flat implement, such as the back of a knife or a spatula. This method is quick and easy. Use the scoop and sweep method for measuring ingredients in measuring spoons. Baking soda, baking powder, spices, and small amounts of ingredients are easy to measure with this method. Many of their containers have a flat edge near the opening for leveling off the measuring spoon.

The spoon-and-sweep method of measuring involves spooning the dry ingredient into the measuring cup and sweeping off the excess at the top with a flat implement. This method tends to add air to the ingredients, and it takes a little longer than the scoop and sweep method (covered in the preceding section).

Brown sugar needs to be packed into the measuring cup to eliminate the air that is trapped between its crystals. This method gives an accurate measure.

Liquid ingredients

Measure liquid ingredients in liquid measuring cups (see Chapter 2). Pour the ingredient into the cup until it reaches the desired level. For accuracy, place the measuring cup on a flat surface and read it at eye level. Pour out any of the ingredient that's over the amount called for in the recipe.

A new type of liquid measuring cup allows you to read the ingredients from above because the lines that mark off the various measurement amounts are slanted. If you have trouble bending over, you may want to try this tool.

Reading Thermometers

I can't state strongly enough the importance of accuracy when you're making chocolate desserts. No one wants to spend time, energy, and ingredients on a dessert that doesn't work out. When cooking sugar mixtures, tempering chocolate, and baking, paying close attention to the temperatures is crucial. Each of these activities has a thermometer that's been specifically designed for that purpose.

Candy thermometer

When you're working with a candy thermometer, make sure the bulb of the candy thermometer is immersed in the sugar mixture. If you have a light over the burners on your stovetop, it helps to have it on while reading the candy thermometer. Tilt the thermometer so you can see the level of the mercury easily. Read the temperature at eye level (see Figure 4-1).

Watch out for steam that rises from the pan of sugar while you try to read the sugar thermometer.

Sugar can change temperature extremely quickly. After you determine that the sugar is at the exact temperature you want, remove the pan from the heat and use it immediately.

Figure 4-1:
Reading
thermo-
meters.

Chocolate thermometer

As with a candy thermometer, the best way to obtain an accurate reading of the temperature of chocolate is to bury the bulb of the thermometer in the center of the bowl or pool of chocolate. This thermometer registers the heat quickly and, because the lines and numbers are easy to read, you can readily see the temperature. Being able to read the temperature easily is important, because 1 or 2 degrees can make a big difference in how chocolate behaves. Tilt the thermometer to a point that it's comfortable for you to see where the mercury is and read it at eye level (refer to Figure 4-1).

Keep a paper towel handy so you can wipe off the bulb of the chocolate thermometer after lifting it out of the bowl or pool of chocolate. If a crust of dried chocolate builds up on the end of the bulb, the thermometer won't be able to take an accurate reading of the chocolate's temperature.

Oven thermometer

Hang your oven thermometer from the center rack of your oven. This will suspend it into the center of your oven and give a true reading of the oven's temperature. As with other thermometers, read the oven thermometer at eye level for a true reading (refer to Figure 4-1).

You may want to move the oven thermometer around periodically to different parts of your oven to check to see if you have any hot or cold spots. Being acquainted with your oven will save you from having any baking disasters.

Using Your Kitchen Scale

If your kitchen scale is a mechanical one, become familiar with how it works and know how to set it to zero. You want to be able to set it to zero when adding a new ingredient to a bowl that already contains other ingredients. Mechanical scales have a platform to hold any type of container you want to use. Adjust the scale to zero after placing the container on the platform, then weigh the ingredients. Reading the numbers on the dial that show the weight is easy. An electronic scale gives a digital readout of the weight of the ingredients. The numbers are usually large and easy to read.

Using Pastry Bags

Pastry bags make life in the chocolate kitchen a snap. They're invaluable for piping out truffle creams, cookie batters, custards, and sauces; for filling cups and other containers with various mixtures; for shaping meringues; and for decorating cakes and other desserts.

Cloth pastry bags

When you buy a new pastry bag, you need to cut off about ½ inch at the pointed end for the pastry tip to fit through (see Figure 4-2). A good way to measure is to drop the pastry tube into the bag, then take a pencil and mark where to make the cut. Back the tube out of the pastry bag and use scissors to make a clean cut over the pencil mark.

Cut only enough off the tip of a pastry bag to fit the smallest tube you plan to use with it. If too much is cut off, the pastry tube may slide out the opening or it may fall out when pressure is applied to the pastry bag. This makes the bag useless and it will have to be discarded.

You can also use a *coupler,* a two-piece cylindrical plastic device with threads in the center that's used to attach a pastry tip to a pastry bag. Its wide top keeps it from falling out of the bag while the bottom protrudes from the tip of the bag. The pastry tip is placed onto the bottom of the coupler and a plastic ring with inside threads fitted over the tip is secured by twisting it so that it holds onto the other half of the coupler.

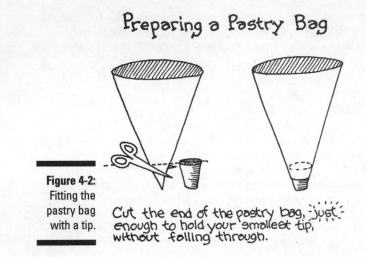

Preparing a Pastry Bag

Figure 4-2:
Fitting the
pastry bag
with a tip.

Cut the end of the pastry bag, just enough to hold your smallest tip, without falling through.

Follow these steps to fill a pastry bag:

1. **Stand the pastry bag in a tall glass, measuring cup, or jar.**

2. **Fold the top edge of the pastry bag out and down a few inches to form a cuff.**

3. **Use a rubber spatula to transfer the filling to the bag, making sure to fill it no more than halfway.**

4. **Unfold the cuff over the filling.**

5. **Holding the pastry bag by the top end, push the filling down in the direction of the tip.**

6. **Twist the pastry bag tightly at the point where the filling ends. Hold the pastry bag between your thumb and forefinger to secure the filling.**

7. **Squeeze a little of the filling back into the bowl to release any air caught in the bag.**

8. **To refill the bag, fold the cuff down and repeat the process.**

To use a pastry bag, hold it about 1 inch above the surface at a slight angle. Apply even pressure with the palm and fingers of the hand holding the bag. Use the fingers of your other hand to steady the bag and help guide it. To stop the filling from coming out of the bag, stop applying pressure with your hand.

To pipe fillings and mounds, hold the pastry bag straight up and down and apply pressure to force the filling out of the bag. Practice piping with a pastry bag to make sure you feel comfortable holding and working with it. Place a piece of waxed paper on a flat work surface to catch the piping.

Paper pastry cones

Paper pastry cones can do the same jobs as pastry bags made from other materials. In addition, they are perfect for piping chocolate to write messages or make fine-line designs. Pastry cones made from parchment paper are disposable. This makes cleanup a breeze. You can buy pre-cut parchment paper triangles or you can cut them yourself from a rectangle or square of parchment. Be sure to cut a triangle with two equal sides and a larger base.

Here's how to form a cone from a parchment paper triangle (see Figure 4-3 for an illustration):

1. **Hold the triangle in front of you with the top point facing down.**

2. **Take the right corner and curve it in, bringing the point down to meet the bottom point.**

3. **Hold the two ends together with your hand. With your other hand, wrap the left point of the triangle around the outside and bring the point down to meet the other points, forming a cone.**

4. **Use a piece of clear tape to secure the back seam and fold the top edges in twice, about ¼ inch each to make the top edge even.**

To fill the paper pastry cone, stand it in a glass, measuring cup, or jar. Pour or place the filling into the pastry cone, filling it no more than halfway. Fold in each side of the top to the center and roll the top down until it meets the filling. Use a pair of scissors to snip off a small opening (about ¼ inch) at the pointed end.

Hold the pastry cone between your thumb and fingers and use the pressure from your fingers to push the filling out the pointed end. Hold the pastry cone about 1 inch above the surface and apply even pressure to release the filling (see Figure 4-4). To stop the flow of the filling, release the pressure on the pastry cone.

Making a Paper Cone for Decorating

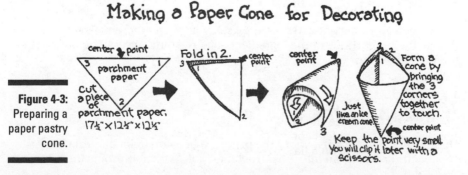

Figure 4-3: Preparing a paper pastry cone.

PIPING AND FILLING SANDWICH COOKIES WITH A PASTRY BAG

1. TO PIPE COOKIES HOLD THE PASTRY BAG ABOUT AN INCH ABOVE THE SURFACE AT AN ANGLE AND APPLY EVEN PRESSURE.

HOLD BAG AT A 45° ANGLE.

2. MOVE THE PASTRY BAG TOWARDS YOU TO FORM A FINGER SHAPE. TO STOP FILLING FROM COMING OUT OF THE BAG, STOP THE PRESSURE FROM YOUR HAND.

3. TO PIPE A MOUND, HOLD THE PASTRY BAG ABOVE THE SURFACE AND KEEP IT STEADY WHILE APPLYING PRESSURE. RELEASE PRESSURE TO STOP FLOW AND PULL BAG AWAY FROM MOUND.

1. TO FILL COOKIES, HOLD BAG STRAIGHT UP AND DOWN. ABOUT AN INCH ABOVE THE SURFACE OF THE COOKIE.

2. HOLD THE BAG STEADY AND APPLY EVEN PRESSURE WITH YOUR HAND TO PUSH OUT THE FILLING ONTO THE COOKIE.

STEADY!

3. RELEASE THE PRESSURE OF YOUR HAND TO STOP THE FILLING FROM FLOWING FROM THE BAG.

Figure 4-4:
Using a paper pastry cone.

To make a disposable plastic pastry bag to pipe out small quantities of an ingredient you can use a plastic bag that zips closed. Cut a small opening in one of the pointed corners of the bag and squeeze the ingredient through this.

Working with Eggs

Eggs are one of the main ingredients used in many chocolate desserts. To get the most out of them, you want to make sure to handle them carefully and correctly. This section covers the techniques you'll need to employ when using eggs.

All the recipes in this book use large eggs. If you use a different size, it will change the proportions of the ingredients and the outcome will be different — and not in a good way.

Handling eggs

There is ongoing concern about the presence of Salmonella bacteria in eggs. This bacteria causes an intestinal tract infection, with symptoms including nausea, vomiting, stomach pain, headache, fever, chills, and diarrhea — not very pleasant. The good news is that salmonella can be treated with antibiotics and has rarely caused death. Very few cases of salmonella have been reported, but knowing the symptoms is a good thing. Follow these precautions in handling eggs and you won't have any problems with salmonella:

- ✔ **Always buy fresh eggs in small quantities that will be used up quickly.**

- ✔ **Keep eggs refrigerated in the coldest part of the refrigerator.** Salmonella grows in the range of 40 to 160 degrees, so you want to store your eggs where the temperature is below 40 degrees. This means storing them towards the back of the refrigerator and not on the door.

- ✔ **Don't use eggs with cracked shells.**

- ✔ **Don't allow eggs to stand at room temperature for more than 2 hours.**

- ✔ **Always wash your hands with warm, soapy before and after handling raw eggs.**

- ✔ **Wash any bowls or utensils that come in contact with raw eggs.**

Check the expiration date on the carton of eggs before you buy them and be sure to use them by this date.

Some recipes in this book use raw eggs. Pregnant and lactating women should be cautious about eating raw eggs, but other people shouldn't have any problems as long as you follow the above instructions on handling eggs.

Adding eggs to a batter or other mixture

Always follow the recipe for when to add eggs to a batter or mixture. *When you add the eggs is as important as the balance of ingredients in the recipe.* If you add the eggs at a different time than what the recipe calls for, your dessert may end up with a completely different texture than planned.

Keep eggs at room temperature before adding to a mixture (but for no more than 2 hours). If the eggs are too cold, they may not blend well and won't have their full ability to help the mixture rise as it bakes.

Here are some tips for adding eggs to batter or other mixtures:

- ✔ **When eggs are added to a butter and sugar mixture, continue mixing and add the dry ingredients, even though the mixture looks curdled.** Continual mixing and the addition of the dry ingredients will smooth out the mixture.

> ✔ **When eggs are added to a creamed butter and sugar mixture, use a rubber spatula to scrape down the sides of the bowl, instead of letting them sit on top of the mixture.** This will help the eggs, butter, and sugar mix together smoothly.
>
> ✔ **Always crack an egg into a separate bowl before adding it to the bowl that contains a batter or mixture.** This technique keeps any spoiled eggs from tainting the mixture. If you crack eggs directly into the mixing bowl, the shells may splinter and scatter into the mixture.

To prevent shell fragments from tainting a mixture, don't crack eggs on the rim of the mixing bowl.

Separating eggs

Many recipes call for eggs to be separated into their two distinct parts of whites and yolks. This is so they can be whipped separately, which adds a great deal of air to a batter or mixture. Sometimes more yolks than whites are called for or more whites than yolks.

If you end up with more egg whites than you need for the recipe at hand, freeze the extra egg whites for later use.

Even a drop of egg yolk that mixes with egg whites will keep the whites from whipping, so keeping egg whites completely free of any egg yolk is crucial. To prevent any contamination of egg white by egg yolks, separate each egg over a small bowl before adding the egg white to the larger bowl.

Egg whites are easier to separate when they're cold, but they whip to their fullest volume when they're at room temperature. Separate them when cold, then cover the bowl tightly with plastic wrap and let them warm up to room temperature for use.

The best way to crack an egg is on a hard, flat surface with a firm hand. With this method the shell won't shatter much.

You can use one of three methods for separating eggs:

> ✔ **The shell-to-shell method:** Crack the egg shell on a sharp surface as close to the center as possible. Pass the egg yolk back and forth from one shell to the other while letting the egg white drop into a bowl directly below your hands (see Figure 4-5).

✔ **The hand method:** Gently crack the egg shell on a sharp surface as close to the center as possible. Break the shell apart and hold the egg in your cupped hand. Slightly separate your fingers and let the egg white drip through into a bowl below. Be sure to wash your hands thoroughly with warm, soapy water after separating each egg, so there's no chance of contamination.

✔ **The egg separator method:** An egg separator is a tool that does the same job as holding the egg in your hand. Place the egg separator over a small bowl and crack the egg into the center of the separator. The white will drip out into the bowl and the yolk will remain in the small center bowl of the egg separator.

How to Separate an Egg

Figure 4-5: Separating eggs.

1. Hold the egg in one hand over two small bowls
2. Crack the shell on the side of one bowl
3. Let the white fall into one of the bowls
4. Pass the yolk back & forth, each time releasing more white
5. When all the white is in the bowl, drop yolk in the other bowl.

Beating eggs to the ribbon stage

Many recipes call for eggs to be beaten to the *ribbon stage*. Just what the heck does this mean? *Ribbon* is the term that's used to describe the consistency of eggs that have been beaten until they're very thick and pale-colored. When the beaters are lifted above the bowl, the batter slowly drops back onto itself in a ribbon-like pattern and holds its shape for a few seconds before it sinks into the mixture (see Figure 4-6). Another way to test the ribbon stage is to draw a line in the middle of the beaten eggs with your finger or a rubber spatula. If the line stays separated, the eggs are at the ribbon stage. Eggs beaten to the ribbon stage have increased their volume several times from their initial quantity.

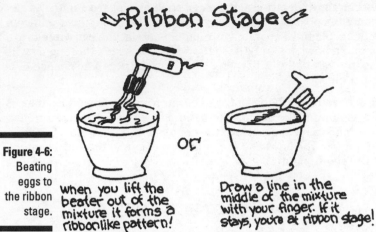

Figure 4-6: Beating eggs to the ribbon stage.

Ribbon Stage

or

when you lift the beater out of the mixture it forms a ribbonlike pattern!

Draw a line in the middle of the mixture with your finger. If it stays, you're at ribbon stage!

Whipping egg whites

Many recipes call for egg whites to be whipped. Whipping increases volume by adding air to the mixtures, which helps the eggs rise as they bake. Whipping egg whites is easiest with an electric mixer and the wire whip attachment, but if you're strong you can whip egg whites by hand with a wire whisk.

Here are some tips for whipping egg whites:

- **Have egg whites at room temperature so they can whip to their fullest volume.** Just don't leave eggs out of the refrigerator for more than 2 hours, or you'll increase your risk of Salmonella poisoning.

- **Make sure all your utensils are completely clean and grease-free.** Any trace of fat or grease will keep the egg whites from whipping.

- **Use beaters with several tines so they incorporate air quickly.**

- **If you're using a hand mixer, move it around the bowl while whipping to incorporate more air.**

- **Add a pinch (about ⅛ teaspoon) of cream of tartar or white vinegar to help stabilize the foam.** Using a copper bowl to beat egg whites produces a similar effect to adding cream of tartar or vinegar. The copper from the bowl combines with the egg whites and helps to stabilize the foam.

- **Don't add salt to egg whites.** Salt has the opposite effect of cream of tartar or white vinegar, causing egg whites to dry out and the stability of the foam to decrease.

✔ **Stop and check the stage of egg whites as you whip them.** Overbeaten egg whites form a lumpy foam that breaks down and becomes watery. Overbeaten egg whites are also difficult to blend with other mixtures.

✔ **If a recipes call for sugar to be added to the egg whites, wait until the whites are frothy before adding the sugar.** This will allow the egg whites to quickly grab onto the sugar and blend well with them before the egg whites dry out. The best type of sugar to add when whipping egg whites is superfine because it dissolves much quicker than regular granulated sugar and leaves no gritty trace behind.

Don't use the ultra-pasteurized liquid egg whites available in cartons when a recipe calls for whipped egg whites. The pasteurization process breaks down their ability to hold air, so they won't whip the same way as fresh or frozen defrosted egg whites.

The recipes in this book call for egg whites whipped to one of two stages, described here:

✔ **Soft peaks:** When egg whites reach this stage, they are fluffy and hold their shape, but the top peaks gently falls over when the beater is removed.

✔ **Firm or stiff peaks:** Egg whites at this stage stand up at attention. They should be glossy and easily hold their shape, but they shouldn't look dry.

Telling what stage egg whites have reached just by looking at them can be difficult. If you're not sure what stage your egg whites are at, stop the mixer and use a rubber spatula to scoop out a small amount of egg whites. Hold the spatula upside down to see what type of peak the egg whites hold. You can always add more whipping time, but you can't rescue overbeaten egg whites.

Going Nuts

All kinds of nuts are used in making chocolate desserts. Chocolate and nuts seem to be a perfect marriage. No matter what type of nuts the recipe calls for, they usually have to be prepared in some way — such as toasting, chopping, or grinding — before they're ready to be added to a recipe. The methods for accomplishing these tasks are the same for all varieties of nuts.

Read through the recipe before starting so you know what preparation is needed for the nuts.

Shelling

Most of the nuts you buy for making chocolate desserts will already be shelled, but occasionally the nuts you want may only be available in their shell. This means you'll have a little work to do to get them ready for baking.

Peanuts are the easiest nuts to shell. Their shell is relatively soft and cracks easily when pressure is applied. Pop peanut shells between your thumb and forefinger, separate the shells, and let the nuts drop out into a bowl or other container.

Other nuts — like hazelnuts, almonds, walnuts, and pecans — have tough, hard shells that need to be cracked with a nutcracker and then separated. This task requires a bit of strength. You may need to use a *pick,* which is a tool with a sharp point and a very thin blade, to remove the nut meat from the shell.

Macadamia nuts are the hardest nuts to crack. These are only cracked commercially and are always available shelled.

Skinning

The skins of almonds and hazelnuts are a bit bitter, so most dessert recipes call for the skins to be removed before using the nuts. The recipe will say to use *blanched almonds* or *skinned hazelnuts.* Spanish peanuts have red skins that have to be removed by hand — this can be very tedious, so try to buy Valencia peanuts, which come without their skins.

The easiest way to skin almonds is to blanch them first. To do this, drop them into a large pot of boiling water for 1 minute. Use a skimmer or slotted spoon to remove them from the boiling water, and immediately transfer them to a bowl of cold water to stop the cooking. Drain them, dry them, and gently squeeze them between your fingers. They'll pop right out of their skins (see Figure 4-7).

HOW TO SKIN NUTS

Figure 4-7: Skinning almonds.

TO SKIN ALMONDS, BLANCH FIRST. DROP THEM INTO A PAN OF BOILING WATER FOR 1 MINUTE.

USE A SLOTTED SPOON OR SKIMMER TO REMOVE THEM. IMMEDIATELY PLACE THEM IN A BOWL OF COLD WATER.

DRAIN THEM, DRY THEM AND GENTLY SQUEEZE BETWEEN YOUR FINGERS. THEY WILL 'POP' OUT OF THEIR SKINS!

To skin hazelnuts, a different method is used. Spread the hazelnuts in a single layer in a jelly roll or cake pan and toast them in a 350-degree oven for 15 to 18 minutes, until the skins split and the nuts turn light golden brown. Remove the pan from the oven and immediately transfer the nuts to a kitchen towel. Fold the towel around the nuts so they're completely enclosed and rub them to remove most of the skins.

Toasting

Toasting definitely brings out the flavor of nuts. Most raw nuts taste fine, but toasted nuts taste *very* good. Spread the nuts in a single layer in a cake or jelly roll pan and toast them in a preheated 350-degree oven (see Figure 4-8). The toasting time is determined by the type of nut. Almonds, walnuts, pecans, and pine nuts toast fairly quickly. Toast them for 5 minutes, then shake or stir the nuts and toast them for another 3 to 5 minutes, until they're light golden in color. Hazelnuts toast for about 15 minutes because they're denser than most other nuts.

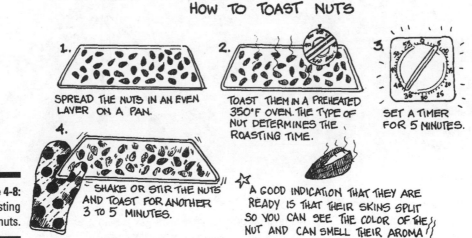

HOW TO TOAST NUTS

1. SPREAD THE NUTS IN AN EVEN LAYER ON A PAN.

2. TOAST THEM IN A PREHEATED 350°F OVEN. THE TYPE OF NUT DETERMINES THE ROASTING TIME.

3. SET A TIMER FOR 5 MINUTES.

4. SHAKE OR STIR THE NUTS AND TOAST FOR ANOTHER 3 TO 5 MINUTES.

☆ A GOOD INDICATION THAT THEY ARE READY IS THAT THEIR SKINS SPLIT SO YOU CAN SEE THE COLOR OF THE NUT AND CAN SMELL THEIR AROMA!!

Figure 4-8: Toasting nuts.

After toasting, remove the pan from the oven and transfer the nuts to a cool pan so they won't continue to brown on the hot baking pan. Place the cool baking pan on a cooling rack.

Nuts don't take long to burn. Check them often as they toast to make sure they're not toasting too quickly. And if you do end up burning nuts, don't even think about using them. They'll spoil the flavor of your chocolate dessert.

You can tell that nuts are ready when their skins split. You'll be able to see the color of the nuts and smell their aroma.

Chopping

Chop nuts with a chef's knife on a cutting board. Be sure to use a sharp knife with a large blade. Place the nuts in the center of the cutting board (as shown in Figure 4-9). Place the edge of the chef's knife across the surface of the nuts with the handle of the knife in one hand. With the other hand resting on the top of the blade, move the knife through the nuts in a curve, rocking the blade up and down. Lift the blade occasionally to gather in more nuts, while continuing to apply the downward pressure. Stop occasionally and gather the chopped nuts into the center. Keep chopping until the nuts are the size you want.

CHOPPING NUTS

1. PLACE THE NUTS ON A WORK SUR-FACE.

2. PLACE THE EDGE OF A HEAVY, SHARP KNIFE BLADE ACROSS THE NUTS. REST ONE HAND ON THE TIP.

3. WITH YOUR OTHER HAND, MOVE YOUR KNIFE THROUGH THE NUTS IN A CURVE, ROCKING THE BLADE UP AND DOWN.

Figure 4-9: Chopping nuts.

Don't try to chop too large a quantity of nuts at one time or you'll find them flying all over the place. A cup is a good quantity to handle easily.

You can also chop nuts in a food processor if you're pressed for time, but the chop is uneven, so only use this as a last resort. Be careful not to over-process the nuts or you'll wind up with nut paste.

Grinding

A food processor is the best way to grind nuts (see Figure 4-10), although you can also grind them in a blender. Use the steel blade and pulse on and off. You can regulate the fineness of the grind by the amount of time. A rough grind usually requires anywhere from 30 seconds to 1 minute; up to 2 minutes produces a very fine grind.

All nuts have a high content of natural oil. As the nuts are ground, the oil releases, which can cause them to be wet and mealy. To prevent this, add 1 tablespoon of sugar for each cup of nuts. The sugar will absorb the oil and make a fluffy, dry grind. For oily nuts, such as hazelnuts, macadamia nuts, and Brazil nuts, add 2 tablespoons of sugar for each cup before grinding.

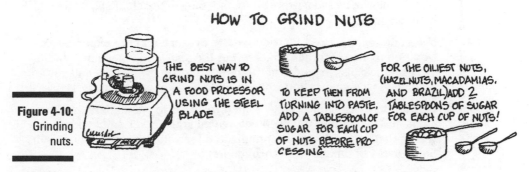

Figure 4-10: Grinding nuts.

Make sure the food processor and steel blade are clean and completely dry before chopping and grinding nuts. You don't want your nuts to taste like onions or to become wet from a wet bowl.

Storing

All nuts have a high oil content, which tends to make them turn rancid quickly at room temperature. For long-term storage, keep nuts in airtight containers or plastic bags in the freezer, which locks out air and freezer smells. Be sure to label and date each container so you know what's inside. Whether they're raw, toasted, chopped, sliced, or ground, most nuts can be frozen for up to a year with no adverse effects.

Be sure to bring nuts to room temperature before grinding. Frozen nuts don't grind as finely as do those at room temperature.

Getting Baking Pointers

Nothing is sweeter than bringing a delicious chocolate dessert that you've made to the table and having your guests *ooh* and *aah* over it. Watching their faces when they take the first bite is a chocolate dessert maker's idea of heaven. But getting to this point takes a little planning and preparation.

Here are some general tips to keep in mind no matter what kind of chocolate dessert you're making:

- ✔ **Start by being sure to choose a chocolate dessert recipe that's appropriate for the occasion and the season.** If it's an informal gathering, choose a recipe that's not too complicated and can be easily transported. You also need to know how many people the dessert is expected to serve. A 9-inch round cake isn't enough to serve 20 people, but two of them are. (With the number of great chocolate dessert recipes in this book, you won't have a problem finding one — the challenge will come in limiting it!)

- ✔ **Set aside time to enjoy your chocolate dessert–making experience.** Don't be rushed by other projects. Let the answering machine handle your phone calls, so you're not tempted to drop everything and get involved in a conversation while in the middle of making dessert.

- ✔ **Be familiar with your recipe.** Read it through so you understand the steps and techniques involved before you start. And don't tackle a recipe that's too difficult or complicated for your skill level unless you have plenty of time to work through it.

- ✔ **Check through your pantry to make sure you have all the ingredients you need.** Nothing is more frustrating than starting to prepare a dessert and finding out you don't have a necessary ingredient.

- ✔ **Measure all the ingredients you need and assemble all the equipment.** This makes working through a recipe without interruptions a cinch.

- ✔ **Be familiar with your oven and how it bakes.** If you haven't used your oven in a long time, do a test run by baking a batch of cookies or brownies to make sure they turn out okay. Be sure to have a reliable oven thermometer in the oven so you know whether it's running hot or cool.

- ✔ **After the dessert is baked, be sure to allow time for it to cool before you serve or store it.**

In the following sections, I provide more specific tips for the wide variety of dessert recipes you'll find in this book.

Cookies

Leave at least 1 inch of space between cookies on the cookie sheet so they'll have room to spread as they bake. Cookies are small and bake quicker than many other desserts. Be sure to read the directions for each particular recipe so you know what to expect in terms of preparation and baking time. Set the timer for the least amount of time called for and check the cookies then.

Most cookies will look set and firm when they're done. With chocolate cookies, you can't really use color as a gauge for when they're done. So touch the top of a cookie with your finger. If the cookie is done, it will stand up to the touch and not collapse. Another way to test for doneness is to use a spatula to remove one from the cookie sheet. Break it open and look at it. If it needs a little more baking time, reset the timer and bake for a few more minutes.

Cookies need to cool completely before they're served or stored. Place cookie sheets on cooling racks so plenty of air can circulate around them.

Storing cookies before they're completely cool results in soft, soggy cookies.

Cakes

There are many different kinds of cakes, so you need to become familiar with the type of cake you're making. Understand the steps and methods involved, so you won't face any last-minute surprises. Many cakes can be baked a day or two in advance of when they'll be served. Take advantage of this to fit cake-making into your busy schedule.

Always use the correct style and size cake pan for the type of cake you're baking. Using another style or size pan will change the result.

Depending on the type of cake the cake pan needs to be prepared before baking. Lightly grease the bottom and sides of the cake pan, then dust the inside with flour and shake out the excess by turning the pan upside down and tapping it against a firm surface. Cut a piece of parchment to fit the bottom of the pan. All this makes it easy for the cake to slip out of the pan without getting stuck.

I like to lightly grease the parchment paper liner in my cake pans. This ensures that the cake will easily come out of the pan. Place the greased side up, so it's against the bottom of the cake. When the cake is turned out of the pan, the parchment paper liner should easily peel off.

Telling when most cakes are done baking is easy. They should have risen to or above the level of the baking pan. The edges of the cake will be starting to pull slightly away from the sides of the pan and the cake will look set and firm. If you touch the top of the cake, it should spring back and not hold the shape of your fingers. Using a cake tester is also an excellent way of determining if a cake is done. Each cake recipe in this book includes guidelines for telling when the cake is done baking.

Opening the oven to check for doneness more than once lowers the oven temperature and can cause a cake to fall.

For cheesecakes, using a cake tester isn't the best way to go. You can usually see that they're done because the sides are set and the center is still slightly wobbly. The cheesecake will firm up as the cake cools and chills.

Be sure to cool all cakes completely before serving and storing them, unless they're supposed to be served warm. Most cakes need to cool for about 20 minutes on a cooling rack before they're turned out of the cake pan.

Turning a cake out of its pan before it's had a chance to cool sufficiently may result in a cake that falls apart.

Pies and tarts

Pies and tarts both have two parts: dough and filling. Most pie and tart doughs need to be chilled before they're rolled out and fitted into the pan. Working with soft dough is difficult because it sticks and tears. Also, you'll have to add too much flour to the dough to make it workable enough to roll out and the excess flour makes the dough tough.

Plan ahead when making pies and tarts. Make the dough enough in advance so that it has time to chill before it's rolled out.

The color of the pie and tart dough is one of the best indications of doneness. The color should be light golden brown. If it becomes much darker, there's a risk that the dough will be over-baked. The filling is also an indication of doneness. If it's a fruit filling, the main problem to avoid is too much liquid, which can make the whole thing soggy. The fruit filling should be bubbling, but not spilling over the edges. A baked filling should look puffed and set.

Place a baking sheet under the pie or tart pan to catch any drips or spills. This also makes transporting the pie or tart to and from the oven easy.

Some tart shells are baked *blind* (that is, without filling, which is added after the shell has cooled). These shells can be baked a day or two in advance and held at room temperature tightly wrapped in foil. Often times the filling can also be made in advance and the tart assembled shortly before serving.

To bake a tart shell blind, line it with foil and fill with tart or pie weights. Bake for 8 to 10 minutes, following the instructions in the recipe. Remove the foil and weights and bake the shell for another 10 to 12 minutes, until light golden brown and set.

The foil and tart or pie weights keep the sides of the tart from collapsing and prevent the bottom from puffing up while the dough sets.

As with other baked goods, pies and tarts need to cool completely before they're served and stored. Cool them on a cooling rack so there's room for air to circulate around them. This eliminates soggy bottoms.

Other desserts

If you're baking a soufflé, the worst thing you can do is open the oven before it's done. This will cause the soufflé to collapse. If you're wondering how the soufflé is doing, turn on the oven light and look through the glass doors, if you have that type of oven. If you don't have a glass door and an oven light, you'll have to be patient and wait until the timer goes off before checking for doneness.

Other desserts, such as baked custards, should look set, yet still be a little wobbly in the center, when they're done. These desserts will continue to firm up as they cool and chill.

Mixing

Mixing is simply the process of combining ingredients in a manner that results in a well-integrated blend. The process of mixing ingredients together takes different forms, depending on the desired outcome. Most chocolate dessert recipes are mixed with an electric mixer, but some can also be mixed by hand.

Beating/whipping

This technique involves incorporating air into a mixture by vigorous mixing. This is best accomplished with an electric mixer, using the wire whip attachment, if available.

Here are the steps for beating/whipping:

1. **Place the ingredient in a mixing bowl.**

2. **Using an electric mixer, beat on medium speed until the mixture becomes frothy.**

3. **Add other ingredients, if there are any.**

4. **Increase the mixer speed to medium-high and continue beating until the desired state is reached.**

You can also beat or whip using a balloon whisk.

Stirring

Stirring is the technique used to combine ingredients together gently but thoroughly. The key is to not mix too much — otherwise, the mixture will become tough.

Stirring is accomplished by mixing ingredients together in a circular motion until they are thoroughly combined. In a mixing bowl, start at the center, using a rubber spatula or wooden spoon, and mix in a circular motion, widening out the motion, moving toward the outer rim of the bowl. Continue until all the ingredients are well blended. An electric mixer accomplishes the task in the same manner.

Creaming

Creaming is an essential technique that's the first step in many dessert recipes. The resulting mixture should be so well combined that you can't distinguish the individual ingredients. This mixture is the base structure for the rest of the ingredients and needs to be strong enough that it won't collapse. Creaming traps air that expands when heated, helping baked goods to rise. Creaming is done most often with butter and sugar as the first step in many dessert recipes.

To get the best results when creaming ingredients together, the fat must be at room temperature.

Here are the steps for creaming:

1. **Place the softened butter or other fat in a mixing bowl.**

2. **Using an electric mixer with the flat beater attachment (if available), or with wire whips, beat the butter at medium speed for 30 seconds to 1 minute, until it becomes fluffy.**

3. **Gradually add the sugar, beating at medium speed.**

4. **After all the sugar is added, beat at medium-high speed for a few minutes, until the mixture begins to hold soft peaks, from 2 to 5 minutes.**

Cutting in

Cutting in is a technique that's used when combining butter or shortening into dry ingredients so that the butter is cut into tiny pieces but still maintains some of it's texture.

Here are the steps for cutting in:

1. **Place the dry ingredients in a large mixing bowl.**
2. **Cut the butter or shortening into small pieces and add to the dry ingredients.**
3. **Use two butter knives, two forks, or a pastry blender tool to work the butter into the dry ingredients.**

   If using two knives or forks, cut in opposite directions from the center of the bowl toward the outer edge. If using a pastry blender, rock it back and forth through the ingredients.

Folding

Folding is used most often to combine a light mixture, such as whipped egg whites and whipped cream, into a heavy mixture, and retain the air that has been beaten into both mixtures. Folding is a delicate process that is always done by hand.

Here are the steps for folding:

1. **In a mixing bowl, place the light mixture on top of the heavier mixture.**
2. **Using a long-handled rubber spatula, cut down through the center of the mixtures, then sweep the spatula around the side and bring it up to the top, turning it over and bringing some of the bottom mixture with it.**
3. **Give the bowl a quarter turn and repeat the folding stroke.**
4. **Repeat this process as many as 15 times until the mixture is thoroughly blended.**

Folding should be done rapidly, but gently.

Be sure to use a bowl that's large enough to hold the mixture and allows room for the spatula to move.

Cutting

After you've made your wonderful chocolate desserts, you need to cut and serve them. Some people have a hard time cutting their work, but I like to think of desserts as edible art. They're made to be eaten and enjoyed. Bon appétit!

A cake into layers

Many cakes that are to be assembled with a filling need to be cut horizontally into two or three layers. Here's how it's done:

1. **Place the cake on a cardboard cake circle that's the same diameter as the cake, then if you have a cake turntable, place the cake on the turntable.**

2. **Decide how many layers you want to cut, then using a small sharp knife, make a mark on one side of the cake where the cuts need to be made.**

3. **Using a long serrated knife, slice about ½ inch into the cake all the way around, turning the turntable slowly.**

   Steady the cake by placing one of your hands on top of it while holding the knife in the other hand.

4. **Continue rotating the turntable slowly while applying pressure to the knife, moving the knife horizontally through the cake, while pushing the cake against the knife.**

5. **Carefully bring the knife out the opposite side from where the cut started.**

   Use a cardboard cake circle to fit underneath the newly cut cake layer to remove it from the cake. Repeat this entire process for the next cake layer.

Cakes, pies, and tarts into serving slices

First decide how many pieces you need to cut from the cake, pie, or tart. Desserts that are 9 or 10 inches in diameter can easily be cut into 8, 10, or 12 serving slices.

In order to cut a cake, pie, or tart into serving pieces without waste, follow these tips:

- ✔ **Use a very sharp knife.** Chef's knives and serrated knives work well for cutting cakes.

- ✔ **In between each cut, dip the knife in hot water and dry it.** This will keep extra crumbs from being dragged from one cut to the other.

To cut the cake, pie, or tart:

1. **Plunge the tip of the knife into the center of the dessert and firmly cut straight down to the bottom.**

2. **Cut the dessert into equal halves, then cut these into halves again (see Figure 4-11).**

3. **For 16 servings, cut each quarter of the dessert into half, and cut that half into half again. For 12 servings, cut each quarter of the dessert into 3 equal pieces.**

Dip the knife into hot water between each cut to clean it off.

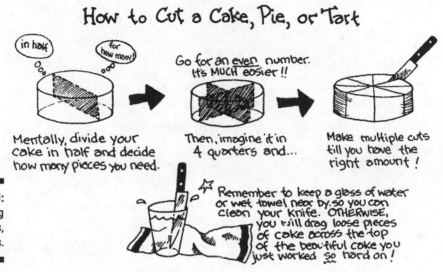

Figure 4-11:
Cutting
cakes, pies,
and tarts.

Chapter 5

Chocolate Care

Chocolate is a sublime substance capable of producing exquisite desserts, pastries, and confections. Like any diva, chocolate has the reputation for being temperamental and requiring special care. If treated with the proper respect and reverence, chocolate will act like a superstar and carry the show. Understanding how to work with chocolate to bring out its best qualities will make your time spent in the kitchen rewarding and exciting.

Chopping Chocolate

If you buy chocolate in bars, it is divided into pieces, which break from the bar easily. These pieces can also be broken into smaller sizes. If you buy chocolate in bulk, you will need to chop it before you can melt it (as shown in Figure 5-1). The easiest way to do this is with a large chef's knife on a cutting board. Chop the chocolate very fine, about the size of matchsticks. The smaller the surface, the quicker it will melt. It will also melt evenly if chopped into tiny pieces and there is little risk of burning the chocolate because less heat is necessary for melting.

Be sure the knife and cutting board used to chop chocolate are completely dry so no moisture comes in contact with the chocolate. I like to keep a cutting board just for chopping chocolate. That way I know that other flavors won't mix with the chocolate.

Don't chop chocolate in a food processor, because the machine beats up the chocolate and the heat of the motor may melt it.

CHOPPING CHOCOLATE

1. LARGE CHUNKS OF CHOCOLATE NEED TO BE CUT INTO SMALL PIECES FIRST, THEN USING A CHEF'S KNIFE WITH A LARGE BLADE ON A CUTTING BOARD....

2. ...CHOP THEM INTO TINY PIECES. WORK WITH A SMALL AMOUNT AT A TIME.

3. TRANSFER THE CHOPPED PIECES TO A BOWL. KEEP THE CUTTING BOARD FREE FOR CHOPPING!

KEEP CHOPPING!

Figure 5-1: Chopping chocolate.

Melting Chocolate

Most chocolate used to make desserts, pastries, and confections needs to be melted before use. But never melt chocolate over direct heat. It's delicate and will burn easily.

There are two main methods for melting chocolate: in the top of a double boiler or in a microwave oven. Both methods are effective, but require that you pay attention. Chocolate can also be melted in a tabletop tempering machine (see the section on tempering later in this chapter for more information).

Be patient when melting chocolate. It takes time and needs to melt slowly over low heat so it won't seize or burn from too much heat. Timing, as they say, is everything. You can't hurry chocolate. It needs time to melt slowly. If you try to hurry it up by adding more heat, you'll wind up burning it. Then you'll have to discard it and start over. Take your time when working with chocolate.

Chocolate's melting point is between 86 and 96 degrees, slightly less than normal body temperature. That's why it melts in the mouth and in your hand.

Keep chocolate in motion as it's melting so it will melt evenly. After chocolate is melted, stir it frequently if it needs to sit for any length of time. This keeps a skin or crust from forming on top.

Milk and white chocolate are more delicate than dark chocolate because they contain milk solids, which coagulate with heat. You may think you need to add more heat to milk or white chocolate because it's not melting down as smoothly as dark chocolate. In fact, what's happened is that the milk solids have congealed, causing the chocolate to look lumpy. Adding more heat will only burn the chocolate. After it's coagulated, there's nothing you can do to bring it back to a smooth texture.

Don't heat dark chocolate over 120 degrees or milk and white chocolate over 115 degrees or it will burn. And burned chocolate doesn't taste good. If you've burned your chocolate, discard it and start over with fresh chocolate.

Double boiler

Melting chocolate in a double boiler cushions the chocolate from coming in contact with direct heat because water is in the bottom pan. Be sure the water level is no higher than an inch, so there's no risk that it will slosh into the top pan holding the chocolate and mix with it. Keep the heat underneath the pan very low. Have the water hot and close to simmering, but not boiling. Be sure to stir the chocolate often as it's melting, so it will melt evenly. I prefer to use a rubber spatula to stir chocolate, because it doesn't hold onto other flavors the way wooden spoons do. Place only enough chocolate in the top pan of the double boiler to ensure that there's enough room for it to melt and to be stirred. If there's too much chocolate, it will be difficult to move around and may melt unevenly.

I like to use a glass double boiler so I can see the water in the bottom pan. If it starts to simmer I know to turn off the heat and stir the chocolate to dissipate the heat.

Don't boil the water in the bottom pan of the double boiler. It will be much too hot and will overheat the chocolate in the top pan.

When chocolate is halfway melted, turn off the heat of the burner. There is enough residual heat in the pan to continue to melt the remaining chocolate. Be sure to stir the chocolate frequently so it melts evenly.

Don't cover the pan of chocolate while it's melting. This will cause moisture to condense on the cover and ruin the chocolate.

Microwave

Microwaving chocolate is easy and clean. Chop or break the chocolate into small pieces and place them in a bowl that's microwave-safe. Use low power for 15– to 30-second bursts. Stir the chocolate in between each burst to make sure it's melting evenly. The microwave melts from the inside out, so it can be deceptive if the chocolate is melted. Unless you stir the chocolate often, you may overheat it thinking it doesn't look melted.

Don't cover the bowl of chocolate when melting it in the microwave. It will generate too much heat and may cause moisture condensation that will ruin the chocolate.

Become familiar with your microwave oven and know its wattage. A few years ago I moved into a new house that had a new microwave oven. I merrily softened butter and melted chocolate for the same amount of time I had done it in my old microwave oven. After melting several pounds of butter and burning lots of chocolate, I realized that my new microwave is much more powerful than my old one was, and I need to use less power for shorter amounts of time.

Paying Attention to the Environment

If you've been reading this chapter from the beginning, you probably realize that chocolate is a bit sensitive. Too much heat isn't good for it nor is too much humidity. Few kitchens have the absolutely ideal conditions for working with chocolate, but you can do very well by making your situation work for you.

Chocolate and moisture: An unhappy couple

Chocolate has a peculiar relationship with water and other liquids. The tiniest bit of liquid that mixes with chocolate can cause it to *seize*, or thicken to the consistency of mud, unable to melt. This is because the cocoa solids and sugar in chocolate are dry and are drawn to the moisture from the liquid. The trick is to add enough liquid to moisten all the dry cocoa and sugar particles and seizing won't happen. Allow at least 1 tablespoon of liquid for every 2 ounces of chocolate when adding liquid to chocolate to prevent seizing.

After removing the top pan or bowl of the double boiler, always wipe the bottom and sides of the bowl very dry. This prevents any stray drops of water from running down the sides of the bowl as it's tilted and mixing with the chocolate.

When a recipe calls for liquid to be combined with chocolate, one good way to do this is to heat the ingredients together. Other ingredients, such as butter, can also be combined with chocolate as it melts.

When adding liquid to melted chocolate, it's best if the liquid is hot. If the liquid is cool or cold, it will cause the chocolate to harden up. If this happens, you may find hard, grainy particles of chocolate in your mixture and there's no way to get rid of them. When you add hot liquid to chopped chocolate, add the liquid at one time, not in small batches, and stir vigorously.

If chocolate begins to thicken too much after you've added hot liquid, it may be necessary to add a little more liquid. Try 1 to 2 more tablespoons and stir vigorously. Be sure what you add is warm so there's no chance of seizing.

Too much moisture in the air can have a definite effect on chocolate, especially if you are working on tempering (see the section on tempering later in this chapter). The excess moisture will interrupt chocolate's ability to set quickly and can cause tempered chocolate to go out of temper. Rainy days are just not the best days for working with chocolate. If you live in the tropics, your chocolate work may be limited to only a few days a year. One remedy for this is to use a dehumidifier in the kitchen. The other is to plan your chocolate-making activities on dry days.

Some people have naturally warm hands. This isn't a problem unless you're rolling truffles by hand. Then you'll find that the heat of your hands will melt the chocolate and you'll have very chocolaty hands. This may not be a bad thing, except it will take a whole lot longer to roll truffles. A good way to deal with this situation is to run your hands under very cold water or dip them in a bowl of ice water and dry them well. Do this several times while rolling truffles.

Storing Chocolate

In order for chocolate to last its maximum time, it needs to be stored in optimum conditions. Stored properly, dark chocolate can last for several years, although it is best used within a few years. Because milk chocolate and white chocolate contain milk solids, which can become rancid, they have a very limited shelf live, about 8 to 10 months. Be sure to buy chocolate from a source with a high turnover so you know the chocolate you're buying is fresh.

Plain chocolate

Store plain chocolate in a cool, dark, dry place. The ideal storage conditions are 65 to 75 degrees with very low humidity. If you're fortunate enough to have a wine cellar, make a little room in it for storing chocolate, because it has just the right conditions. Most people do just fine storing their plain chocolate in the kitchen pantry. Keep it away from light, heat, and moisture. Wrap plain chocolate in foil or brown paper. If plastic wrap is used, it will cause moisture to stick to the chocolate, which will cause problems when the chocolate is melted. Chocolate is like a sponge, easily picking up other flavors, so be sure to store it away from strongly flavored foods.

I keep one side of my kitchen pantry set aside for storing chocolate and other dessert-making ingredients. This way I know my chocolate won't be exposed to flavors that will contaminate it.

Don't store chocolate in the refrigerator or freezer. It will pick up moisture that will mix with the chocolate when it melts, causing it to seize. Also, temperature changes can cause unpleasant changes in chocolate's flavor and texture.

Chocolate desserts

Store finished chocolate desserts, pastries, and confections in the refrigerator, tightly covered or wrapped, to protect against moisture. If the chocolate is shiny, as for dipped chocolate truffles, refrigeration will cause the sheen to dull. Take care where you place the chocolate in the refrigerator so it won't taste like other food. Some chocolate desserts can be stored at room temperature for a short period of time. (Be sure they are tightly wrapped to protect from air and from picking up other flavors.) Some chocolate candies and confections can be frozen. To do this, place them in airtight containers and wrap with several layers of foil and plastic wrap. Defrost them in the refrigerator for at least 24 hours before letting them stand at room temperature.

Rapid temperature changes will cause the outer coating of chocolate on candies and confections to crack.

Chocolate tastes best at room temperature. Leave enough time for your chocolate desserts, candies, and confections to warm up to room temperature before serving so their full flavor can be appreciated.

Tempering Chocolate: Why Bother?

Tempering is a process of heating, cooling, and stirring chocolate to achieve a balance that holds cocoa butter at its most stable point. All chocolate comes from the factory tempered, which is why it has a shiny, smooth, evenly colored appearance. Well-tempered chocolate sets quickly with a glossy sheen and smooth texture. It has an overall even color without streaks or dots and breaks with a clean, crisp snap. When chocolate is melted, it goes out of temper, and must be tempered before use for dipping, molding, and decorating. Chocolate does not have to be tempered when used in baking, truffle centers, and other candies and confections.

If chocolate is in temper, it doesn't have to be heated to an exact temperature when melting. However, if chocolate is out of temper (it's been used previously and cooled), it must be heated to 115 degrees before tempering, to completely melt all the cocoa butter crystals.

There are several methods of tempering chocolate. You can temper any amount of chocolate with the following methods.

Quick tempering

This method is also called the *pot method* of tempering. Although accuracy is important when tempering chocolate, this method doesn't rely on an exact temperature. I recommend this method (shown in Figure 5-2) if you're just getting started tempering chocolate.

1. **Chop 1 pound of chocolate very finely.**

2. **Place two-thirds of the chocolate in the top of a double boiler and melt over low heat, stirring the chocolate frequently with a rubber spatula to ensure even melting.**

   Alternatively, melt the chocolate in a microwave oven on low power for 15– to 30-second intervals. Stir the chocolate between each interval.

3. **Remove the chocolate from the double boiler (if using) and wipe the bottom and sides very dry. If melting the chocolate in a microwave oven, remove the bowl and stir the chocolate to make sure it's completely melted.**

4. **Stir in the remaining third of finely chopped chocolate in 3 batches.**

   Make sure each batch is melted before adding the next. The chopped chocolate will absorb the heat of the melted chocolate and cool it.

5. **When all the chopped chocolate has been added, test the temperature of it by placing a dab of chocolate below your lower lip.**

   It should feel comfortable — not too hot or too cool. If it's still too warm, add more chopped chocolate to cool it down. If it's too cool, place the bowl or pan of chocolate over warm water briefly to bring the temperature up.

For this method of tempering to be successful, you must start with tempered chocolate. Untempered chocolate pieces that are stirred into the melted chocolate will cause the batch to be untempered.

QUICK TEMPERING

STIR GRATED OR FINELY CHOPPED CHOCOLATE INTO THE WARM CHOCOLATE IN SEPARATE BATCHES.

THE CHOCOLATE THICKENS WHEN ENOUGH GRATED CHOCOLATE HAS BEEN ADDED. THEN, REHEAT THE CHOCOLATE *GENTLY!*

Figure 5-2: Quick tempering.

Chunk tempering

Chunk tempering is a variation of the quick tempering method:

1. **Chop 1 pound of chocolate very finely.**

2. **Place two-thirds of the chocolate in the top of a double boiler and melt over low heat, stirring the chocolate frequently with a rubber spatula to ensure even melting.**

   Alternatively, melt the chocolate in a microwave oven on low power for 15– to 30-second intervals. Stir the chocolate between each interval.

3. **Remove the chocolate from the double boiler (if using) and wipe the bottom and sides very dry. If melting the chocolate in a microwave oven, remove the bowl and stir the chocolate to make sure it's completely melted.**

4. **Add a large chunk of chocolate to the bowl and stir continuously until the chocolate is cool.**

   Test the temperature of it by placing a dab of chocolate below your lower lip. It should feel comfortable — not too hot or too cool. If it's still too warm, keep stirring to cool it down. If it's too cool, place the bowl or pan of chocolate over warm water briefly to bring the temperature up.

5. **Remove the chunk from the liquid chocolate, dry it, wrap it well, and store it for future use.**

Classic tempering

This method (shown in Figure 5-3) involves using a chocolate thermometer (see Chapter 2) to test for accurate temperature of the chocolate at the stages of the tempering process.

1. **Chop and melt 1 pound of chocolate.**

2. **Place two-thirds of the chocolate in the top of a double boiler and melt over low heat, stirring often with a rubber spatula while melting.**

3. **Remove the top pan or bowl from the double boiler (if using) and wipe the bottom and sides very dry. If melting the chocolate in a microwave oven, remove the bowl and stir the chocolate to make sure it's completely melted.**

4. **Pour two thirds of the melted chocolate onto a marble slab, and spread it from one side to the other with an offset spatula. Then gather the chocolate into the center with a plastic scraper.**

   Repeat this process several times until the chocolate thickens noticeably.

Maintaining chocolate's temper

After chocolate is tempered it must be held at the same temperature while dipping truffles or any other confections. Place the bowl of tempered chocolate in a pan of water that is 2 degrees warmer than the chocolate. It will be necessary to check the temperature of the water and refresh it occasionally. Make sure the bowl fits snugly over the pan of water so no water sloshes into the chocolate. Don't use the same thermometer to check the temperature of the water in the pan and the temperature of the chocolate. Doing so makes it too easy to mix water with the chocolate. Stir the chocolate frequently as you're working with it. Chocolate against the sides of the bowl will begin to cool and set up quicker than the body of chocolate, so stir it into the mass often. Don't stir cooled chocolate from the sides of the bowl into the mass of chocolate. This will cause it to go out of temper.

5. **Use a chocolate thermometer to take the temperature of the chocolate, which should read between 78 and 80 degrees.**

6. **Scrape this chocolate into the bowl with the remaining third of the melted chocolate and stir together for a couple of minutes until thoroughly blended.**

The temperature of the chocolate should be between 89 and 91 degrees for dark chocolate, and 85 to 88 degrees for milk and white chocolate. If the temperature is below this, reheat the chocolate carefully over the pan of warm water or in the microwave until it reaches the correct temperature. If the chocolate is too warm it will be necessary to repeat the process.

Chocolate can be fairly forgiving. If you're not successful at tempering chocolate the first time, simply melt the chocolate and try again. As with everything else, the more you temper chocolate, the better you will be at it.

CLASSIC TEMPERING

1. WITH AN OFFSET SPATULA, SPREAD THE CHOCOLATE OUT ONTO A MARBLE SURFACE. SPREAD INTO RECTANGLE.

2. USE A PLASTIC SCRAPER TO SCRAPE IT UP INTO A 'POOL' IN THE CENTER. REPEAT THESE STEPS 3 OR 4 TIMES.

3. TAKE THE TEMPERATURE OF THE CHOCOLATE USING A CHOCOLATE THERMOMETER. THE TEMPERATURE SHOULD READ BETWEEN 78°-80° F.

Figure 5-3: Classic tempering.

Using a tempering machine

This is a foolproof method of tempering chocolate that is about as easy as it gets. The machine melts and tempers the chocolate and holds it at the correct temperature for dipping. Simply turn on the machine, put in the finely chopped chocolate, and set the temperature mode according to the type of chocolate you're using, following the manufacturer's instructions. When the chocolate is tempered, the machine sounds a signal and you're ready to go.

To test if chocolate is tempered, place a small spoonful on a piece of aluminum foil or waxed paper, then place this in the refrigerator to set up for a few minutes. If it is tempered, the chocolate will set quickly, be shiny, and have an overall even appearance. If the chocolate is dull and cloudy with streaks or dots, it isn't tempered and you'll have to start the tempering process again.

Chapter 6

Dipping, Molding, and Decorating

● ●

In This Chapter

▶ Dipping truffles in chocolate

▶ Molding chocolate

▶ Making your chocolate desserts look spectacular

Recipes in This Chapter

▶ Chocolate Ribbons

● ●

Any type of chocolate (dark, milk, or white) can be used for dipping, molding, and decorating. The best chocolate to use, however, is *couverture,* because it's formulated for these specific uses. The extra cocoa butter in couverture gives it more fluidity, so it makes thin outer coatings on dipped truffles and molds beautifully. Couverture is also great to use for decorating, because it flows smoothly and there's not as much risk of encountering lumps as there is with baking chocolate.

Molding chocolate is fun and easy. There are so many molds to choose from that you're sure to find one that's perfect for your needs. And creating chocolate decorative touches sends the message that you care enough to do just a little bit more than the ordinary. As with anything, the more you practice dipping, molding, and decorating, the better you get — and you and your loved ones can enjoy the fruits of your labor along the way.

Dipping in Chocolate

A smooth chocolate coating improves the appearance and taste of many desserts. Truffles and other candies are the desserts most often dipped in chocolate, but cookies and both fresh and dried fruit also benefit from being dipped in chocolate.

When you're dipping in chocolate, keep the following tips in mind:

✔ **Use couverture chocolate for dipping because it makes a smooth, thin coating.**

✔ **Temper the chocolate you use for dipping so it will set quickly with a shiny appearance and adhere to the piece.**

✔ **Use plenty of chocolate for dipping so there is room for the centers or other pieces to swim around.** Using twice what the recipe recommends as a good general rule. You can save any extra chocolate and use it another time.

✔ **Have all items to be dipped at room temperature.** If the centers or other pieces are too cold, the chocolate coating will crack as it dries because of the rapid temperature change.

✔ **Always let the excess chocolate drip off the dipped item so that when it's set down onto paper, a puddle (called a *foot*) doesn't form underneath it.** The foot isn't attractive — it's a sign of an inexperienced chocolate dipper.

Using dipping tools

Dipping tools make coating truffle centers and other items with tempered chocolate easy. Here's how to use them (see Figure 6-1):

1. **Drop a truffle center or other item into a bowl of tempered chocolate or use a dipping tool to lower it into the chocolate.**

2. **Slide the dipping tool under the center and retrieve it from the chocolate.**

USING DIPPING TOOLS

1. USE YOUR DIPPING TOOL TO GENTLY LOWER THE CANDY INTO THE TEMPERED CHOCOLATE.

2. REMOVE THE CANDY AND 'SKIM' THE SURFACE OF THE CHOCOLATE TO REMOVE THE DRIP.

3. GENTLY 'DROP' THE CANDY ONTO A PIECE OF PARCHMENT PAPER.

YOU CAN USE THE TOOL TO DRIZZLE A PATTERN ON TOP!

Figure 6-1:
Using
dipping
tools.

3. **Hold the dipping tool over the bowl of chocolate and let the excess chocolate drip off, then lightly tap or skim the tool against the side of the bowl.**

4. **Gently turn the tool upside down over a piece of parchment or waxed paper and let the center drop off the dipper onto the paper.**

Wipe off the dipping tool with a paper towel after dipping two or three centers. This keeps the tool from becoming coated with hardened chocolate, which makes it difficult to release dipped centers.

Hand dipping

Hand dipping is for anyone who really likes to get her hands into chocolate. It's a fun and rewarding way to dip truffles and other items. In order to enjoy yourself, remember to get everything set up and organized before you start.

Here are the steps for hand dipping (see Figure 6-2):

1. **Clear a large area on your kitchen counter or tabletop.**

   Place the tray of truffle centers on your left. Leave space in the center for the bowl of tempered chocolate. Place a baking sheet lined with parchment or waxed paper on your right (reverse the order if you're left-handed). Also, have paper towels handy.

2. **Melt and temper the chocolate for dipping.**

   Place the bowl of tempered chocolate over a pan of water a couple of degrees warmer than the chocolate to hold it at the correct temperature.

3. **Working from the left, pick up a truffle center and drop it into the bowl of chocolate.**

   Move the center around so it is completely coated.

4. **Use two fingers of your right hand to slide underneath the center and retrieve it from the chocolate.**

   Holding the two fingers slightly apart, balance the truffle center on them and let the excess chocolate drip off.

5. **Transfer the candy to the lined baking sheet and gently turn your hand over, letting the truffle drop onto the paper.**

6. **As you lift up your hand, let the string of chocolate create a design on top of the candy.**

Making your own dipping tool

If you'd like to try your hand at dipping before buying dipping tools, you can easily create your own. Take a heavy-duty plastic fork and break out the two middle tines, as shown below. This makes a dipping tool that is just the right size for dipping truffles. The truffle balances on the two outer tines, which leaves plenty of room for excess chocolate to drip off.

MAKING YOUR OWN DIPPING TOOL

BREAK OFF THE CENTER TYNES OF A PLASTIC FORK AND YOU HAVE MADE A DIPPING TOOL!

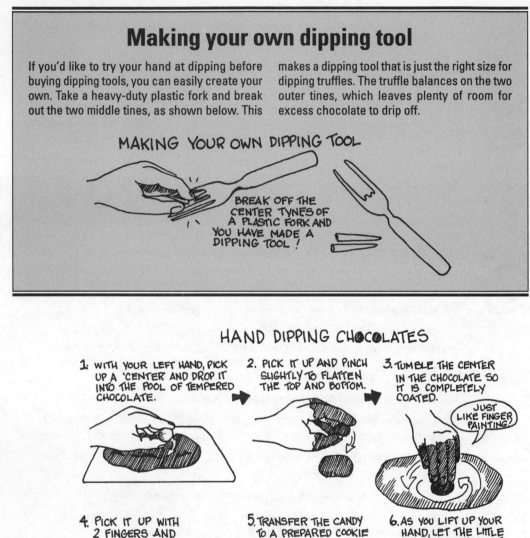

HAND DIPPING CHOCOLATES

1. WITH YOUR LEFT HAND, PICK UP A 'CENTER' AND DROP IT INTO THE POOL OF TEMPERED CHOCOLATE.

2. PICK IT UP AND PINCH SLIGHTLY TO FLATTEN THE TOP AND BOTTOM.

3. TUMBLE THE CENTER IN THE CHOCOLATE SO IT IS COMPLETELY COATED.

JUST LIKE FINGER PAINTING.

4. PICK IT UP WITH 2 FINGERS AND SHAKE TO REMOVE EXCESS CHOCOLATE.

5. TRANSFER THE CANDY TO A PREPARED COOKIE SHEET (GENTLY LET IT ROLL OFF YOUR FINGERS).

6. AS YOU LIFT UP YOUR HAND, LET THE LITTLE STRING OF CHOCOLATE CREATE A DESIGN ON TOP OF THE CANDY.

Figure 6-2: Hand dipping chocolates.

Another way to hand dip is to place a small pool of chocolate in the palm of your hand and coat the truffle center by rolling it around your palm. The only drawback to this method is that if you have warm hands, they will soon be completely coated in chocolate.

If you have very warm hands, you can wear tight-fitting latex gloves for hand dipping.

If you're partially dipping cookies or small pastries in chocolate, hold the item between your thumb and forefinger and dip the end up to halfway in chocolate. Let the excess chocolate drip off, then place on waxed or parchment paper, and chill for 15 minutes to set the chocolate.

Molding chocolate

Molded chocolates always look so perfect and beautiful. The secret is that the mold does all the work. Molds are available in just about any shape you can imagine. Many are seasonal, such as hearts for Valentine's Day, rabbits and eggs for Easter, stars and trees for Christmas, to name just a few. There are also molds that make chocolate bowls as containers for other desserts. Imagine serving a delicious white chocolate mousse in a dark chocolate molded container. Yum! Any type of chocolate can be molded, but couverture works best because of its high cocoa butter content.

There are two types of molds used for chocolate. Flexible flat plastic molds are flat on one side with three-dimensional cavities that extend to the other side of the mold. The size of the cavities varies depending on their shape. Two-part molds are used primarily for hollow molding. These molds have two parts that have the identical shapes, so they create a three-dimensional object when unmolded. The molds are often held together with a hinge or clip.

A very attractive way to present molded chocolates is to wrap them individually in colored foil. Red or gold foil looks great wrapped around hearts. Blue and silver foil makes a beautiful addition to molded chocolate stars. There are many creative ways to wrap and package molded chocolates. Let your imagination go and see how creative you can be.

When you're making molded chocolate, following these suggestions:

- **Always use tempered chocolate so it will dry quickly, shrink from the sides of the molds, and release easily.**

- **Always melt and temper more chocolate than needed for the molds.** This makes it easy to ensure you have enough. Work with at least 1 pound of chocolate. Any leftover chocolate can be stored at room temperature and used again.

✔ **Make sure the molds are completely dry and have no scratches so there's no chance of the chocolate seizing or of becoming caught in the grooves.**

✔ **Have the molds at room temperature.** If they're too warm, the chocolate won't set properly. If they're too cold, the chocolate will set too quickly.

✔ **Gently butt the inside of chocolate molds with a clean, dry cloth to create a shiny surface.**

✔ **After filling the mold with chocolate, gently tap it on a flat surface to release any air bubbles, which will make holes in the chocolate when it dries.**

To make the chocolate molding process go smoothly, it's best to have more than one mold of each type. Otherwise, you have to wait for each mold to set up before proceeding.

Solid molding

You create solid molds with flexible, flat plastic molds, which are very easy to use:

1. **Melt and temper the chocolate.**

2. **Stand two or three large parchment paper pastry cones in glasses and fill each partway with the chocolate.**

   Fold down the tops snugly and snip an opening at the pointed end of one of the cones.

3. **Squeeze chocolate into each cavity of the mold just up to, but not over, the top edge.**

   Repeat with as many molds and paper pastry cones as needed. Gently tap each mold on a flat surface to eliminate any air bubbles.

4. **Place the molds on a flat baking sheet and place the sheet on a flat surface in the freezer for at least 15 minutes, until the bottom of the mold looks frosted.**

   Remove the molds and hold them upside down over waxed paper on a flat surface.

5. **Holding opposite corners of the mold, gently twist it in opposite directions.**

   The molded chocolates should easily drop out of the molds. If they don't, return the molds to the freezer for a few more minutes and try again.

Hollow molding

You make hollow molds with two-part metal or plastic molds, which requires coating each side of the mold with thin layers of chocolate, then sticking them together to set up.

1. **Melt and temper the chocolate.**

2. **Spoon or pour the chocolate into one side of the mold, filling it completely.**

3. **Let the chocolate stand for 30 seconds, then turn the mold upside down over the bowl of chocolate and shake the mold to allow the chocolate to drip out.**

   This will leave a thin coating of chocolate on the mold. Repeat this process with the other side of the mold and again with each side of the mold.

4. **Assemble the mold and attach the clips or hinges so it is secure.**

   Chill the mold in the freezer for 20 minutes the mold to set the chocolate firmly. If using a plastic mold it will look frosted when the chocolate is completely set.

5. **Carefully unmold the chocolate.**

   Use a very sharp knife to trim the seams and remove any excess chocolate. These molded items are delicate and must be handled carefully so they don't break.

Start working with small hollow molds and become accomplished at them before moving on to large molds.

Collecting chocolate molds

Myriad chocolate molds are available in hundreds of shapes and sizes. Occasionally, you can find antique molds at flea markets and estate sales. I always look for chocolate molds when I'm traveling in Europe. Chocolate molds are not only fun to have for molding chocolate, but I like to use them for decorating my kitchen. I can change them according to the season and my whims. And I often get inspired to mold chocolate just by looking at my collection. Many of my friends give me unusual chocolate molds as gifts, too. In return, I sometimes bring a chocolate mold along with a bar of chocolate as a hostess gift when I'm invited for dinner. When you focus on collecting chocolate molds, you'll realize that they seem to be everywhere. There are no rules to collecting, except to have fun!

Decorating with Chocolate

Making your chocolate desserts look sensational is as easy as adding a decorative touch. You can make many decorations in advance to have on hand for last-minute touches. Any of these decorative touches make your chocolate desserts look like a professional made them and add lots of extra pizzazz.

Combing chocolate

A cake comb or serrated knife can be used to make very interesting textural designs on cakes. To make wavy designs on the surface of a cake that is covered with buttercream, use a cake comb. Dip the edge of the comb in hot water and dry it thoroughly. Hold it against the side of the cake that is on a decorating turntable. Slowly turn the turntable while applying slight pressure to the cake comb. Or you can make a wavy design on the side of the cake by moving the comb in a zigzag.

To make similar designs on *top* of a cake it's better to use a serrated knife to cover the larger surface. Dip the blade of the knife in hot water and dry well. Hold the knife at a slight angle to the top of the cake at the edge farthest from you. Gently pull the knife toward you while slightly moving it back and forth to create a wavy pattern.

You can create the same design on top of frosted brownies or even on a cake glazed with chocolate. Just be sure to work quickly before the glaze sets up.

Piping and writing with chocolate

Piping fine-line decorative designs or writing with chocolate are two ways of adding artistic touches to your chocolate desserts. *Happy Birthday* written in chocolate on top of a cake is always appreciated. You can also decorate a plate with piped chocolate designs before serving dessert.

The best vehicle for holding piping chocolate is a pastry cone made from parchment paper (see Chapter 4 for information on how to make a paper pastry cone). It's a good idea to have extra paper pastry cones on hand when working with piping chocolate, just in case one breaks, or in case you have more decorating to do and the filling in the pastry cone runs out.

You can pipe or write with dark, milk, or white chocolate. A contrasting color stands out against the background. Try using milk or white chocolate piping on a dark chocolate surface.

Use the quick tempering method for piping chocolate. In most cases, you'll be using a small amount (4 ounces) and it's easier to temper using the quick method.

Here are the steps for piping and writing with chocolate:

1. **Melt and temper the chocolate.**

2. **Stand a parchment paper pastry cone in a glass or measuring cup.**

3. **Pour the chocolate into the cone filling it only halfway.**

4. **Fold the top down tightly. Snip off a very small opening at the pointed tip (¼-inch or less).**

   Hold the paper pastry cone at least 1 inch above the surface to be decorated so the chocolate will flow out smoothly.

5. **Use one hand to hold the pastry cone and apply pressure to push the chocolate out and use the other hand to steady the cone.**

   This will make your designs and writing smooth and even.

Snip a very tiny opening in the pointed end of the cone to start. You can make it larger if necessary. If the chocolate flows out too quickly, the opening is too large.

If the chocolate comes out of the cone very slowly, there may be an obstruction blocking the opening. Pinch the tip to remove the object or snip off a tiny bit more of the cone. The chocolate may also be too cool to flow. Warm the pastry cone in a microwave oven on low power for a few seconds.

You can make piped designs to have on hand to decorate desserts. To do this, draw designs on paper. Place a sheet of waxed paper over the paper and trace the designs with piping chocolate. Let the piped designs set until firm, then gently release them with a flexible-blade spatula. Store the designs between layers of waxed paper in an airtight container at room temperature for a few months.

Practice piping and writing with chocolate on waxed paper before working on desserts. If you make any mistakes, you can easily fix them when practicing. This will give you confidence when piping and writing on desserts.

Creating chocolate shavings and curls

Shavings and curls are quick and easy chocolate decorations — and they dress up any dessert. You can use any type of chocolate to make shavings and curls, and you can make them in advance and store them at room temperature in an airtight container away from light and heat.

Work with at least a ½-pound bar or block of chocolate. The chocolate should be at room temperature. If it's cool, warm the chocolate in a microwave oven for a 3-second burst on high heat to make it pliable enough to produce curls. If the chocolate is too cold, you'll get very brittle pieces flying everywhere. Hold the chocolate with a paper towel so the heat of your hands doesn't melt it. Use a vegetable peeler or a small sharp knife to make shavings. Working on the thin side of the bar or block, pull the vegetable peeler or knife down — away from you — applying pressure to the chocolate, causing it to curl up. (See Figure 6-3 for an illustration.)

You can also use a melon ball scoop to make shavings and curls. To do this, place the chocolate bar or block on a flat surface covered with waxed paper and hold it in place with a paper towel. Scrape the melon ball scoop over the surface to make rounded curls and shavings.

Use a small metal spatula to move the shavings and curls. Handle them as little as possible. They are delicate and fragile and will easily break apart and melt.

☺Making Chocolate Curls☺

With a potato peeler....   or   With a french knife...
                                                    wedge against a the
                                                    hard surface like wall!
                                                    flat side up!!

Figure 6-3: On a stable block of chocolate,   Using only a small part
Making   narrow edge up, push the   of the knife (1" to 4" from
chocolate peeler, using pressure. This will   the point) push away from
curls.   make your curl!!   you to form your curl!

Coming up with chocolate cutouts

You can make just about any shape decoration you desire by using cookie cutters or a template to cut designs out of chocolate. You can make your own template by cutting a shape out of lightweight cardboard (see Figure 6-4).

1. **Line a baking sheet with parchment or waxed paper.**

2. **Melt and temper 8 to 10 ounces of chocolate (see Chapter 5).**

3. **Spread the chocolate onto the paper or a marble board.**

   If using the paper, hold opposite ends of it and gently shake to release any air bubbles.

4. **Place the pan in the refrigerator for 15 minutes to set the chocolate, then rest at room temperature for 3 to 4 minutes.**

5. **Use a cookie cutter or template with a sharp knife to cut through the chocolate.**

   Dip the end of the cutter in warm water and dry thoroughly before cutting the chocolate.

6. **Use a flexible blade metal spatula to lift the cutouts off of the paper.**

   Handle as little as possible so you don't leave fingerprints on the chocolate.

CHOCOLATE CUTOUTS

1. USE A METAL SPATULA TO SPREAD A LAYER OF CHOCOLATE ONTO A PIECE OF PARCHMENT (OR MARBLE)

2. LET IT SET. USE A COOKIE CUTTER OR SHARP KNIFE TO CUT SHAPES THROUGH THE CHOCOLATE.

3. USE A METAL SPATULA TO LIFT OFF THE PIECES OR TURN THE PARCHMENT ON TO A SECOND PIECE, PEEL OFF THE TOP LAYER AND....

...REMOVE SHAPES!

Figure 6-4: Chocolate cutouts.

Chocolate cutouts can be made in advance and stored in airtight containers between layers of waxed paper at room temperature for several months.

Making chocolate leaves

Leaves made from chocolate are beautiful additions to many desserts. Chocolate leaves can be made in advance so they're ready to be used when you need them. The best leaves to use for making chocolate leaves are thick, shiny ones with prominent veins, such as Camellia and Gardenia leaves. Just be sure that the leaves you use are nontoxic, and thoroughly wash and dry the leaves before using.

1. **Line a baking sheet with waxed paper.**

2. **Melt and temper 8 ounces bittersweet or semisweet chocolate (see Chapter 5 for information on tempering).**

3. **Holding a leaf by its stem, use a spoon to coat the underside with a thin layer of chocolate.**

   Be careful not to drip the chocolate onto the top part of the leaf. Let the excess chocolate drip off, then place each leaf on the lined baking sheet, chocolate side up.

4. **Chill in the refrigerator until the chocolate is set, about 15 minutes.**

   Let the leaves stand at room temperature for a few minutes.

5. **Starting at the stem, carefully peel the real leaf from the chocolate.**

   Handle the chocolate side of the leaves as little as possible so you don't leave fingerprints on the leaves.

Store the chocolate leaves between layers of waxed paper in an airtight container at room temperature for several weeks.

Tying chocolate ribbons

You can make ribbons out of chocolate modeling paste, also called chocolate plastic. Chocolate plastic is a mixture of chocolate and corn syrup that is pliable. It's kind of like working with the sandy textured dough you played with as a kid, but this is smooth and completely edible. Its texture is similar to marzipan. To make your own, follow the recipe in this section.

Ribbons of any size can be cut from chocolate plastic. Use small ribbons to shape into bows to adorn the top of individual desserts.

Chocolate Ribbons

Use chocolate plastic to make ribbons to wrap the outside of cakes or to use for other decorative touches.

Preparation time: *2 hours and 15 minutes, includes resting time*

Cooking time: *15 minutes*

Yield: *Eight 10-inch long ribbons or Twenty 5-inch long ribbons*

8 ounces dark chocolate, finely chopped   ¼ cup light corn syrup

1 Melt the chocolate in the top of a double boiler over hot water or in a microwave oven on low power for 30-second bursts. Stir the chocolate often with a rubber spatula to ensure even melting. Remove the top pan of the double boiler (if using) and wipe the bottom and sides very dry. Add the corn syrup and stir together well. Pour the mixture out onto a large piece of plastic wrap, form it into a flat disc, cover tightly, and leave to set up at room temperature until firm but pliable, about 2 hours.

2 Knead the mixture on a smooth, flat work surface until pliable before using. Store the mixture in an airtight container at room temperature for up to a month.

3 To make chocolate ribbons, roll out the chocolate plastic mixture on a smooth, flat work surface dusted with cocoa powder to a large rectangle with a thickness of about ⅛ inch. Use a sharp knife or pizza cutter to cut out ribbons of any width and length you desire. Use a flexible-blade metal spatula to slide underneath a ribbon so you can gently pick it up.

4 Carefully transfer the ribbon to the outside of a cake covered with frosting. Wrap the ribbon around the cake and firmly but gently pat it against the cake so it will stick. Trim off any excess where the edges meet using scissors.

Per serving (1 ribbon): Calories 185 (From Fat 83); Fat 9g (Saturated 6g); Cholesterol 0mg; Sodium 14mg; Carbohydrate 25g (Dietary Fiber 1g); Protein 1g.

Dusting and stenciling

A sprinkling of cocoa powder or confectioners' sugar or a mixture of both adds an extra-special touch to many chocolate desserts. You can use a stencil to create a unique and unusual design to decorate a dessert (see Figure 6-5).

Paper doilies offer a quick and easy stencil. Simply hold it over the top of the dessert to be decorated and dust heavily with either cocoa powder or confectioners' sugar or a combination (see Figure 6-5). Carefully remove the doily so none of the mixture escapes and mars the design.

Figure 6-5:
Dusting and
stenciling
your
desserts.

You can buy stencils in shops that specialize in cake decorating supplies, or you can make your own stencil to decorate desserts. Draw a design of your choice onto a piece of lightweight cardboard. Carefully cut out the design using very sharp scissors. Hold this stencil over a dessert and dust with you choice of materials.

If the top of the dessert is sticky, hold the stencil slightly about it, so the stencil doesn't get dirty. You can use stencils over and over, as long as they don't become dirty and crusty from coming in contact with tacky substances, like chocolate glaze or buttercream.

An interesting way to decorate a dessert is to first dust the entire top with cocoa powder or confectioners' sugar, then place a stencil over this and dust with the contrasting material (confectioners' sugar on top of cocoa powder or vice versa). This makes a dramatic presentation.

For a very professional looking presentation, stencil a design on a dessert plate, then place a slice of cake or a portion of dessert in the center of the plate.

Practice dusting and stenciling over waxed paper before decorating your dessert. An easy way to get even coverage is to place the cocoa powder or confectioners' sugar in a dredger or a fine mesh strainer.

Glazing cakes with chocolate

A smooth, shiny chocolate glaze surrounding a cake makes an elegant presentation. This is easy to do, but you must work quickly and focus on what you're doing.

Here are some tips for success with chocolate glazing:

✔ **Make sure the surface of the cake to be glazed is very smooth.** This is best accomplished by coating the cake with a layer of whipped ganache (see Queen of Sheba cake in Chapter 17) or buttercream. Let this coating set in the refrigerator until very firm.

✔ **Make sure the cake or other dessert to be glazed is at the proper temperature before it is glazed.** If the dessert is too cold, the glaze will crack when it comes in contact with the outer coating. On the other hand, if the dessert is too warm, the glaze won't adhere to it and will run off.

✔ **The glaze should be warm and fluid but not hot.** Stir it for a couple of minutes before pouring over the cake.

✔ **Line a baking sheet with parchment or waxed paper and center a cooling rack over the paper.** Center the cake on the cooling rack.

✔ **Hold the bowl or pan of glaze a couple of inches above the cake.** Starting at the center of the cake pour the glaze quickly over the surface, moving toward the outer edges.

✔ **Use a dry flexible-blade spatula and, working quickly, push the glaze over the top and edges of the cake.** Use only two or three strokes over the top of the cake. Any more than this and the spatula marks will show and mar the surface of the glaze.

✔ **If you notice bare spots on the sides of the cake, scoop up a small amount of glaze from the paper with the tip of the spatula and gently touch it to the spot.**

✔ **Let the glazed cake stand at room temperature until the glaze has set.** This time will vary depending on the temperature of the room and the dessert. In some cases it's okay to set the glaze by refrigerating the cake. The only drawback to this method is that the glaze will lose some of its sheen.

Part III
Baked Chocolate Goodies

The 5th Wave By Rich Tennant

"WHY DO I SENSE YOU'RE UPSET? BECAUSE
YOU'RE PIPING THAT CAKE WITH HAND
GRENADES INSTEAD OF ROSETTES."

In this part . . .

This is where your chocolate dreams become reality. In this part, you go into the kitchen to bake all kinds of chocolate goodies. I start you off with cookies and brownies, then move on to quick breads, muffins, and scones. All types of chocolate cakes come next, followed by chocolate pies and tarts. You'll find lots of variations, so there's something for everyone. Jump around and try any recipe you like. Why not make two while you're at it? (Your family and friends will thank you for it!)

Chapter 7

Me Like Cookies: Satisfying the Cookie Monster in You

*E*arly on in this book, I ask the question, "Who doesn't like chocolate?" Here, I ask, "Who doesn't like cookies?" The answer to both these questions is probably, "Nobody." When you use chocolate to make cookies, you have the best of both worlds.

Cookies are a hands-on dessert. They're very easy to eat — you can eat them standing still or while you're on the move. Although they require no formality, cookies can be eaten in a more formal manner during afternoon tea or as a dessert.

One of the many reasons I like cookies so much is because they're not only easy to make but also guaranteed to be a big hit — especially if they're made with chocolate. With the recipes in this chapter, you can't go wrong.

Identifying the Different Types of Cookies

Cookies are divided into categories based on how they're made. Here are the main types of cookies you'll encounter:

- **Bar cookies:** These cookies are baked and then cut when cool into bars or squares in the same pan.

- **Drop cookies:** These are dropped from a spoon or ice cream scoop (as shown in Figure 7-1) onto the cookie sheet. This type of cookie needs a firm dough that will hold its shape as it's dropped.

- **Filled cookies:** These cookies have dough wrapped around an inside filling.

- **Hand-formed cookies:** These are shaped by hand into a ball or other shape before baking.

- **Molded cookies:** These cookies are baked in the mold or are shaped by a mold before baking.

- **Refrigerator cookies:** These cookies are formed into a log-shaped cylinder that is chilled before the cookies are sliced off.

- **Rolled cookies:** These cookies are so named because the dough is rolled out on a flat surface with a rolling pin. Cookie cutters are used to cut out a variety of shapes from the dough.

- **Sandwich cookies:** These consist of two cookies that enclose a filling between them.

Figure 7-1:
An easy way to shape drop cookies is with an ice cream scoop.

USE AN ICE CREAM SCOOP TO SHAPE DOUGH!

Trying Your Hand at the Easiest Cookies in the World

Drop cookies and refrigerator cookies are the easiest kinds of cookies to make. All you do for drop cookies is mix the dough and then drop them onto the cookie sheet by the spoonful. For refrigerator cookies, you mix the dough and shape it into a log, chill it for a short while, and then slice the cookies off the log, and bake. Refrigerator cookies are great because you can keep the logs in the freezer, so you're ready to bake cookies whenever anyone drops in unexpectedly or when the kids come home from school.

Chocolate Chip–Walnut Cookies

These are classic American cookies that you probably grew up eating. They're the first cookies I ever baked when I was 5 years old, and I still love to make them. If you want to try different flavors, you can substitute milk-chocolate baking chips for the semisweet variety, and you can also try using different types of nuts.

Preparation time: *1½ hours (includes chilling)*

Baking time: *10 minutes*

Yield: *5 dozen*

2½ cups flour	*¾ cup sugar*
1 teaspoon baking soda	*2 teaspoons vanilla extract*
½ teaspoon salt	*2 eggs*
1 cup (2 sticks) butter, softened	*2 cups chocolate chips*
1 cup light brown sugar	*1 cup roughly chopped walnuts*

1 Combine the flour, baking soda, and salt in a mixing bowl. Set aside.

2 Using a mixer, beat the butter in a large mixing bowl until fluffy, about 2 minutes. Add the brown sugar, sugar, and vanilla, and mix together.

3 Add the eggs, one at a time, stopping to scrape down the sides of the bowl with a rubber spatula after each addition.

4 Blend in the flour mixture in three stages. Stir in the chips and nuts.

5 Cover the bowl tightly with plastic wrap, and chill for 30 minutes.

6 Line a cookie sheet with parchment paper. Scoop out walnut-sized mounds of the cookie dough and place on the cookie sheet, leaving 2 inches of space between the mounds. Chill the cookies for 30 minutes.

7 While the cookies are chilling, preheat the oven to 375 degrees.

8 Bake for 10 to 12 minutes, until golden. Remove the cookie sheet from the oven and transfer the cookies from the parchment to cooling racks. Store in an airtight container at room temperature for up to a week. Freeze for longer storage.

Per serving: Calories 112 (From Fat 56); Fat 6g (Saturated 3g); Cholesterol 15mg; Sodium 45mg; Carbohydrate 14g (Dietary Fiber 1g); Protein 1g.

Place cookies of the same size together on the cookie sheet so they will bake uniformly.

White Chocolate Chunk–Dried Cherry–Oatmeal Cookies

White chocolate adds extra sweetness and flavor to these yummy cookies. Dried cherries are a nice surprise that add extra zing. For a variation, try dried cranberries.

Preparation time: 10 minutes

Baking time: 10 minutes

Yield: 5 dozen

1⅔ cup flour	1 cup light brown sugar
1½ cup old-fashioned rolled oats	1 egg
¾ teaspoon baking soda	2 teaspoons vanilla extract
½ teaspoon baking powder	10 ounces (1½ cups) white chocolate, coarsely chopped, or white baking chips
½ teaspoon salt	¾ cup dried cherries
1 cup (2 sticks) butter, softened	

1 Preheat the oven to 375 degrees. Line a cookie sheet with parchment paper.

2 Combine the flour, oats, baking soda, baking powder, and salt in a mixing bowl. Set aside.

3 Using a mixer, beat the butter in a large mixing bowl until fluffy, about 2 minutes. Add the brown sugar and mix together until smooth.

4 Add the egg and vanilla. Stop to scrape down the sides of the bowl with a rubber spatula. Blend in the flour mixture in three stages. Stir in the white chocolate and dried cherries.

5 Scoop out walnut-sized mounds of the cookie dough and place on the cookie sheet, leaving 2 inches between the mounds. Bake for 10 to 12 minutes, until the cookies are light golden. Remove the cookie sheet from the oven, and transfer the cookies from the parchment to cooling racks. Store in an airtight container at room temperature for up to a week. Freeze for longer storage.

Per serving: Calories 96 (From Fat 45); Fat 5g (Saturated 3g); Cholesterol 13mg; Sodium 47mg; Carbohydrate 12g (Dietary Fiber 1g); Protein 1g.

To prevent your cookies from spreading into each other, allow adequate space between them on the cookie sheet. If you're at all concerned about your cookies' distance from each other, it's better to leave more space than you need.

Chocolate–Peanut Butter Coins

These delicious cookies work best with a natural-style or freshly ground peanut butter. They can be made even more special by half-dipping them in chocolate or drizzling chocolate on top.

Preparation time: *15 minutes*

Baking time: *10 minutes*

Yield: *3½ to 4 dozen*

½ cup (1 stick) butter, softened	*½ cup natural cocoa powder*
1 cup light brown sugar	*½ teaspoon baking soda*
1 egg	*Pinch of salt*
1 teaspoon vanilla extract	*½ cup creamy peanut butter*
1½ cups flour	

1 Using a mixer and mixing bowl, beat the butter until fluffy, about 2 minutes. Add the sugar and mix together until smooth. In a small bowl, stir the egg with the vanilla and add to the butter mixture, blending well.

2 Sift together the flour, cocoa powder, baking soda, and salt, and add to the mixture in three stages. Add the peanut butter and blend well.

3 Divide the dough in half. Place each piece on a large rectangle of waxed paper and roll each into a cylinder 8 to 10 inches long and 1 inch thick. Wrap the cylinders in the waxed paper, wrap again in plastic wrap, and chill for at least 2 hours, until firm. The cylinders can be frozen at this point. If frozen, defrost overnight in the refrigerator before using.

4 Preheat the oven to 350 degrees. Line a cookie sheet with parchment paper. Cut each cylinder into ¼-inch-thick slices. Place on the cookie sheet with 2 inches between them.

5 Bake for 10 minutes or until firm. Remove the cookie sheets from the oven and transfer to cooling racks for a few minutes. Then transfer the cookies from the cookie sheet to the cooling racks to cool completely. Store in an airtight container at room temperature up to a week. Freeze for longer storage.

Per serving: Calories 68 (From Fat 32); Fat 4g (Saturated 2g); Cholesterol 9mg; Sodium 32mg; Carbohydrate 9g (Dietary Fiber 1g); Protein 1g.

The word *cookie* comes from the Dutch work *koekje,* meaning "small cake."

Chocolate-Cinnamon Coins

Very chocolaty is the best way to describe these. The crystal sugar on the outside adds extra crunch and is a great flavor enhancer, with cinnamon adding its own special touch. Crystal sugar is white sugar that has been processed into small oblong pellets that are about four to six times larger than grains of regular sugar. It's used for garnishing and decorating and can be colored with food coloring. You can find crystal sugar in the baking aisle of the supermarket or through the sources in Chapter 19.

Preparation time: *1 hour (includes chilling)*

Baking time: *10 minutes*

Yield: *About 3 dozen*

2¼ cups flour	1 egg
1 cup sugar	2 teaspoons vanilla extract
⅓ cup unsweetened Dutch-processed cocoa powder	4 ounces bittersweet chocolate, finely chopped
½ teaspoon baking powder	1 egg yolk
2 teaspoons ground cinnamon	¼ cup crystal sugar
1 cup (2 sticks) butter, cold	

1 Combine the flour, sugar, cocoa powder, baking powder, and cinnamon in the work bowl of a food processor fitted with a steel blade. Pulse briefly to blend.

2 Cut the butter into small pieces and add. Pulse until the butter is cut into tiny pieces, about 1 minute.

3 Add the egg and vanilla, and pulse until the dough is well blended, about 30 seconds. Add the chopped chocolate and pulse to blend well, another 30 seconds to a minute.

(If not using a food processor, soften the butter briefly in a microwave oven or let it stand at room temperature. Using a mixer and mixing bowl, beat the butter until fluffy, about 2 minutes. Add the sugar, and cream together well. Mix the flour with the cocoa powder and cinnamon and add to the butter mixture in three stages, stopping to scrape down the sides of the bowl after each addition. Add the egg and vanilla and mix well, then add the chopped chocolate and mix until well blended.)

4 Divide the dough in half and place each half on a large sheet of waxed paper. Use the waxed paper to shape each into a log about 8 inches long and 2 inches wide. Wrap the logs in the waxed paper and chill in the freezer for about 40 minutes or in the refrigerator for several hours, until firm enough to slice.

5 Preheat the oven to 350 degrees. Line a cookie sheet with parchment paper.

6 Lightly beat the egg yolk in a small bowl. Use a pastry brush to coat the outside of each log with egg yolk. Divide the crystal sugar in half and roll each log in the sugar, coating the outside completely.

7 Cut each cylinder into ½-inch-thick slices. Place the slices on the cookie sheet with an inch of space between the slices.

8 Bake for 10 to 11 minutes, until set. Remove the cookie sheet from the oven and let it cool on a rack for several minutes. Transfer the cookies from the cookie sheet to the cooling rack to cool completely. Store in an airtight container at room temperature for up to a week. Freeze for longer storage.

Per serving: Calories 136 (From Fat 67); Fat 8g (Saturated 5g); Cholesterol 29mg; Sodium 10mg; Carbohydrate 16g (Dietary Fiber 1g); Protein 2g.

Creating Classy Cookies

A classy cookie is, quite simply, one that's a little fancier than other cookies. You may not want to make classy cookies on a daily basis — but if they're your favorites, there's no reason you can't. Classy cookies work well for special occasions, and they're wonderful to give as gifts. Next time you're invited to a dinner party or any other get-together, bring some of these and you'll be the most popular one there. In this section, you'll find recipes for sandwich, hand-formed, molded, and filled cookies. These may take a little more effort to make, but the rewards are great.

The appeal of cookies

One reason that cookies are so popular is that, because of the variety of cookies you can make, they meet the needs of everyone's taste. If you're having guests and you aren't sure which cookies to serve, the best bet is to make two or three different types. This way you're sure they will all be eaten.

Cookies are also popular because they work for just about any occasion. They're great for a picnic, a potluck gathering, a dinner party, or an afternoon tea, to name just a few. Cookies also make wonderful gifts. Plus, they're convenient. No formal etiquette is required — just put them on a plate and watch them disappear. And if you happen to have some left over, they're great for a midnight snack or the next day's lunch.

Double-Chocolate Sandwich Cookies

This recipe is a way to double your cookie-eating pleasure. With these you get two dark-chocolate wafers and a rich-chocolate, frosting-like filling. You can use this filling with just about any cookies — either as a filling for sandwich cookies or as a topping.

Preparation time: 35 minutes (includes melting)

Baking time: 18 minutes

Yield: About 20 sandwiches

Chocolate Buttercream Filling (see the following recipe)

1 cup flour

½ teaspoon baking soda

¼ teaspoon salt

¼ cup natural cocoa powder

½ cup (1 stick) butter, softened

⅔ cup light brown sugar

1 egg

1 teaspoon vanilla extract

1 Preheat oven to 325 degrees. Line a cookie sheet with parchment paper.

2 Sift together the flour, baking soda, salt, and cocoa powder. Set aside.

3 Using a mixer, beat the butter in a large mixing bowl until fluffy, about 2 minutes. Add the brown sugar, and mix together until smooth. In a separate bowl, blend the egg with the vanilla, and add to the butter mixture. Stop and scrape down the sides of the bowl with a rubber spatula.

4 Add the dry ingredients to the butter mixture in three stages, stopping to scrape down the sides of the bowl after each addition. Blend thoroughly.

5 Fit a 12– or 14-inch pastry bag with a ½-inch plain round tip (#5). Fill the bag partway with batter. On the cookie sheet, pipe out 1-inch-thick mounds, leaving 2 inches between them. You can also scoop out mounds of dough using an ice cream scoop or a spoon. Bake for 18 to 20 minutes, until set. Remove the cookie sheet from the oven and transfer the cookies from the parchment paper to cooling racks.

6 For each sandwich cookie, place a tablespoon of filling on the flat side of one cookie. Place a second cookie on top and gently press together until the filling spreads to the sides. Wipe off any filling that drips or spills over the sides. Store at room temperature in a single layer covered with foil for 2 days. The cookies can be kept up to 5 days in an airtight container at room temperature without the filling.

Chocolate Buttercream Filling

3 ounces bittersweet or semisweet chocolate, finely chopped

3 tablespoons butter

¼ cup cream

2 cups confectioners' sugar, sifted

1 Melt the chopped chocolate and butter together in the top of a double boiler over warm water. Stir frequently with a rubber spatula to ensure even melting.

2 Remove the top pan of the double boiler and wipe the bottom and sides dry. Pour the cream into the chocolate/butter mixture and stir until thoroughly blended.

3 Stir in the confectioners' sugar in three stages, blending well after each addition.

Per serving: Calories 186 (From Fat 84); Fat 9g (Saturated 5g); Cholesterol 32mg; Sodium 69mg; Carbohydrate 25g (Dietary Fiber 1g); Protein 2g.

Cocoa Shortbread Fingers

You're probably familiar with shortbread cookies, but this recipe takes the old standby to new heights. The addition of cocoa powder adds rich depth of flavor that is very satisfying. I guarantee these will disappear quickly, so you may want to make an extra batch. For extra added chocolate flavor, drizzle some melted chocolate on top after the shortbread is cool.

Preparation time: *2¼ hours (includes chilling)*

Baking time: *40 minutes*

Yield: *60 fingers, 1 x 2 inches each*

2 cups (4 sticks) butter, softened	*½ cups unsweetened Dutch-processed cocoa powder*
1 cup sugar	
½ teaspoon salt	*3½ cups flour*

1 Using a mixer, beat the butter in a large mixing bowl until fluffy, about 2 minutes. Add the sugar and mix together until smooth.

2 Combine the salt, cocoa powder, and flour together. Stir to blend well. Add to the butter mixture in 4 stages, stopping to scrape down the sides of the bowl after each addition. After all the dry ingredients are added, continue to mix for another 2 to 3 minutes, until the dough is smooth and soft.

3 Lightly flour a 9-x-13-inch baking pan. Dust your fingertips with flour and press the dough evenly into the baking pan. Use a ruler to score the dough into bars that are 1 inch wide and 2 inches long. Use a fork to pierce each bar on the diagonal two times. Cover the pan tightly with plastic wrap and chill for at least 2 hours.

4 Preheat the oven to 275 degrees. Line a cookie sheet with parchment paper. Cut through the scored lines on the chilled dough and place the bars on the cookie sheet, leaving 2 inches between them.

5 Bake for 40 minutes, until set. Remove the cookie sheet from the oven and transfer the cookies to racks to cool. Store in an airtight container at room temperature for up to a week. Freeze for longer storage.

Per serving: *Calories 95 (From Fat 57); Fat 6g (Saturated 4g); Cholesterol 17mg; Sodium 21mg; Carbohydrate 9g (Dietary Fiber 0g); Protein 1g.*

Cookie troubleshooting

Always bake cookies for the least amount time called for in the recipe. You can easily add more time if necessary, but it's impossible to subtract it if the cookies are overbaked. If your cookies are too dry, it's a result of overbaking.

If the cookie dough is too soft or sticky when it's rolled out, it's either too warm and needs to be chilled, or it doesn't have enough flour. Be sure to double check the recipe to make sure you measured the correct amount of flour.

If the cookie dough is too dry and crumbly when it's rolled out, it doesn't have enough liquid or fat, or it has too much flour. Sometimes the dough is too cold to roll out. Let it stand briefly at room temperature until it becomes pliable enough to work with or warm it in a microwave oven for 5– to 10-second intervals on low power.

A few different factors contribute to cookies spreading too much as they bake:

✔ **The cookie sheet may be overgreased.** The best solution to this is to line the cookie sheet with parchment paper or a nonstick liner.

✔ **The cookie dough may have been placed on a hot cookie sheet.** Cookie dough on a hot cookie sheet will start to spread before it reaches the oven. Let the cookie sheet cool between batches.

✔ **The cookie dough may have been sitting at room temperature too long.** Letting a cookie sheet of dough sit at room temperature while waiting to go into the oven isn't a good idea. Instead, keep waiting cookie dough in the refrigerator.

✔ **The cookies may have too much fat or liquid, which causes them to spread.** Cookies made with butter spread more than those made with shortening.

If the bottom of your cookies is too crisp or dark, the oven temperature may be too hot or the cookie sheet may be too close to the source of heat. Bake cookies on the center rack of the oven and check your oven temperature.

If you notice that your cookies break when you move them from the cookie sheet to the cooling rack, they need to cool slightly before they're moved. When you take the cookie sheet out of the oven, place it on the cooling rack and let the cookies stand for 3 to 5 minutes before transferring them to the rack.

If your cookies stick to the cookie sheet, it's due to one of several reasons:

✔ The cookie sheet wasn't prepared correctly.

✔ The cookie sheet wasn't covered with parchment paper or a nonstick liner.

✔ The cookies cooled too long on the cookie sheet before being transferred to the cooling rack.

If your cookies bake unevenly on the cookie sheet, either the dough was rolled or shaped unevenly or the oven has hot spots. To remedy hot spots, rotate the cookie sheets partway through the baking process.

Have space set aside and your cooling racks ready for your cookies when they come out of the oven. There's nothing more frustrating than juggling hot cookie sheets.

French-Style Chocolate Macaroons

These are the type of macaroons found in elegant French pastry shops. They're different from American-style macaroons because they're filled with ganache, a velvety smooth mixture of chocolate and cream. Try them with afternoon coffee or tea or whenever you want a sophisticated cookie.

Tools: *Jelly roll pan*

Preparation time: *1½ hours (includes chilling)*

Baking time: *14 minutes*

Yield: *About 30 assembled cookies*

Ganache (see the following recipe)

4 egg whites at room temperature

⅓ teaspoon cream of tartar

1⅓ cups confectioners' sugar, sifted

Pinch of salt

¼ cup unsweetened Dutch-processed cocoa powder, sifted

1½ cups finely ground almonds or almond flour

1 teaspoon vanilla extract

1 Preheat the oven to 350 degrees. Line a cookie sheet with aluminum foil, shiny side up.

2 Using a mixer, whip the egg whites in a large mixing bowl until they are frothy, about 1 minute. Add the cream of tartar and continue to whip on medium speed. Slowly add the sugar and whip until the whites hold firm peaks. Set aside.

3 In a separate bowl, combine the salt, cocoa powder, and ground almonds. Toss to blend well. Fold in to the egg whites in three stages, blending well after each addition. Add the vanilla and mix well.

4 Fit a 14-inch pastry bag with a ½-inch plain round tip (#5) and fill partway with the mixture. Hold the pastry bag 1 inch above the cookie sheet and pipe out 1-inch mounds, leaving 2 inches between the mounds.

5 Bake for 14 to 15 minutes, until set. Remove the cookie sheet from the oven and place on a cooling rack. Immediately lift up a corner of the foil and carefully pour ¼ cup water under the foil to make steam, which makes removing the macaroons from the foil easy. Let cool completely, then remove the macaroons from the foil.

6 Using a mixer whip the Ganache in a mixing bowl until it holds soft peaks, about 1 minute. Fit a 14-inch pastry bag with a ½-inch plain round tip (#5) and fill partway with the whipped Ganache.

7 Pipe a small mound (about 2 teaspoons of Ganache) on the flat side of one of the cookies. Place a second cookie on top and gently press together until the Ganache spreads to the sides. Wipe off any Ganache that spills over the sides. Store in a single layer, tightly covered, in the refrigerator for up to 2 days. They will soften slightly but remain delicious.

Tip: Don't get carried away and pipe out big mounds of the cookie mixture. They need to stay small and flat on top to resemble the French originals. The mounds will spread a bit as they bake.

Ganache

4 ounces bittersweet or semisweet chocolate,   ½ cup heavy cream
very finely chopped

Melt the chocolate in the top of a double boiler over warm water or in a microwave oven on low power for 30 second bursts. Stir often with a rubber spatula. In a separate small saucepan, bring the cream to a boil. Remove the top pan of the double boiler and wipe the bottom and sides very dry. Pour the cream into the chocolate and stir to blend thoroughly. Transfer the mixture to another bowl, cover tightly with plastic wrap, and cool to room temperature. Refrigerate until thick, but not stiff, about an hour.

Per serving: Calories 142 (From Fat 90); Fat 10g (Saturated 2g); Cholesterol 6mg; Sodium 10mg; Carbohydrate 11g (Dietary Fiber 2g); Protein 4g.

Double-Chocolate Biscotti with Pistachios and Dried Cranberries

Biscotti has become an all-American favorite. Cocoa powder and chopped chocolate are used to give these a powerful chocolate flavor. The addition of pistachios and dried cranberries make them an absolute winner. They keep well and are perfect to pack in lunches.

Preparation time: *15 minutes*

Baking time: *1 hour and 5 minutes (includes resting)*

Yield: *About 3 dozen*

½ cup (1 stick) butter, softened

1½ cups flour

½ cup unsweetened Dutch-processed cocoa powder

2 teaspoons baking soda

¼ teaspoon salt

½ cup sugar

⅓ cup light brown sugar

2 eggs

1½ teaspoons vanilla extract

½ teaspoon chocolate extract (optional)

3 ounces (⅔ cup) bittersweet or semisweet chocolate, chopped into small chunks

1 cup shelled, toasted pistachio nuts

1 cup dried cranberries

1 Preheat the oven to 350 degrees. Line a cookie sheet with parchment paper.

2 Melt the butter in a small saucepan or in the microwave.

3 In a large mixing bowl, sift together the flour, cocoa powder, baking soda, and salt. Add the sugar and stir to blend well.

4 In a separate bowl, whisk the eggs with the vanilla and chocolate extract (if using). Add to the dry ingredients along with the melted butter. Using a mixer, blend on low speed until thoroughly combined. Blend in the chocolate chunks, pistachios, and dried cranberries.

5 Divide the dough in half. Dust your hands with flour and shape each half of the dough into a log about 8 inches long by 2 inches wide by ¾ inch high. Center a log on the cookie sheet. Keep the remaining dough covered with plastic in the refrigerator, or you can bake two logs on one sheet.

6 Bake for 28 minutes, until set. Remove the cookie sheet from the oven and rest for 30 minutes. Lower the oven temperature to 325 degrees.

7 Transfer the log to a cutting board. Cut the log on the diagonal into ½-inch-thick slices and place the slices on their sides (see Figure 7-2). Bake for 16 to 18 minutes, until firm. Remove the cookie sheet from the oven and transfer the cookies to racks to cool. Store in an airtight container at room temperature for up to 3 weeks. Freeze for longer storage.

Per serving: Calories 110 (From Fat 49); Fat 5g (Saturated 3g); Cholesterol 19mg; Sodium 91mg; Carbohydrate 14g (Dietary Fiber 1g); Protein 2g.

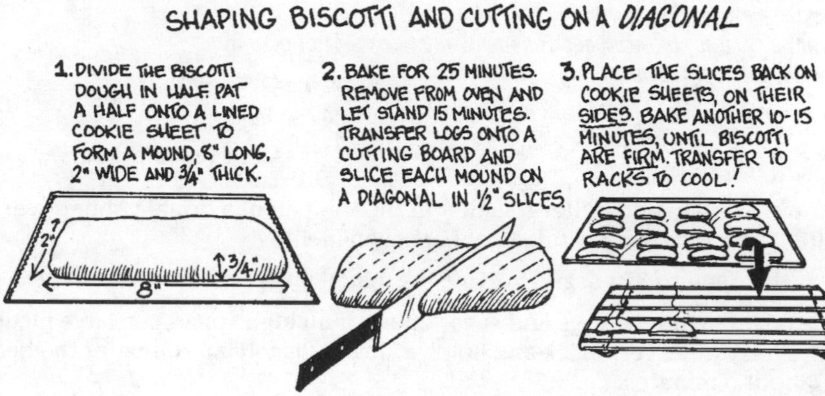

SHAPING BISCOTTI AND CUTTING ON A *DIAGONAL*

Figure 7-2: Shaping biscotti and cutting on the diagonal.

1. DIVIDE THE BISCOTTI DOUGH IN HALF. PAT A HALF ONTO A LINED COOKIE SHEET TO FORM A MOUND, 8" LONG, 2" WIDE AND ¾" THICK.

2. BAKE FOR 25 MINUTES. REMOVE FROM OVEN AND LET STAND 15 MINUTES. TRANSFER LOGS ONTO A CUTTING BOARD AND SLICE EACH MOUND ON A DIAGONAL IN ½" SLICES.

3. PLACE THE SLICES BACK ON COOKIE SHEETS, ON THEIR SIDES. BAKE ANOTHER 10-15 MINUTES, UNTIL BISCOTTI ARE FIRM. TRANSFER TO RACKS TO COOL!

Chocolate Madeleines

If you like a cake-like cookie, these are the way to go. The hint of vanilla helps to intensify the chocolate flavor. I love the shell shape of these that results from the pan they're baked in. If you don't have a madeleine pan, you can use a mini-muffin pan. A madeleine pan is a flat rectangular pan with shell-shaped indentations that give the baked cookies their characteristic ribbed scallop-shell shape. The pans come in different sizes with a variety of indentations, but the most common size holds 12 cookies that measure 3 inches by 1¾ inches by ½ inch deep.

Tools: *Two 12-cavity madeleine pans*

Preparation time: *25 minutes (includes melting)*

Baking time: *12 minutes*

Yield: *2 dozen*

2½ ounces (½ cup) bittersweet or semisweet chocolate, finely chopped

6 tablespoons (¾ stick) butter, cut into pieces

2 eggs

⅓ cup sugar

⅛ teaspoon salt

½ cup flour

½ teaspoon vanilla extract

1 Melt the chocolate and butter together in the top pan of a double boiler over hot water. Stir often with a rubber spatula to ensure even melting.

2 Preheat the oven to 350 degrees. Place the madeleine pans on cookie sheets.

3 Using a mixer, whip the eggs and sugar on medium-high speed in a large mixing bowl until the mixture is very thick and holds a slowly dissolving ribbon as the beater is lifted, about 5 minutes.

4 In a separate mixing bowl, blend the salt into the flour and add to the eggs in 3 stages. Stop and scrape down the sides of the bowl with a rubber spatula after each addition. Add the chocolate and butter mixture and blend in thoroughly. Blend in the vanilla.

5 Transfer the mixture to a 2-cup liquid measuring cup. Spray the cavities of two 12-cavity madeleine pans with non-stick cooking spray. Pour the batter into each cavity of the pans, filling them three-fourths full. Bake for 12 to 15 minutes, until the madeleines are set and the tops spring back when lightly touched.

6 Remove the cookie sheets from the oven and turn the madeleine pans upside down onto cooling racks. Gently shake the pans to remove the madeleines. Cool completely on the racks. Store in an airtight container at room temperature for up to 3 days. Freeze for longer storage.

Per serving: *Calories 69 (From Fat 39); Fat 4g (Saturated 3g); Cholesterol 26mg; Sodium 18mg; Carbohydrate 7g (Dietary Fiber 0g); Protein 1g.*

Chocolate-Apricot Rugelach

This is a special Eastern European cookie that involves a little more effort, but it's well worth it. A cream cheese and butter dough is rolled out, cut into pie-shaped wedges, and wrapped around a delicious filling of nuts, dried apricots, chocolate, and cinnamon. The final shape looks like a croissant, but the taste and texture are totally different — crispy and crunchy.

Preparation time: *1½ hours (includes chilling)*

Baking time: *20 minutes*

Yield: *4 dozen*

½ pound cream cheese, softened

1 cup (2 sticks) butter, softened

1 teaspoon vanilla extract

2⅔ cups flour

¼ cup confectioners' sugar

¼ teaspoon salt

¾ cup walnuts

½ cup dried apricots, chopped

½ cup plus 6 tablespoons sugar

2 tablespoons plus 2 teaspoons ground cinnamon

¾ cups semisweet chocolate chips

1 egg beaten with 1 teaspoon water

1 For the dough, combine the cream cheese and butter in a large mixing bowl. Using a mixer, beat together until smooth. Blend in the vanilla. Sift together the flour, confectioners' sugar, and salt. Add to the cream cheese mixture in 3 stages, stopping to scrape down the sides of the bowl after each addition. Blend thoroughly. Divide the dough into 6 equal pieces. Shape each piece into a flat disk about 5 inches round. Cover with plastic wrap and chill for at least an hour, until firm.

2 For the filling, combine the walnuts, dried apricots, ½ cup sugar, and 2 tablespoons cinnamon in the work bowl of a food processor fitted with a steel blade. Pulse until the mixture is finely chopped, about 30 seconds. Add the chocolate chips and pulse for about 15 seconds again to chop them.

3 Preheat the oven to 350 degrees. Line a cookie sheet with parchment paper.

4 To assemble, work with one piece of dough at a time while keeping the others chilled. Roll each piece on a floured surface into a circle about 10 inches round (see Figure 7-3). Sprinkle one-sixth of the filling over the dough. Press it into the dough by rolling over it with the rolling pin. Cut each circle into 8 even pie-shaped pieces. Starting from the wide end, roll each piece toward the point into a tight sausage shape. Place each piece on the cookie sheet, leaving 1 inch between each cookie. Mix together the 6 tablespoons sugar and the 2 teaspoons cinnamon. Brush the top of each cookie with the beaten egg and sprinkle with the cinnamon sugar.

5 Bake for 20 to 25 minutes, until light golden brown. Remove the cookie sheet from the oven, and transfer the cookies to racks to cool. Store in an airtight container at room temperature for up to a week. Freeze for longer storage.

Per serving: *Calories 121 (From Fat 67); Fat 8g (Saturated 4g); Cholesterol 20mg; Sodium 29mg; Carbohydrate 13g (Dietary Fiber 1g); Protein 2g.*

FILLING AND SHAPING RUGELACH

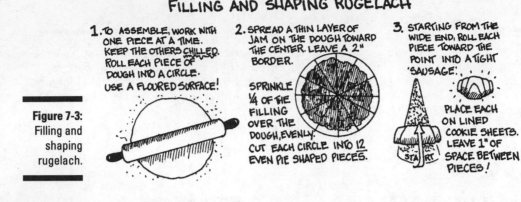

Figure 7-3: Filling and shaping rugelach.

1. TO ASSEMBLE, WORK WITH ONE PIECE AT A TIME. KEEP THE OTHERS CHILLED. ROLL EACH PIECE OF DOUGH INTO A CIRCLE. USE A FLOURED SURFACE!

2. SPREAD A THIN LAYER OF JAM ON THE DOUGH TOWARD THE CENTER. LEAVE A 2" BORDER.

   SPRINKLE ¼ OF THE FILLING OVER THE DOUGH, EVENLY. CUT EACH CIRCLE INTO 12 EVEN PIE SHAPED PIECES.

3. STARTING FROM THE WIDE END, ROLL EACH PIECE TOWARD THE POINT INTO A TIGHT 'SAUSAGE'.

   PLACE EACH ON LINED COOKIE SHEETS. LEAVE 1" OF SPACE BETWEEN PIECES!

   START

Chapter 8

Brownies You Can't Eat Just One Of

*J*ust hearing the word *brownies* causes most people to think of a wonderful taste experience. I can't think of anyone who doesn't like brownies. Most people were raised eating them — and they weren't store-bought. After all, when it comes to brownies, homemade is the only way to go.

A brownie is, quite simply, a cross between a cake and a cookie. Now think about it for a minute: Most people like cookies and most people like cake. So when the two are brought together, it's bliss. What you end up with is a texture that is usually more dense than a cake, but not as crispy or crunchy as many cookies.

Another thing that's great about brownies is that they're easy to handle. Like cookies, they're finger food. With a brownie, however, you usually get a little more than with a cookie — of course, this depends on how you cut them. Also, brownies can be baked, cut, and stored in the same pan. Brownies are also very easy to transport and are perfect for packing into lunch bags and picnic baskets.

Having Fun with Fudgy Brownies

Fudgy brownies have a very moist texture. When a cake tester or toothpick is inserted in the center, moist crumbs cling to it. You won't find a fudgy brownie that's dry inside. If they *are* dry, they won't have their typical gooey texture, because they've most likely been overbaked. Fudgy brownies have a pronounced chocolate flavor. Often, they're made using unsweetened chocolate or a combination of unsweetened and bittersweet or semisweet (dark) chocolate. Fudgy brownies are classics. They normally don't need any enhancements. You simply bake them and eat them. These are the type of brownies you probably think of when you have a brownie craving. Although I like other types of brownies, fudgy brownies are my favorite.

Follow the instructions and use the exact ingredients in each brownie recipe, because they've been formulated carefully to produce particular results. If you change methods and ingredients, you may have a different outcome than you expect.

To easily cut brownies and remove them from the baking pan, line the pan with foil that hangs about 2 inches over the edges. The overhang can be used like a handle to lift the entire batch of brownies from the pan. Gently peel the foil away from the sides of the brownies and cut them cleanly into squares.

Be sure to wipe the bottom and sides of the top pan of the double boiler very dry when it's removed from the water. If any stray drops of water run down the sides of the pan and mix with the chocolate as it's poured out, the chocolate will *seize,* or thicken like mud.

Super-Fudgy Brownies

These are the quintessential fudgy brownie, with deep chocolate flavor. Either a cold glass of milk or a cup of steaming hot coffee is the perfect accompaniment to these rich and decadent treats. A scoop of vanilla ice cream goes well with them, too.

Preparation time: *25 minutes (includes melting)*

Baking time: *35 minutes*

Yield: *Sixteen 2-inch squares*

1 tablespoon butter, softened, for the pan	*1½ cups sugar*
4 ounces unsweetened chocolate, finely chopped	*1 teaspoon vanilla extract*
3 ounces bittersweet chocolate, finely chopped	*¾ cup plus 1 tablespoon flour*
¾ cup (1½ sticks) butter, cut into small pieces	*2 tablespoons unsweetened Dutch-processed cocoa powder*
2 eggs and 1 egg yolk	*⅛ teaspoon salt*

1 Preheat the oven to 350 degrees. Line an 8-inch square baking pan with a large piece of aluminum foil, letting it hang over the edges about 2 inches. Butter the foil lightly with the tablespoon of butter.

2 Place the unsweetened chocolate, bittersweet chocolate, and butter in the top of a double boiler over hot water. Or combine the chocolates and butter in a microwave-proof bowl and melt in a microwave on low for 30 second bursts. Stir often with a rubber spatula to ensure even melting. Remove the top pan of the double boiler and wipe the bottom and sides very dry. Let stand to cool for 10 minutes, stirring often to prevent a skin from forming on top.

3 Using a mixer whip the eggs and egg yolk together in a large mixing bowl. Add the sugar and whip until the mixture is very pale and thick and holds a slowly dissolving ribbon as the beater is lifted. Blend in the vanilla.

4 Sift the flour, cocoa powder, and salt onto a piece of waxed paper.

5 Add the melted chocolate mixture to the egg and sugar mixture, and blend thoroughly. In three stages, add the flour and cocoa mixture to the batter, blending well after each addition.

6 Transfer the batter to the prepared baking pan. Bake the brownies for 35 minutes, until a tester inserted in the center comes out with a few moist crumbs clinging to it. Remove the pan from the oven and transfer it to a cooling rack to cool completely.

7 To cut the brownies, lift them from the baking pan by holding onto the edges of the aluminum foil, and place on a cutting board. Peel the foil away from the sides of the brownies. Cut into 4 rows in each direction with a knife dipped in hot water and dried between cuts. Store in an airtight container between layers of waxed paper at room temperature for up to 4 days. Freeze for longer storage.

Per serving: Calories 260 (From Fat 145); Fat 16g (Saturated 10g); Cholesterol 65mg; Sodium 30mg; Carbohydrate 29g (Dietary Fiber 2g); Protein 3g.

Don't overbake your brownies or they'll dry out and lose their fudginess.

Brownies: What's in a name?

Where did the name *brownies* come from? No one is exactly sure. Some speculate that the name comes from their brown color. Others say that they were named after a girl with the nickname "Brownie." We may never know where the name comes from, but that doesn't stop us from loving them. Brownies are an all-American creation and have been around for over a century. From their current popularity, it looks as though they'll be with us into the next century and beyond.

Checkerboard Brownies

White chocolate frosting is the crowning touch on these yummy double-chocolate brownies. You can bake the brownies a day or two in advance and hold them at room temperature tightly wrapped in aluminum foil before adding the frosting.

Preparation time: *30 minutes (includes melting)*

Baking time: *25 minutes*

Yield: *Sixteen 2-inch brownies*

White Chocolate Frosting (see the following recipe)

1 tablespoon butter, softened, for the pan

½ cup flour

¼ teaspoon baking soda

¼ teaspoon salt

¾ cup (1½ sticks) butter, cut into small pieces

3 ounces bittersweet chocolate, finely chopped

1 cup light brown sugar

2 eggs

1 teaspoon vanilla extract

3 ounces bittersweet chocolate, cut into small chunks

1 Preheat the oven to 350 degrees. Line an 8-inch square baking pan with a large piece of aluminum foil, letting it hang over the edges about 2 inches. Butter the foil lightly with the tablespoon of butter.

2 Sift the flour, baking soda, and salt together onto a piece of waxed paper.

3 Melt the butter in a 2-quart saucepan over medium heat. Remove the pan from the heat and use a wooden spoon to stir in the 3 ounces finely chopped chocolate. Stir to melt the chocolate completely and cool the mixture. Blend in the brown sugar thoroughly.

4 Add the eggs one at a time, blending well after each addition. Stir in the vanilla. Blend in the flour mixture in two stages, mixing well after each addition. Stir in the chocolate chunks.

5 Transfer the batter to the prepared baking pan. Bake 25 to 30 minutes, until a tester inserted in the center comes out with moist crumbs clinging to it. Remove the pan from the oven and cool on a rack.

6 Use a small metal icing spatula to spread the White Chocolate Frosting evenly over the top of the brownies. Chill for 15 minutes to set the frosting, then cut into squares by cutting four rows in each direction. Store the brownies in a single layer, tightly wrapped with plastic wrap, in the refrigerator for up to 4 days.

White Chocolate Frosting

4 ounces white chocolate, finely chopped   *½ cup confectioners' sugar, sifted*

7 ounces cream cheese, softened

1 Melt the white chocolate in the top pan of a double boiler over warm water. When the chocolate is almost melted, remove the top pan of the double boiler and wipe the bottom and sides completely dry. Stir the white chocolate until it's smooth.

2 Using a mixer, beat the cream cheese in a large mixing bowl until it's smooth and fluffy, about 2 minutes. Add the white chocolate and the confectioners' sugar, and beat until the mixture is well blended.

Per serving: Calories 314 (From Fat 184); Fat 21g (Saturated 12g); Cholesterol 67mg; Sodium 115mg; Carbohydrate 30g (Dietary Fiber 1g); Protein 3g.

Wait until your brownies are completely cool before cutting them, or they may fall apart.

The best way to cut brownies is to use a knife that has been run under hot water and dried. This will make a clean cut without dragging extra crumbs along.

Be sure to separate layers of brownies with waxed paper in their storage container or they'll stick together.

You can cut your brownies into smaller squares by cutting five rows in each direction, making 1½-inch squares.

Gianduia Brownies

Gianduia (pronounced john-DOO-yah) is a blend of chocolate and hazelnuts that was created in the Piedmont region of Italy in the early 19th century. It's easy to produce the wonderful flavor of gianduia by combing hazelnuts and chocolate together. This recipes also call for Nutella, a creamy Italian hazelnut-chocolate spread that can be found in most supermarkets and specialty food shops. Nutella adds another flavor dimension to these delicious treats. When you make these, you'll be hooked on gianduia. They're my all-time favorite brownies.

Preparation time: *30 minutes (includes melting)*

Baking time: *35 minutes*

Yield: *Sixteen 2-inch brownies*

1 tablespoon butter, for the pan	½ cup (1 stick) butter, cut into small pieces
1½ cups toasted, partially skinned hazelnuts	¼ cup Nutella
1 tablespoon plus ½ cup flour	½ teaspoon baking powder
4 ounces bittersweet chocolate, finely chopped	⅛ teaspoon salt
3 ounces milk chocolate, finely chopped	½ cup sugar
	2 eggs

1 Preheat the oven to 350 degrees. Line an 8-inch square baking pan with a large piece of aluminum foil, letting it hang over the edges about 2 inches. Butter the foil lightly with the tablespon of butter.

2 Place the hazelnuts and 1 tablespoon of the flour in the work bowl of a food processor fitted with a steel blade, in a clean coffee grinder, or a blender. Pulse to chop the nuts fairly finely, about 30 seconds.

3 Melt the chopped chocolates, butter, and Nutella in the top pan of a double boiler over warm water. Stir often with a rubber spatula to ensure even melting. Remove the top pan and wipe the bottom and sides completely dry. Let stand to cool for 10 minutes, stirring often to prevent a skin from forming on top.

4 Sift together the ½ cup flour, baking powder, and salt. Stir the sugar into the chocolate mixture, blending thoroughly. Add the eggs and stir until the mixture is smooth.

5 Add the flour mixture and the hazelnuts and stir to blend well.

6 Transfer the batter to the prepared pan. Bake 35 to 40 minutes, until a tester inserted in the center comes out with moist crumbs clinging to it. Remove the pan from the oven and cool on a rack.

7 Cut the brownies into squares by cutting 4 rows in each direction. Store in an airtight container between layers of waxed paper at room temperature for up to 4 days. Freeze for longer storage.

Per serving: Calories 273 (From Fat 180); Fat 20g (Saturated 7g); Cholesterol 46mg; Sodium 47mg; Carbohydrate 21g (Dietary Fiber 2g); Protein 4g.

Almond-Amaretto Brownies

These brownies are rich and chewy. Amaretto is an Italian almond-flavored liqueur. It does a great job of enhancing the almond flavor of these yummy brownies. A small square will satisfy even the most demanding brownie lover. You can decorate these by dusting with confectioners' sugar, cocoa powder, or with a dollop of whipped cream.

Preparation time: _20 minutes_

Baking time: _30 minutes_

Yield: _Sixteen 2-inch squares_

1 tablespoon butter, softened, for the pan

7 ounces bittersweet or semisweet chocolate, finely chopped

¾ cup (1½ sticks) butter, cut into small pieces

4 eggs

1 cup sugar

1 teaspoon almond extract

1 tablespoon Amaretto

⅓ cup flour

Pinch of salt

1 cup sliced almonds, roughly chopped

_1_ Preheat the oven to 350 degrees. Line an 8-inch square baking pan with a large piece of aluminum foil, letting it hang over the edges about 2 inches. Butter the foil lightly with the tablespon of butter.

_2_ Melt the chocolate and butter together in the top pan of a double boiler over warm water. Stir often with a rubber spatula to ensure even melting.

_3_ Using a mixer, beat the eggs and sugar together in a large mixing bowl until they are thick, pale colored, and hold a slowly dissolving ribbon when the beaters are lifted, about 5 minutes. Blend in the almond extract and the Amaretto.

_4_ Combine the flour with the salt and add slowly to the egg mixture, with the mixer at low speed. Stop and scrape down the sides of the bowl with a rubber spatula and mix again.

_5_ Remove the top pan of the double boiler and wipe the bottom and sides very dry. Let stand to cool for 10 minutes, stirring often to prevent a skin from forming on top. Pour into the egg mixture and blend thoroughly. Add the chopped almonds and mix briefly to blend.

_6_ Pour the batter into the prepared pan. Bake for 30 to 35 minutes, until a tester inserted 2 inches in from the edge has moist crumbs clinging to it. The center will be very moist.

_7_ Remove the pan from the oven and cool completely on a rack. Cut the brownies into squares by cutting 4 rows in each direction. Store in an airtight container between layers of waxed paper at room temperature for up to 4 days. Freeze for longer storage.

Per serving: _Calories 268 (From Fat 163); Fat 18g (Saturated 9g); Cholesterol 79mg; Sodium 28mg; Carbohydrate 23g (Dietary Fiber 2g); Protein 4g._

Creating Chewy and Cake-Like Brownies

Chewy brownies are moist and soft on the inside with a thin crust. They're usually taller than fudgy brownies. Also, although they have good chocolate flavor, it's not quite as intense as fudgy brownies. Cake-like brownies have the lightest texture of all. They usually have a smooth top with a light, bouncy texture that springs back when touched. They go very well with frosting.

Butterscotch and Dark-Chocolate-Chunk Brownies

Sometimes called Blondies because of their light color, these brownies have a rich, deep flavor that comes from brown sugar. The dark-chocolate chunks add their special quality to an already delicious brownie.

Preparation time: 20 minutes

Baking time: 25 minutes

Yield: Sixteen 2-inch squares

1 tablespoon butter, softened, for the pan	*1 cup flour*
½ cup (1 stick) butter, softened	*1 teaspoon baking powder*
1 cup light brown sugar	*¼ teaspoon salt*
1 egg	*4 ounces bittersweet or semisweet chocolate, cut into small chunks*
1 teaspoon vanilla extract	

1 Preheat the oven to 350 degrees. Line an 8-inch-square baking pan with a large piece of aluminum foil, letting it hang over the edges about 2 inches. Butter the foil lightly with the tablespon of butter.

2 Melt the butter in a 2-quart saucepan over medium heat. Add the brown sugar and stir until the mixture bubbles, about 1 minute. Remove from the heat and cool until the mixuture is lukewarm. Add the egg and vanilla and blend together well.

3 Add the flour, baking powder, and salt, and stir to blend completely. Stir in the chocolate chunks.

4 Transfer the batter to the prepared pan. Bake for 25 to 30 minutes, until a tester inserted in the center comes out with moist crumbs clinging to it. Remove the pan from the oven and cool on a rack.

5 Cut the brownies into squares by cutting 4 rows in each direction. Store in an airtight container between layers of waxed paper at room temperature for up to 4 days. Freeze for longer storage.

Per serving: Calories 182 (From Fat 83); Fat 9g (Saturated 6g); Cholesterol 31mg; Sodium 71mg; Carbohydrate 23g (Dietary Fiber 1g); Protein 2g.

Top: Cheesecake Brownies (Chapter 8); Bottom: Super-Fudgy Brownies (Chapter 8)

Chocolate-Chunk Scones (Chapter 9); Spiced Hot Chocolate (Chapter 15)

Chocolate-Spice Bundt Cake with Orange-Ginger Caramel Sauce (Chapter 10)

Devil's Food Cake with Vanilla Buttercream (Chapter 10)

**Solid Molded Chocolates (Chapter 13);
White Chocolate-Peppermint Candy Bark (Chapter 13)**

Chocolate Crème Brûlée (Chapter 12)

Marble Two-Chocolate Tart (Chapter 11)

Chocolate Hazelnut Dacquoise (Chapter 17)

Cheesecake Brownies

A creamy cheesecake layer tops a dense chocolate brownie. It's hard to get much better!

Preparation time: *30 minutes (includes melting)*

Baking time: *45 minutes*

Yield: *Sixteen 2-inch square brownies*

Topping (see the following recipe)	*⅔ cup sugar*
1 tablespoon butter, softened, for the pan	*2 teaspoons vanilla extract*
6 ounces semisweet or bittersweet chocolate, finely chopped	*¾ cup flour*
	½ teaspoon baking powder
4 tablespoons (½ stick) butter, cut into small pieces	*⅛ teaspoon salt*
	2 eggs

1 Preheat the oven to 350 degrees. Line an 8-inch-square baking pan with foil, letting it hang over the edges about 2 inches. Butter the foil lightly with the tablespoon of butter.

2 Melt the chopped chocolate and butter together in the top of a double boiler over warm water or in a microwave on low for 30-second bursts. Stir frequently with a rubber spatula. Remove the top pan of the double boiler; wipe the bottom and sides very dry. Let stand to cool for 10 minutes, stirring often. Lower the oven temperature to 325 degrees. Add the sugar and stir to blend well. Add the vanilla and mix well.

3 In a separate bowl, combine the flour, baking powder, and salt. Toss to blend well, then fold in to the chocolate mixture in three stages, blending well after each addition.

4 In a separate bowl, lightly beat the eggs. Add to the mixture; blend well. Transfer the batter to the prepared pan; bake for 10 minutes. Remove from the oven. Cool on a rack.

5 Transfer the Cheesecake Topping to the pan of brownies and use a rubber spatula to spread it evenly over the top. Bake for 35 minutes, until the top begins to turn light golden and the sides pull away from the pan. Remove from the oven and cool completely on a rack. Chill the brownies before cutting into 2-inch squares. Store tightly covered in the refrigerator for up to 3 days. Freeze for longer storage.

Topping

12 ounces cream cheese, softened	*½ teaspoon finely grated lemon zest*
½ cup sugar	*1 teaspoon vanilla extract*
2 eggs	*1 tablespoon flour*

Using a mixer, beat the cream cheese in a large mixing bowl until fluffy, about 2 minutes. Add the sugar and beat together well. Add the eggs one at a time, stopping to scrape down the sides of the bowl with a rubber spatula after each addition. Add the lemon zest and vanilla and blend well. Stir in the flour and mix completely.

Per serving: Calories 257 (From Fat 149); Fat 17g (Saturated 10g); Cholesterol 86mg; Sodium 110mg; Carbohydrate 25g (Dietary Fiber 1g); Protein 5g.

Chocolate-Spice Brownies
with Ganache Frosting

A blend of spices adds warm depth, and the Ganache Frosting gives these a sophisti-cated elegance. Try serving these as dessert after your next dinner party. Your guests will be impressed, and you'll receive more praise than you think you deserve.

Preparation time: *1½ hours, includes chilling*

Baking time: *35 minutes*

Yield: *Sixteen 2-inch brownies*

Ganache Frosting (see the following recipe)

1 tablespoon butter, softened, for the pan

½ cup flour

2 teaspoons ground cinnamon

½ teaspoon ground ginger

¼ teaspoon ground nutmeg

⅛ teaspoon salt

6 ounces bittersweet or semisweet chocolate, finely chopped

¾ cup (1½ sticks) butter, softened, cut into small pieces

4 eggs

1 cup sugar

1 teaspoon vanilla extract

1 cup walnuts, roughly chopped

1 Preheat the oven to 350 degrees. Line an 8-inch square baking pan with a large piece of aluminum foil, letting it hang over the edges about 2 inches. Butter the foil lightly with the tablespon of butter.

2 On a piece of waxed paper or in a small bowl, mix together the flour, cinnamon, ginger, nutmeg, and salt.

3 Melt the chocolate and butter together in the top pan of a double boiler over warm water or in a microwave oven on low power for 30-second bursts. Stir often with a rubber spatula to ensure even melting. Remove the top pan of the double boiler and wipe the bottom and sides very dry. Let stand to cool for 10 minutes, stirring often to prevent a skin from forming on top.

4 Using a mixer, beat the eggs and sugar in a large mixing bowl until pale-colored and the mixture holds a slowly dissolving ribbon as the beater is lifted, about 5 minutes. Add the vanilla and blend well.

5 Add the flour mixture in two stages, blending well after each addition.

6 Pour the melted chocolate and butter into the mixture and blend thoroughly. Add the walnuts and stir briefly.

7 Transfer the batter to the prepared pan. Bake for 35 minutes, until a tester instered in the center comes out with moist crumbs clinging to it. Remove the pan from the oven and cool on a rack.

8 Using a small metal cake spatula, spread the Ganache Frosting evenly over the top of the brownies. Chill for 15 minutes to set the ganache, then cut into squares by cutting 4 rows in each direction. Store the brownies in a single layer, tightly wrapped with plastic wrap, in the refrigerator for up to 3 days.

Ganache Frosting

6 ounces bittersweet or semisweet chocolate, finely chopped

¼ cup whipping cream

3 tablespoons butter, softened

1 Melt the chocolate and cream together in the top of a double boiler over warm water or in a microwave oven on low power for 30-second bursts. Stir often with a rubber spatula to ensure even melting. When the mixture is smooth, remove the top pan of the double boiler and wipe the bottom and sides very dry. Transfer the mixture to another bowl, cover tightly with plastic wrap, and chill until thick, but not stiff, about 1 hour.

2 Using a mixer, beat the butter in a mixing bowl until fluffy, about a minute. With the mixer on low speed add the chocolate and cream mixture in two stages. Blend for no longer than 1 minute or the chocolate may curdle.

Per serving: Calories 357 (From Fat 229); Fat 25g (Saturated 13g); Cholesterol 90mg; Sodium 38mg; Carbohydrate 29g (Dietary Fiber 2g); Protein 5g.

TIP

Dressing up your brownies

Sometimes an occasion calls for decorating your brownies. Here are a few quick and easy ways you can make them look special:

✔ Dust the top with confectioners' sugar.

✔ Dust the top with cocoa powder.

✔ Mix equal parts of confectioners' sugar and cocoa powder together. Place a stencil over the top of the brownies and dust with the mixture. Carefully lift the stencil off, so you don't disturb the mixture.

✔ Drizzle the tops of the brownies with a contrasting color of melted chocolate, like milk or white chocolate.

✔ Use your favorite frosting or icing to spread over the tops of the brownies. Or place the frosting in a pastry bag fitted with a large star tip. Pipe rosettes, shells, or stars on top. Chill briefly to set the topping, then cut into squares.

✔ Take the frosting or icing one step further and sprinkle chocolate shavings or curls on top. Or try sprinkling the top with chopped nuts, crystal sugar, sprinkles, or nonpareils.

✔ Cut a brownie and arrange it on a dessert plate. Pour hot fudge over the top of the brownie and place a couple of small scoops of ice cream next to it.

✔ Cover a dessert plate with a pool of raspberry sauce. Place a brownie on top of the sauce, then arrange fresh raspberries around the brownie.

✔ Whip cream to soft peaks. Fit a pastry bag with a large star tip. Pipe the top of each brownie with a star or rosette, then top with a chocolate cut-out, fresh berries, or finely chopped toasted nuts.

✔ Use any shape cookie cutter to cut out the brownies. For example, for Valentine's Day use a heart-shaped cutter or during the fall use a leaf-shaped cutter.

What to do with the leftover brownies after cutting them with a cookie cutter? Gather the scraps together and press into balls. Roll the balls in cocoa powder, confectioners' sugar, or ground, toasted nuts, then place them into paper candy cups. They resemble truffles with a unique taste and texture.

Turn to Chapter 6 for specific chocolate-decorating techniques.

Tiger Brownies

I named these brownies after my cat, Tiger, because their marble appearance looks like him. A rich cream-cheese layer mixed with toasted hazelnuts is swirled between two layers of hazelnut brownie batter. I love the look these create, and the taste is a delicious surprise.

Preparation time: 25 minutes (includes melting)

Baking time: 40 minutes

Yield: Sixteen 2-inch brownies

Cream Cheese–Hazelnut Layer (see the following recipe)

1 tablespoon butter, softened, for the pan

4 ounces bittersweet or semisweet chocolate, finely chopped

4 tablespoons (½ stick) butter

¾ cup flour

2 tablespoons unsweetened Dutch-processed cocoa powder

½ teaspoon baking powder

¼ teaspoon salt

2 eggs

⅔ cup sugar

1 teaspoon vanilla extract

⅔ cup roughly chopped, toasted hazelnuts

1 Preheat the oven to 350 degrees. Line an 8-inch-square baking pan with a large piece of aluminum foil, letting it hang over the edges about 2 inches. Butter the foil lightly with the tablespon of butter.

2 Melt the chopped chocolate and butter together in the top of a double boiler over warm water or in a microwave oven on low power for 30-second bursts. Stir frequently with a rubber spatula to ensure even melting.

3 Remove the top pan of the double boiler and wipe the bottom and sides dry. Let stand to cool for 10 minutes, stirring often to prevent a skin from forming on top.

4 Over a piece of waxed paper or in a medium bowl, sift together the flour, cocoa powder, baking powder, and salt.

5 Using a mixer, beat the eggs and sugar together in a large mixing bowl until pale-colored and thick, about 3 minutes. Add the vanilla and blend well.

6 Add the melted chocolate and butter and blend thoroughly.

7 Add the dry ingredients from Step 3 in two stages, blending well after each addition. Stop and scrape down the sides of the bowl with a rubber spatula.

8 Stir in the hazelnuts and blend well.

9 Transfer half of the brownie batter into the prepared pan. Use a rubber spatula to spread the batter evenly into the corners. Spread the Cream Cheese–Hazelnut Layer over the brownie batter, then dot the remaining brownie batter evenly over the cream-cheese batter. Use a rubber spatula to pull through the batters to marbleize them.

10 Bake for 40 minutes, until a tester inserted in the center comes out with moist crumbs clinging to it. Remove the pan from the oven and cool on a rack.

11 Cut the brownies into squares by cutting 4 rows in each direction. Store in an airtight container between layers of waxed paper at room temperature for up to 4 days. Freeze for longer storage.

Cream Cheese–Hazelnut Layer

4 ounces cream cheese, softened	*2 teaspoons lemon juice*
¼ cup sugar	*1 teaspoon vanilla extract*
1 egg	*⅓ cup toasted hazelnuts, finely ground*

1 Using a mixer, beat the cream cheese in a large mixing bowl until fluffy, about 2 minutes. Add the sugar and beat until smooth.

2 In a small bowl combine the egg, lemon juice, and vanilla and stir to blend well. Add to the cream-cheese mixture and beat well. Stop and scrape down the sides and bottom of the bowl with a rubber spatula. Blend in the hazelnuts and mix well.

Per serving: Calories 232 (From Fat 132); Fat 15g (Saturated 6g); Cholesterol 58mg; Sodium 82mg; Carbohydrate 22g (Dietary Fiber 2g); Protein 4g.

Chapter 9

Quick Breads, Muffins, and Scones

*Q*uick breads definitely fit into the category of comfort food. They're just what their name implies — quick. Because they're made without yeast, you don't have to spend time waiting for them to rise. Instead, baking powder or baking soda is used to give them a lift as they bake. The liquid in the batter and the heat from the oven react with the leavening to raise them rapidly. Quick breads are perfect to whip up and serve when someone drops in unexpectedly. Even though they're called *bread,* quick breads have a tender, moist, cake-like texture. But they're less elaborate than most cakes, making them good for many informal situations. Muffins and scones are types of quick bread. Muffins are made from a drop batter. Scones are made from a soft dough made with butter cut into the dry ingredients, which is then rolled out and cut into triangles or rounds.

TIP

If you want to have a quick bread, muffin, or scone for breakfast, but you don't have the time to spend in the kitchen in the morning, you can mix the dry and wet ingredients separately the night before. Stir them together in the morning, spread the mixture in the pan, or roll out the dough and cut, then bake it while you're getting dressed. Yum! Warm and fresh treats are great for breakfast.

Quick breads, muffins, and scones store well at room temperature tightly wrapped for a few days. They also freeze very well, so it's easy to bake them to have on hand for any occasion or for everyday.

Leavening is a substance (such as baking powder or baking soda) that results in the lightening and raising of a dough or batter. When mixed with liquid, leavening agents produce carbon dioxide gas that causes the dough or batter to rise before and/or during baking.

Short Order Cake–Like Sweets

When you don't have much time to spend in the kitchen making sweets, quick breads come to the rescue. This collection has some of the easiest and fastest recipes you can make. Plus, they're fairly forgiving, so you can make them up a couple of days in advance and they'll be as tasty as they are when they're freshly baked. Quick breads also freeze beautifully, making it easy to plan in advance.

One of things I especially like about quick breads is that no fuss is required for serving them. They don't need much at all in the way of decoration, and they slice into easily varied serving pieces. Although they can be eaten with utensils, they also can be served on a napkin and eaten with your fingers. A little whipped cream or butter and jam served alongside any of these quick breads is always a welcome addition.

Chocolate Gingerbread

How can you make gingerbread any better than it already is? Add chocolate, of course! Rich, deep, dark, with intense spicy flavor, is the best way to describe chocolate gingerbread.

Preparation time: *25 minutes (includes melting)*

Baking time: *45 minutes*

Yield: *Sixteen 2-inch squares*

1 tablespoon butter, softened, for the pan

2½ ounces (½ cup) bittersweet or semisweet chocolate, finely chopped

2½ cups flour

2 teaspoons baking soda

1 tablespoon ground ginger

1 teaspoon ground cinnamon

½ teaspoon ground cloves

¼ teaspoon freshly ground or grated nutmeg

¼ teaspoon salt

6 tablespoons (¾ stick) butter, softened

¼ cup light brown sugar

¼ cup sugar

2 eggs, lightly beaten

1 cup dark molasses

1 cup boiling water

½ cup heavy whipping cream

2 teaspoons confectioners' sugar

½ teaspoon vanilla extract

1 Preheat the oven to 350 degrees. Line an 8-inch square baking pan with a large piece of aluminum foil, letting it hang over the edges about 2 inches. Butter the foil lightly with the tablespoon of butter.

2 Melt the chopped chocolate in the top of a double boiler over hot water or in a microwave oven on low power for 30-second bursts. Remove the top pan of the double boiler and wipe the bottom and sides very dry. Cool for about 10 minutes, stirring occasionally to prevent a skin from forming on top.

3 Sift the flour, baking soda, spices, and salt together over a large piece of wax paper or into a mixing bowl.

4 Using a mixer, beat the butter in a large mixing bowl until fluffy, about 2 minutes. Add the brown sugar and granulated sugar and cream together well.

5 Blend in the eggs and molasses, beating well, then add the boiling water and the melted chocolate. Stop and scrape down the sides of the mixing bowl with a rubber spatula. Add the dry ingredients in 3 stages, blending well after each addition.

6 Transfer the batter to the prepared pan and bake for 45 minutes, until the top springs back when lightly touched and a cake tester inserted into the center comes out clean. Remove from the oven and cool completely on a rack. Cut into squares by cutting 4 rows in each direction.

7 For the garnish, use a mixer to whip the cream in a mixing bowl until it is thick. Add the confectioners' sugar and vanilla and whip until the mixture holds soft peaks. Serve a square of gingerbread with a dollop of whipped cream.

8 Store the gingerbread tightly wrapped in aluminum foil at room temperature for up to 3 days or freeze for longer storage.

Per serving: Calories 258 (From Fat 91); Fat 10g (Saturated 6g); Cholesterol 51mg; Sodium 215mg; Carbohydrate 39g (Dietary Fiber 1g); Protein 3g.

 Any quick bread or loaf cake can be baked in a muffin pan. Line the cavities of a muffin pan with muffin papers or coat with a nonstick spray. Reduce the baking time to approximately half the amount called for. Be sure to check with a tester for doneness, which should come out clean when inserted in the center.

Chocolate-Apricot-Ginger Loaf Cake

Deep, dark chocolate, plump dried apricots, and two kinds of ginger — ground and crystallized — combine to create a moist, very flavorful loaf. This recipe is one of my favorites. You'll have a hard time eating just one piece of this treat.

Preparation time: *20 minutes (includes melting)*

Baking time: *1 hour*

Yield: *1 loaf (12 servings)*

1 tablespoon butter, softened, for the pan	4 eggs
5 tablespoons butter, softened	½ cup flour
½ cup sugar	1¼ teaspoons ground ginger
¼ cup light brown sugar	¼ cup crystallized ginger, chopped
½ pound bittersweet or semisweet chocolate, finely chopped	⅔ cup dried apricots, cut into chunks

1 Preheat the oven to 350 degrees. Line a 9-x-5-inch loaf pan with a large piece of aluminum foil, letting it hang over the edges about 1 inch. Butter the foil lightly with the tablespoon of butter.

2 Melt the chocolate in the top of a double boiler over hot water or in a microwave oven on low power for 30-second bursts. Remove the top pan of the double boiler and wipe the bottom and sides very dry. Cool for about 10 minutes, stirring occasionally to prevent a skin from forming on top.

3 Using a mixer, beat the butter in a large mixing bowl, until fluffy. Add the sugar and brown sugar and cream together well. Add the melted chocolate and blend thoroughly.

4 Add the eggs one at a time, beating well after each addition. Combine the flour, ground ginger, and crystallized ginger and add to the mixture in two stages. Stop and scrape down the sides of the bowl with a rubber spatula after each addition and blend well. Add the chopped dried apricots and mix well.

5 Transfer the batter to the prepared loaf pan, using a rubber spatula to spread it evenly. Bake for 1 hour to 1 hour and 10 minutes, until a cake tester inserted in the center comes out clean. Remove the pan from the oven and cool completely on a rack.

6 Invert the loaf pan to remove the cake. Store the cake tightly wrapped in plastic wrap at room temperature for up to 4 days. Freeze for longer storage.

Per serving: *Calories 279 (From Fat 125); Fat 14g (Saturated 8g); Cholesterol 87mg; Sodium 28mg; Carbohydrate 35g (Dietary Fiber 2g); Protein 4g.*

Chocolate–Peanut Butter Loaf

Chocolate and peanut butter are made for each other. The combination creates a moist, dense loaf with lots of flavor. Use a natural style or freshly ground peanut butter for the most moisture. Both chocolate chunks and chunky peanut butter give this loaf lots of texture.

Preparation time: *10 minutes*

Baking time: *50 minutes*

Yield: *1 loaf (12 servings)*

1 tablespoon butter, softened, for the pan	*¼ teaspoon salt*
1¾ cups flour	*⅔ cup chunky peanut butter*
¼ cup unsweetened Dutch-processed cocoa	*1 cup milk*
½ cup light brown sugar	*1 egg, lightly beaten*
2 teaspoons baking powder	*¾ cup semisweet chocolate chunks*

1 Preheat the oven to 350 degrees. Line a 9-x-5-inch loaf pan with a large piece of aluminum foil, letting it hang over the edges about 1 inch. Butter the foil lightly with the tablespoon of butter.

2 Combine the flour, cocoa powder, brown sugar, baking powder, and salt in a large mixing bowl. Toss to blend. Add the peanut butter, milk, and egg, and mix together well. Add the chocolate chunks and blend.

3 Transfer the batter to the prepared pan. Use the rubber spatula to spread the batter evenly. Bake for 50 to 55 minutes, until a tester inserted in the center comes out clean. Remove the pan from the oven and cool completely on a rack.

4 Store the loaf tightly wrapped in plastic wrap at room temperature for up to 4 days. Freeze for longer storage.

Per serving: Calories 263 (From Fat 111); Fat 12g (Saturated 4g); Cholesterol 23mg; Sodium 201mg; Carbohydrate 34g (Dietary Fiber 3g); Protein7g.

 Be sure to use the size of pan called for in the recipe, or you may wind up with a quick bread that's either over– or underbaked.

Banana-Chocolate Quick Bread

Bananas and chocolate are a great combination. Together they bring out the best in each other and make a moist, flavorful quick bread. One bite reveals the chunky texture of the walnuts and chocolate chunks.

Preparation time: *10 minutes*

Baking time: *50 minutes*

Yield: *1 loaf (12 servings)*

1 tablespoon butter, softened, for the pan

1¾ cups flour

¼ cup unsweetened Dutch-processed cocoa powder

1 teaspoon baking powder

¼ teaspoon baking soda

⅛ teaspoon salt

½ cup (1 stick) butter, softened

½ cup sugar

⅓ cup light brown sugar

2 large eggs

1 cup mashed ripe bananas (2 large)

Zest of 1 large orange, finely minced

¾ cup walnuts, roughly chopped

½ cup (3 ounces) semisweet chocolate chunks

1 Preheat the oven to 350 degrees. Line a 9-x-5-inch loaf pan with a large piece of aluminum foil, letting it hang over the edges about an inch. Butter the foil lightly with the tablespoon of butter.

2 Sift together the flour, cocoa powder, baking powder, baking soda, and salt onto a large piece of wax paper or in a large mixing bowl.

3 Using a mixer beat the butter in a large mixing bowl until fluffy, about 2 minutes. Add the sugar and brown sugar, and cream together well. Add the eggs one at a time, beating well after each addition. Stop and scrape down the sides of the bowl with a rubber spatula. Add the mashed bananas and orange zest, and blend well.

4 Add the dry ingredients in three stages, blending well after each addition. Stir in the walnuts and chocolate chunks.

5 Transfer the batter to the pan and use a rubber spatula to spread it evenly. Bake for 50 minutes to 1 hour, until a tester inserted in the center comes out clean.

6 Remove the pan from the oven and cool completely on a rack. Store the loaf tightly wrapped in plastic wrap at room temperature for up to 4 days. Freeze for longer storage.

Per serving: Calories 296 (From Fat 140); Fat 16g (Saturated 8g); Cholesterol 59mg; Sodium 98mg; Carbohydrate 39g (Dietary Fiber 2g); Protein 5g.

Don't overmix the batter for quick breads, or they may end up too heavy.

Chocolate Chunk–Walnut– Sour Cream Loaf Cake

Sour cream gives this loaf cake moisture and a hint of tang in the flavor while the chocolate chunks and walnuts provide great crunchy texture. This is delicious served warm for breakfast — or anytime for that matter!

Preparation time: *10 minutes*

Baking time: *40 minutes*

Yield: *1 loaf (12 servings)*

1 tablespoon butter, softened, for the pan	*1½ cups flour*
5 tablespoons butter, melted	*1 teaspoon baking soda*
½ cup sugar	*½ teaspoon baking powder*
⅓ cup light brown sugar	*¼ teaspoon salt*
1 cup sour cream	*¾ cup semisweet chocolate, chopped into small chunks, or chocolate chips*
1 large egg	
1 teaspoon vanilla extract	*½ cup walnuts, roughly chopped*

1 Preheat the oven to 350 degrees. Line a 9-x-5-inch loaf pan with a large piece of aluminum foil, letting it hang over the edges about 1 inch. Butter the foil lightly with the tablespoon of butter.

2 Place the melted butter in a large mixing bowl and stir in the sugar and brown sugar until smooth. Add the sour cream, egg, and vanilla extract, and blend together well.

3 Sift together the flour, baking soda, baking powder, and salt. Add to the mixture in three stages, stirring well after each addition. Stir in the chocolate and the walnuts.

4 Transfer the batter to the pan and use a rubber spatula to spread it evenly. Bake for 40 to 45 minutes, until a tester inserted in the center comes out clean.

5 Remove the pan from the oven and cool completely on a rack. Store the loaf tightly wrapped in plastic wrap at room temperature for up to 4 days. Freeze for longer storage.

Per serving: Calories 289 (From Fat 156); Fat 17g (Saturated 9g); Cholesterol 42mg; Sodium 187mg; Carbohydrate 33g (Dietary Fiber 1g); Protein 4g.

No Utensils Required

Muffins and scones are practically finger food. They can be eaten on the run, and they pack well in lunch bags and picnic baskets. They also fit in a more proper setting, like afternoon tea, where they can be served with butter and jam. They're quick and easy to make, and they freeze well, so you can make them up in advance. Having muffins and scones on hand for unexpected guests is convenient. Just pop them out of the freezer, reheat, and serve. The added bonus here will be the wonderful aroma of almost freshly baked muffins and scones.

Chocolate-Chunk Muffins

Use any chocolate you like — dark, milk, or white chocolate — for this recipe. Or try a combination. Any way you mix it up, these are delicious muffins. I especially like them warm.

Preparation time: 10 minutes

Baking time: 20 minutes

Yield: 12 muffins

2 cups flour	1 cup milk
1 tablespoon baking powder	¼ cup (½ stick) butter, melted
¼ teaspoon salt	1 teaspoon vanilla extract
¾ cup light brown sugar	¾ cup chocolate cut into small chunks, or
2 eggs	chocolate chips

1 Preheat the oven to 350 degrees. Line a 12-cavity muffin tin with muffin papers.

2 In a large mixing bowl, combine the flour, baking powder, salt, and brown sugar, and toss to blend well.

3 In another bowl combine the eggs, milk, butter, and vanilla extract. Add the wet ingredients to the dry ingredients, and stir just until the dry ingredients are wet. Stir in the chocolate.

4 Spoon the batter into the muffin tin, filling each cavity three-fourths full. Bake for 20 to 24 minutes, until a tester inserted in the center comes out with moist crumbs clinging to it. Remove the pan from the oven and cool on a rack. Turn the pan upside down to release the muffins.

5 Store in an airtight container between layers of wax paper in the refrigerator for up to 4 days. Freeze for longer storage.

6 Reheat the muffins in a 325-degree oven for 10 minutes to serve warm.

Per serving: Calories 247 (From Fat 82); Fat 9g (Saturated 5g); Cholesterol 49mg; Sodium 171mg; Carbohydrate 36g (Dietary Fiber 1g); Protein 5g.

TIP

Don't overfill the cavities of the muffin pan with batter because they will spread too much out of the cavities and into each other.

Double-Chocolate-Chunk Muffins

The texture of these muffins is close to cake. They have a full-bodied chocolate flavor that comes from the use of both cocoa and chocolate chunks. For a variation, use white-chocolate or milk-chocolate chunks.

Preparation time: *10 minutes*

Baking time: *20 minutes*

Yield: *15 muffins*

½ cup (1 stick) butter, softened

⅔ cup sugar

2 eggs

⅔ cup milk or cream

1 teaspoon vanilla

1¼ cups flour

¼ cup unsweetened Dutch-processed cocoa powder

1½ teaspoons baking soda

2 teaspoons baking powder

⅛ teaspoon salt

¾ cup (3 ounces) bittersweet or semisweet chocolate, chopped into small chunks

1 Preheat the oven to 350 degrees. Line the cavities of a 12-cup muffin tin with muffin papers, or spray each cavity with a nonstick spray.

2 Using a mixer beat the butter in a large mixing bowl until fluffy, about a minute. Add the sugar, and cream together well. Add the eggs, one at a time, beating well after each addition. Add the milk or cream and vanilla and blend well.

3 Sift together the flour, cocoa powder, baking soda, baking powder, and salt and add to the butter mixture in three stages, stopping to scrape down the sides of the bowl with a rubber spatula after each addition. Stir in the chocolate chunks.

4 Spoon the batter into the muffin tin, filling each cavity three-fourths full. Bake for 20 to 25 minutes, until a tester inserted in the center comes out clean. Remove the pan from the oven and cool on a rack. Turn the pan upside down to remove the muffins.

5 Store in an airtight container between layers of wax paper in the refrigerator for up to 4 days. Freeze for longer storage.

6 Reheat the muffins in a 325-degree oven for 10 minutes to serve warm.

Per serving: Calories 179 (From Fat 84); Fat 9g (Saturated 6g); Cholesterol 47mg; Sodium 241mg; Carbohydrate 22g (Dietary Fiber 1g); Protein 3g.

Be sure to let your muffins cool completely before peeling the paper off the outside, or the paper will take chunks of the muffin with it.

If there isn't enough batter to fill all the cavities of your muffin tin, fill the empty ones with water so the tin won't warp as it bakes.

Chocolate-Chunk Scones

The chocolate chunks are a nice surprise in these scones. Although they're delicious on their own, they are superb served warm with butter and jam.

Preparation time: *15 minutes*

Baking time: *12 minutes*

Yield: *Twelve 3-inch triangular scones or sixteen 2½-inch round scones*

2½ cups flour

1 tablespoon baking powder

1 tablespoon plus 1 teaspoon sugar

⅛ teaspoon salt

6 tablespoons (¾ stick) butter, chilled

¾ cup (3 ounces) bittersweet or semisweet chocolate, chopped into small chunks

2 eggs

¾ cup heavy whipping cream

Egg Wash:

1 egg yolk

2 tablespoons cream

2 teaspoons sugar

1 Preheat the oven to 400 degrees. Line two baking sheets with parchment paper.

2 In the work bowl of a food processor fitted with a steel blade, combine the flour, baking powder, sugar, and salt. Pulse briefly to blend. Cut the butter into small pieces and add. Pulse until the butter is cut into tiny pieces, 30 seconds to 1 minute.

3 Add the chopped chocolate and blend briefly.

4 In a small bowl beat the eggs lightly. Add the cream and blend well. Pour the mixture through the feed tube with the machine running and process until the dough forms a ball, about 30 seconds.

(If not using a food processor, follow this procedure: Soften the butter to room temperature, then beat in a mixing bowl until fluffy. Add the sugar and cream together well. Lightly beat together the eggs and cream and add. Stop occasionally and scrape down the sides of the bowl with a rubber spatula. Combine the flour, baking powder, and salt together. Add to the mixture in 3 stages, stopping to scrape down the sides of the bowl after each addition. Add the chopped chocolate and blend.)

5 Turn the dough out onto a lightly floured surface. Using a rolling pin, roll the dough or pat it with your fingertips into a large rectangle with a thickness of about ¾ inch. Brush off any excess flour. Use a 6-inch diameter round cutter to cut out large circles. To form triangles, cut each circle into quarters. To make round scones, use a 2½-inch round cutter. Transfer the scones to the lined baking sheets, leaving at least 2 inches space between them. Gather the scraps together, re-roll and cut into scones.

6 For the egg wash, beat the egg yolk lightly in a small bowl with the cream. Brush the top of each scone with the egg wash, then sprinkle with sugar. Bake for 12 to 14 minutes, until light golden. Remove from the oven and cool completely on a rack.

7 Store the scones tightly wrapped in aluminum foil at room temperature for up to 3 days. Freeze for longer storage. Warm the scones in a 300-degree oven for 10 minutes before serving.

Per serving: Calories 271 (From Fat 145); Fat 16g (Saturated 10g); Cholesterol 93mg; Sodium 138mg; Carbohydrate 27g (Dietary Fiber 1g); Protein 5g.

Making variations of Chocolate-Chunk Scones is easy. All you do is add one or two ingredients to the main recipe. Here are several of my favorite variations.

- **Chocolate Chunk–Orange:** Add the zest of one large orange to the dry ingredients.

- **Chocolate Chunk–Cherry–Almond:** Add ⅓ cup chopped dried cherries and ⅓ cup sliced almonds to the dough when adding the chocolate chunks.

- **Chocolate Chunk–Nut:** Add ⅔ cup toasted nuts (such as walnuts, hazelnuts, or pecans) to the dough when adding the chocolate chunks.

- **Chocolate Chunk–Apricot:** Add ⅔ cup chopped dried apricots to the dough when adding the chocolate chunks.

- **Chocolate Chunk–Cranberry:** Add ⅔ cup chopped dried cranberries to the dough when adding the chocolate chunks.

- **Chocolate Chunk–Date:** Add ⅔ cup chopped pitted dates to the dough when adding the chocolate chunks.

- **Chocolate Chunk–Ginger:** Add 1 teaspoon ground ginger to the dry ingredients and add ⅓ cup chopped crystallized ginger to the dough when adding the chocolate chunks.

- **Chocolate Chunk–Spice:** Replace ¼ cup of the flour with ¼ cup unsweetened Dutch-processed cocoa powder. Add 1¼ teaspoons ground cinnamon, ¾ teaspoon ground ginger, ½ teaspoon ground nutmeg, and ¼ teaspoon ground cloves to the dry ingredients.

Chapter 10

Let Them Eat Chocolate Cake

In This Chapter

▶ Getting acquainted with different types of cakes
▶ Assembling layer cakes
▶ Making delectable cheesecakes

Although cakes are a tradition for celebrations, like birthdays and anniversaries, you don't need a special occasion to bake a cake. Chocolate cakes are the top of the cake pyramid. In my house, chocolate cakes are the only kind of cakes that I bake. The only problem I have is deciding which chocolate cake to bake — because there are so many delicious ones to choose from.

One thing that I like about chocolate cakes is that they always bring *oohs* and *aahs* from the people who eat them. The *oohs* come when they see the cake, and the *aahs* follow shortly after, as they taste it. And when you're cutting the cake and serving it, you're guaranteed to hear people say, "Just a tiny piece for me" — but they always ask for a second serving.

All the Satisfaction, without All the Effort

You're not alone if your idea of making a chocolate cake involves buying a box mix from the grocery store. But you can make your very own homemade chocolate cake without much more effort — and the results are definitely worth it. When you stop and think about it, baking a chocolate cake from scratch is really just a matter of mixing all the ingredients together, pouring them in a pan, and baking. It's hard to make a mistake — in fact, the only mistake you may make is not making enough.

The best part about the easy recipes in this section is this: You can whip them up in a jiffy. And that means you can bake the cake and serve it fairly quickly, even if it's a little warm. Oh, yum!

Cocoa Angel Food Cake

Angel food cake is typically light and airy and contains no fat at all. This one is no different, except that the cocoa gives it a definite chocolate flavor. It's delicious served with fresh fruit, such as strawberries or raspberries, with raspberry sauce, caramel sauce (see Chapter 15 for sauces), or ice cream.

Tools: *10-x-4-inch tube pan with removable bottom*

Preparation time: *15 minutes*

Baking time: *40 minutes*

Yield: *14 to16 servings*

¾ cup cake flour	12 egg whites, at room temperature
¼ cup unsweetened natural cocoa powder	1 teaspoon cream of tartar
¼ teaspoon salt	2 teaspoons vanilla extract
1½ cups superfine sugar	1 teaspoon chocolate extract (optional)

1 Preheat the oven to 325 degrees. Over a large piece of wax paper, sift together the cake flour, cocoa powder, and salt. Stir in ¾ cup of the sugar, and set aside.

2 In a large mixing bowl, using a mixer, whip the egg whites on medium speed until they're frothy, about 1 minute. Add the cream of tartar. Increase the mixer speed to medium-high, and whip the egg whites, sprinkling on the remaining sugar, 2 tablespoons at a time, until the mixture holds firm, but not dry, peaks, about 5 minutes. Add the vanilla and chocolate extracts.

3 Using a rubber spatula, fold the dry ingredients into the whipped egg whites in 4 batches.

4 Transfer the batter to the pan, using the rubber spatula to smooth and even the top. Tap the pan gently on the countertop to eliminate air bubbles. Bake the cake for 40 minutes, until a tester inserted near the center comes out clean.

5 Remove the cake from the oven and invert it over a cooling rack onto its feet or hang it by the center tube over a large funnel. The cake should come out of the pan on its own. If it doesn't release from the pan, run a thin-bladed knife or spatula around the rim of the pan and gently push the bottom of the pan up. Then run the knife or spatula between the bottom of the cake and the cake pan. Let the cake cool completely at room temperature.

6 Store the cake well wrapped in plastic at room temperature for up to 3 days or freeze for up to 4 months.

Tip: Don't grease the pan when making this recipe. If you do, the batter won't be able to "grab" and climb up the sides of the pan.

Per serving: Calories 103 (From Fat 0); Fat 0g (Saturated 0g); Cholesterol 0mg; Sodium 78mg; Carbohydrate 23g (Dietary Fiber 1g); Protein 3g.

Chocolate Chiffon Cake

Chiffon cake has a light texture and contains very little cholesterol due to the use of vegetable oil. This cake has deep flavor that comes from the cocoa powder. It's great dusted lightly with confectioners' sugar, but you can also serve it with ice cream or a sauce and fresh fruit.

Tools: *10-x-4-inch tube pan with removable bottom*

Preparation time: *10 minutes*

Baking time: *1 hour 5 minutes*

Yield: *14 to 16 servings*

½ cup unsweetened Dutch-processed cocoa powder

¾ cup boiling water

2 teaspoons pure vanilla extract

1¾ cups cake flour

1 tablespoon baking powder

½ teaspoon salt

1⅔ cups sugar

½ cup vegetable oil

6 eggs at room temperature, separated

½ teaspoon cream of tartar

Confectioners' sugar, for garnish

1 Preheat the oven to 325 degrees. In a small bowl, combine the cocoa powder and boiling water. Stir until the mixture is smooth, about 3 minutes. Let cool, then add the vanilla extract and stir to blend.

2 In a large mixing bowl, sift together the cake flour, baking powder, and salt. Add 1⅓ cups of the sugar to the flour mixture. Stir to blend well, then make a well in the center of the ingredients. Add the oil, egg yolks, and chocolate mixture. Stir together until well blended.

3 In a large mixing bowl, using an electric mixer, whip the egg whites with the cream of tartar until frothy. Slowly add the remaining ⅓ cup sugar, and whip until the egg whites hold firm, but not dry, peaks, about 5 minutes.

4 Fold the egg whites into the chocolate mixture in 4 stages, blending well after each addition. Transfer the batter to the tube pan.

5 Bake 60 to 65 minutes, until a cake tester inserted near the center comes out clean and the cake springs back when touched on top. Remove the cake pan from the oven and invert it onto a funnel to hang until cool. To release the cake from the pan, use a thin-bladed knife or spatula to run around the sides, being careful not to tear the cake. Use a very thin knife or spatula to remove the bottom and center core of the pan. Invert the cake onto a rack, and re-invert onto a plate of cardboard cake round.

6 Dust the cake lightly with confectioners' sugar before serving. Store the cake tightly wrapped in plastic at room temperature for up to 3 days, or freeze for up to 4 months.

Tip: *Don't grease the pan when making this recipe. If you do, the batter won't be able to "grab" and climb up the sides of the pan.*

Per serving: *Calories 220 (From Fat 82); Fat 9g (Saturated 1g); Cholesterol 80mg; Sodium 169mg; Carbohydrate 32g (Dietary Fiber 1g); Protein 4g.*

You can easily make variations of Cocoa Angel Food Cake or Chocolate Chiffon Cake by adding an ingredient or two:

- ✔ **Chocolate Chip (or Chunk) Angel Food or Chiffon Cake:** Add 1 cup dark chocolate chips or finely chopped dark chocolate chunks to the dry ingredients.

- ✔ **Chocolate-Lemon Angel Food or Chiffon Cake:** Replace the vanilla extract with lemon extract, and add 1 tablespoon finely minced lemon zest to the dry ingredients.

- ✔ **Chocolate-Orange Angel Food or Chiffon Cake:** Replace the vanilla extract with orange extract, and add 1 tablespoon finely minced orange zest to the dry ingredients.

- ✔ **Chocolate-Spice Angel Food or Chiffon Cake:** Add a blend of 1 teaspoon ground cinnamon, ½ teaspoon ground ginger, and ¼ teaspoon grated nutmeg to the dry ingredients.

- ✔ **Chocolate Five-Spice Angel Food or Chiffon Cake:** Add 1½ teaspoons five-spice powder to the dry ingredients.

- ✔ **Chocolate-Nut Angel Food or Chiffon Cake:** Add 1¼ cups roughly chopped nuts to the dry ingredients. Use any nut or a combination of nuts.

- ✔ **Chocolate–Dried Fruit Angel Food or Chiffon Cake:** Add 1¼ cups finely chopped dried fruit to the dry ingredients and toss together. Try dried apricots, peaches, pears, dates, figs, or raisins.

- ✔ **Chocolate-Coconut Angel Food or Chiffon Cake:** Add 1¼ cups shredded coconut to the dry ingredients.

The easiest way to cut angel food and chiffon cakes is with a serrated knife, using a back-and-forth motion. Using a regular knife pushes the cake down and flattens it.

Chocolate Pound Cake

Pound cake originated in England. The name comes from the traditional ingredients: a pound each of butter, flour, eggs, and sugar. As you can imagine, this cake is rich, but it's not too sweet. Chocolate pound cake is wonderful on its own, but it's also delicious served with fresh fruit; a sauce, such as fruit sauce, fudge sauce, or caramel sauce (see Chapter 15 for sauces); or ice cream.

Preparation time: *20 minutes*

Baking time: *1 hour and 10 minutes*

Yield: *10 to 12 servings*

1 tablespoon butter, softened, for the pan	1 cup (2 sticks) unsalted butter, softened
2 teaspoons cake flour, for the pan	1½ cups superfine sugar
⅓ cup unsweetened Dutch-processed cocoa powder	4 eggs
4 tablespoons hot water	1⅔ cups cake flour
2 teaspoons pure vanilla extract	1 teaspoon baking powder
	¼ teaspoon salt

1 Preheat the oven to 325 degrees. Use the tablespoon of butter to generously butter the inside of a 9-x-5-inch loaf pan. Dust the inside of the pan with flour, and shake out the excess.

2 Place the cocoa powder in a small mixing bowl. Add the hot water, and stir until it is a smooth paste. Then blend in the vanilla.

3 Using a mixer, beat the butter in a large mixing bowl until fluffy, about a minute. Gradually add the sugar and continue to beat to cream together well. Stop and scrape down the sides of the bowl with a rubber spatula.

4 Add the eggs one at a time, beating well after each addition. Add the cocoa mixture from Step 2 and blend well.

5 Mix together the cake flour, baking powder, and salt and add to the dry ingredients in 3 stages, beating well after each addition. Transfer the batter to the prepared pan. Use the rubber spatula to spread it smoothly and evenly. Bake the cake for 1 hour and 10 minutes, until a tester inserted in the center comes out clean. Remove the pan from the oven and cool on a rack for 15 minutes. Turn the cake out of the pan and cool on the rack completely.

6 Store the cake tightly wrapped in aluminum foil at room temperature for up to 4 days, or freeze for up to 4 months.

Note: *Pound cake typically splits down the center of the top. This is the result of steam that is released during baking.*

Per serving: *Calories 322 (From Fat 166); Fat 18g (Saturated 11g); Cholesterol 115mg; Sodium 104mg; Carbohydrate 38g (Dietary Fiber 1g); Protein 4g.*

You can easily make variations of pound cake by adding an ingredient or two:

- **Chocolate Chip (or Chunk) Pound Cake:** Add 1 cup dark-chocolate chips or finely chopped dark-chocolate chunks to the batter after adding the dry ingredients.

- **Double-Chocolate Pound Cake:** Add 4 ounces melted and cooled bittersweet or semisweet chocolate after adding the dry ingredients.

- **Chocolate-Lemon Pound Cake:** Eliminate the vanilla extract and add 2 teaspoons lemon extract and 1 tablespoon finely minced lemon zest after adding the dry ingredients.

- **Chocolate-Orange Pound Cake:** Eliminate the vanilla extract and add 2 teaspoons orange extract and 1 tablespoon finely minced orange zest after adding the dry ingredients.

- **Chocolate-Spice Pound Cake:** Add a blend of 1 teaspoon ground cinnamon, ½ teaspoon ground ginger, and ¼ teaspoon grated nutmeg after adding the dry ingredients.

- **Chocolate Five-Spice Pound Cake:** Add 1½ teaspoons five-spice powder after adding the dry ingredients.

- **Chocolate-Nut Pound Cake:** Add 1¼ cups roughly chopped nuts after adding the dry ingredients. Use any nut or a combination of nuts.

- **Chocolate–Dried Fruit Pound Cake:** Add 1¼ cups finely chopped dried fruit to the dry ingredients and toss together. Try dried apricots, peaches, pears, dates, figs, or raisins.

- **Chocolate-Coconut Pound Cake:** Add 1¼ cups shredded coconut after adding the dry ingredients.

Individual Chocolate-Spice Cakes with Mocha Sauce

These little cakes look like they take a lot of work to make, but they're surprisingly easy . . . and delicious! The blend of spices enhances the chocolate flavor.

Preparation time: *20 minutes (includes melting)*

Baking time: *15 minutes*

Yield: *Eight 3-inch cakes*

Mocha Sauce (see Chapter 15)	*⅛ teaspoon ground ginger*
1 tablespoon butter, for the pan	*⅛ teaspoon ground cloves*
1 tablespoon flour, for the pan	*⅛ teaspoon freshly grated nutmeg*
2 ounces bittersweet or semisweet chocolate, finely chopped	*⅛ teaspoon salt*
3 tablespoons butter, softened	*2 egg whites at room temperature*
¼ cup flour	*⅛ teaspoon cream of tartar*
¼ teaspoon ground cinnamon	*6 tablespoons sugar*

1 Preheat the oven to 375 degrees. Butter the inside of 8 cavities of a muffin pan; dust with flour and shake out the excess. Or spray the cavities with a nonstick baking spray. Melt the chocolate and butter together in the top of a double boiler over hot water, stirring often with a rubber spatula or in a microwave on low for 30-second bursts.

2 Sift together the flour, cinnamon, ginger, cloves, nutmeg, and salt. In a large mixing bowl, whip the egg whites with an electric mixer until they are frothy. Add the cream of tartar and continue whipping until they begin to mound. Sprinkle the sugar on slowly, and whip the egg whites until they hold firm, but not stiff, peaks.

3 Fold the flour mixture into the egg whites. Remove the top pan of the double boiler, and wipe the bottom and sides very dry. Fold the chocolate into the mixture in two stages, blending well. Divide the batter evenly between the 8 cavities of the prepared muffin pan. Fill the remaining cavities of the muffin pan with water. Bake the cakes for 15 minutes, until the tops spring back when touched. Remove from the oven and cool on a rack for 5 minutes. Pour the water out of the muffin cups carefully, so the cakes don't get wet, then invert the pan to release the cakes or use a small, thin metal spatula to gently lift the cakes from the pan. Let the cakes cool completely. Store the spice cakes tightly wrapped in aluminum foil at room temperature for up to 3 days. Freeze for longer storage. Serve each spice cake in a pool of Mocha Sauce.

Per serving: Calories 261 (From Fat 120); Fat 13g (Saturated 8g); Cholesterol 18mg; Sodium 57mg; Carbohydrate 32g (Dietary Fiber 2g); Protein 3g.

Chocolate-Spice Bundt Cake with Orange-Ginger Caramel Sauce

A blend of warm spices gives extra zip to this cake. Because of the lovely shape the Bundt pan gives, the cake needs no decoration. Note that this recipe calls for a 10-cup Bundt pan, and the standard size is a 12-cup size. If you have a 12-cup Bundt pan, you can use it, but your cake will be a bit flatter.

Tools: *10-cup Bundt pan or Kugelhupf mold*

Preparation time: *15 minutes*

Baking time: *1 hour and 20 minutes*

Yield: *14 to 16 servings*

Orange-Ginger Caramel Sauce (see Chapter 15)	*2 teaspoons ground cinnamon*
5 ounces unsweetened chocolate, finely chopped	*1½ teaspoons ground ginger*
2 tablespoons butter, for the pan	*1¼ teaspoons freshly grated nutmeg*
2 tablespoons flour, for the pan	*1 cup (2 sticks) plus 1 tablespoon butter, softened*
3¼ cups flour	*1 cup light brown sugar*
½ cup unsweetened natural cocoa powder	*½ cup sugar*
1½ teaspoons baking powder	*⅔ cup molasses*
½ teaspoon baking soda	*6 eggs*
¼ teaspoon salt	*2 teaspoons pure vanilla extract*

1 Melt the chocolate in the top of a double boiler over hot water. Stir often with a rubber spatula to ensure even melting. Preheat the oven to 325 degrees. Use the 2 tablespoons of butter to grease the inside of a 10-cup Bundt pan. Dust the pan with the 2 tablespoons of flour and shake off the excess.

2 In a 2-quart bowl or over a large piece of wax paper, sift together the flour, cocoa powder, baking powder, baking soda, salt, cinnamon, ginger, and nutmeg.

3 Using a mixer, beat the butter in a large mixing bowl until fluffy, about 1 minute. Gradually add the brown sugar and sugar and continue to beat to cream together well. Stop and scrape down the sides of the bowl with a rubber spatula. Add the molasses and blend well. Add the eggs, one at a time, beating well after each addition.

4 Add the vanilla and the melted chocolate and blend well. Add the dry ingredients in 3 stages, blending well after each addition.

5 Transfer the batter to the prepared pan. Use the rubber spatula to smooth and even the top. Bake the cake for 1 hour and 10 minutes, until a tester inserted in the center comes out with a few crumbs clinging to it. Remove the pan from the oven and cool on a rack for 15 mintues. Invert the cake pan to remove the cake. The cake is best served warm. It can be baked in advance and kept at room temperature tightly wrapped in aluminum foil for up to 3 days. Or freeze for up to 4 months. The cake can be warmed in a 325-degree oven for 10 to 15 minutes before serving. Serve slices of the cake in a pool of the warm Orange-Ginger Caramel Sauce.

Per serving: Calories 522 (From Fat 228); Fat 25g (Saturated 15g); Cholesterol 131mg; Sodium 156mg; Carbohydrate 72g (Dietary Fiber 3g); Protein 7g.

Chocolate-serving etiquette

To make your chocolate experience the very best it can be, here are a few general guidelines for serving:

✔ **Bring the entire chocolate dessert to the table so everyone can see how beautiful it is.** You can then serve it right from the table if there's enough room. If not, take it back to the kitchen and cut serving pieces, then bring the individual plates to the table.

✔ **If you're setting the chocolate dessert into a sauce, make sure to put the sauce on the plate first, then set a slice of the dessert on top of the sauce.**

✔ **Leave room on the plate for any other garnishes that may be used, such as cookies or fruit.**

✔ **Wait five to ten minutes after everyone finishes their meal before you serve dessert.** This allows everyone's palate to be ready.

✔ **Have plenty of fresh drinking water available to keep everyone's palate clear so they can completely appreciate the full flavor of the chocolate dessert.**

Look-at-Me Chocolate Cakes

All chocolate cakes are wonderful, but some take on a little more panache. The recipes in this section have various components, which can be made in advance. You can assemble and decorate them shortly before serving.

Trying your hand at layer cakes

Layer cakes are usually the ones people think of when they want a celebration cake. Layer cakes are put together with butter cream, frosting, or whipped cream and decorated with nuts or shaved chocolate.

Lining layer cake pans with buttered parchment paper makes removing the cake from the pan a cinch.

Any cake batter can be made easily into cupcakes. To do this, line two 12-cup cupcake pans with baking cups. Fill each cup three-fourths full with the batter. Bake for approximately half the time called for, until a tester inserted in the center comes out clean. Remove the pans from the oven and cool completely on racks. For frosting or icing, use half the amount called for in the Chocolate Cream Frosting recipe (later in this chapter), or use sweetened whipped cream.

No matter what kind of layer cake you're making, the assembly process is essentially the same. Figure 10-1 shows how to slice a cake into layers. Figure 10-2 shows how to put the layers together.

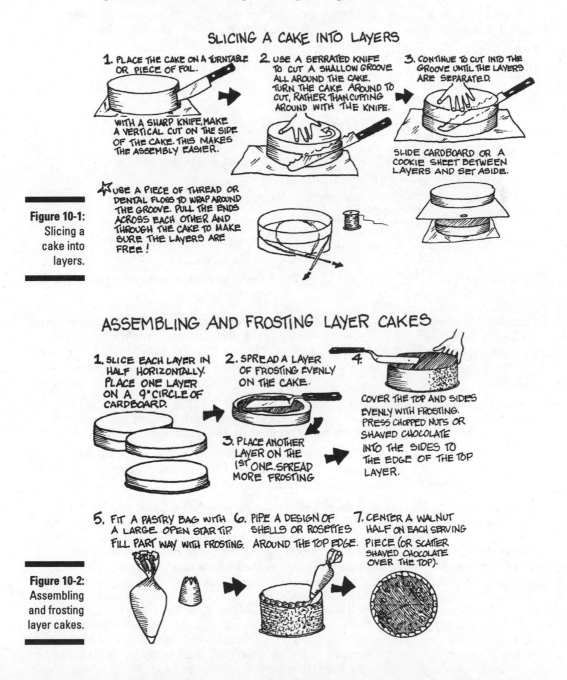

SLICING A CAKE INTO LAYERS

1. PLACE THE CAKE ON A TURNTABLE OR PIECE OF FOIL.

WITH A SHARP KNIFE, MAKE A VERTICAL CUT ON THE SIDE OF THE CAKE. THIS MAKES THE ASSEMBLY EASIER.

2. USE A SERRATED KNIFE TO CUT A SHALLOW GROOVE ALL AROUND THE CAKE. TURN THE CAKE AROUND TO CUT, RATHER THAN CUTTING AROUND WITH THE KNIFE.

3. CONTINUE TO CUT INTO THE GROOVE UNTIL THE LAYERS ARE SEPARATED.

SLIDE CARDBOARD OR A COOKIE SHEET BETWEEN LAYERS AND SET ASIDE.

USE A PIECE OF THREAD OR DENTAL FLOSS TO WRAP AROUND THE GROOVE. PULL THE ENDS ACROSS EACH OTHER AND THROUGH THE CAKE TO MAKE SURE THE LAYERS ARE FREE!

Figure 10-1:
Slicing a cake into layers.

ASSEMBLING AND FROSTING LAYER CAKES

1. SLICE EACH LAYER IN HALF HORIZONTALLY. PLACE ONE LAYER ON A 9" CIRCLE OF CARDBOARD.

2. SPREAD A LAYER OF FROSTING EVENLY ON THE CAKE.

3. PLACE ANOTHER LAYER ON THE 1ST ONE. SPREAD MORE FROSTING

4. COVER THE TOP AND SIDES EVENLY WITH FROSTING. PRESS CHOPPED NUTS OR SHAVED CHOCOLATE INTO THE SIDES TO THE EDGE OF THE TOP LAYER.

5. FIT A PASTRY BAG WITH A LARGE OPEN STAR TIP. FILL PART WAY WITH FROSTING.

6. PIPE A DESIGN OF SHELLS OR ROSETTES AROUND THE TOP EDGE.

7. CENTER A WALNUT HALF ON EACH SERVING PIECE (OR SCATTER SHAVED CHOCOLATE OVER THE TOP).

Figure 10-2:
Assembling and frosting layer cakes.

The World's Best Chocolate Layer Cake

I named this cake "the world's best" because it has what I like in a chocolate cake: a deep, full-bodied chocolate flavor and great texture. You can't ask for anything more!

Preparation time: *1 hour*

Baking time: *30 minutes*

Yield: *12 to 14 servings*

Chocolate Cream Frosting (see the following recipe)

1 tablespoon butter, for the pans

1 tablespoon cake flour, for the pans

1¼ cups walnuts plus 12 walnut halves or 1¼ cups finely shaved semisweet or bittersweet chocolate (for assembly)

4 ounces unsweetened chocolate, finely chopped

1¾ cups cake flour

1 teaspoon baking soda

½ teaspoon salt

½ cup (1 stick) butter, softened

1 cup sugar

⅔ cup light brown sugar

2 eggs

2 teaspoons pure vanilla extract

1 cup sour cream

1 teaspoon instant espresso powder dissolved in ¼ cup hot water

1 Preheat the oven to 350 degrees. Cut two rounds of parchment to fit the bottom of two 9-x-2-inch round cake pans. Grease the inside of the two cake pans and the tops of the parchment paper rounds with the tablespoon of butter. Dust the inside of the pans with the flour; shake out the excess. Place the parchment paper in the bottom of each cake pan, butter side up.

2 If using the walnuts for assembly, place them in a single layer in a separate cake pan and toast at 350 degrees for 5 to 8 minutes, until light colored. Remove and cool. Set aside 12 walnut halves for decoration and finely chop the remainder.

3 Melt the chocolate in the top of a double boiler over hot water, stirring often with a rubber spatula or in a microwave on low for 30-second bursts. Over a large piece of wax paper, sift together the cake flour, baking soda, and salt.

4 In a large mixing bowl, beat the butter with an electric mixer until fluffy. Add the sugar and brown sugar and cream together well. In a small bowl, lightly beat together the eggs and vanilla and add to the mixture. Stop and scrape down the sides of the bowl with a rubber spatula occasionally. Remove the top pan of the double boiler and wipe the bottom and sides very dry. Add the chocolate to the mixture and blend well. Add the dry ingredients alternately with the sour cream in 3 stages. Blend well after each addition. Stir in the espresso and blend well. Divide the mixture evenly between the two cake pans. Use the rubber spatula to smooth and even the tops. Bake for 30 to 35 minutes, until a cake tester inserted in the center comes out clean. Remove the pans from the oven. Cool on racks. Invert the cake pans to remove the layers; peel the parchment paper off the back. Re-invert onto cardboard cake circles or plates. Store the cakes tightly wrapped in plastic at room temperature for up to 2 days. Freeze for longer storage.

5 To assemble the cake, slice each layer in half horizontally (refer to Figure 10-1). Place one layer on a 9-inch cardboard circle. Set aside ½ cup of the Chocolate Cream Frosting for decoration. Spread a layer of Chocolate Cream Frosting about ¼-inch thick, evenly on the cake. Place another cake layer on top of the frosting. Repeat with the remaining cake layers. Cover the top and sides with frosting, smoothing it evenly. (Refer to Figure 10-2 for an illustration of how to assemble the layer cake.) Press the chopped walnuts or shaved chocolate into the sides of the cake up to the top edge. Fit a 12– or 14-inch pastry bag with a large, open star tip and fill partway with the ½ cup frosting you set aside. Pipe a design of shells or rosettes around the top outer edge of the cake. Center a walnut half on each serving piece. If using the shaved chocolate, scatter it across the top of the cake. Refrigerate the cake, well covered with aluminum foil, until 20 minutes before serving. Store the cake well covered in the refrigerator for up to 4 days.

Chocolate Cream Frosting

1 pound semisweet or bittersweet chocolate, finely chopped

1½ cups (3 sticks) unsalted butter, softened

2 tablespoons light corn syrup

1 tablespoon pure vanilla extract

5 cups confectioners' sugar, sifted

1 Melt the chocolate in the top of a double boiler over hot water, stirring often with a rubber spatula or in a microwave oven on low power for 30-second bursts.

2 In a large mixing bowl, beat the butter with an electric mixer until fluffy, about 2 minutes. Add the corn syrup and vanilla and blend well. Remove the top pan of the double boiler and wipe the bottom and sides very dry. Pour the chocolate into the butter mixture and blend well. Add the confectioners' sugar in 3 stages, stopping to scrape down the sides of the bowl. Blend each addition well before adding the next. If the frosting is too firm, stir in a tablespoon of water.

Per serving: Calories 850 (From Fat 473); Fat 53g (Saturated 28g); Cholesterol 111mg; Sodium 208mg; Carbohydrate 99g (Dietary Fiber 4g); Protein 7g.

Serving chocolate at the correct temperature

Chocolate tastes best at room temperature. Like a good cheese, if a chocolate dessert is too cold, its delicious flavor won't come through. Any chocolate dessert that has been chilled needs to stand at room temperature for at least 20 minutes before it's served. This is especially important for chocolate desserts that have been frozen and defrosted or those that have been in the refrigerator for several hours. In some seasons, it may take longer than 20 minutes for a dessert to warm up to room temperature.

TIP

Chocolate Truffle Torte with Raspberry Sauce

Eating this cake is like eating a chocolate truffle. It's rich and very tasty with a wonderful texture. The Raspberry Sauce (in Chapter 15) goes with it perfectly.

Preparation time: *25 minutes*

Baking time: *25 minutes*

Yield: *14 to 16 servings*

Raspberry Sauce (see Chapter 15)	4 eggs
Truffle Cream (see the following recipe)	½ cup sugar
1 tablespoon butter, softened, for the pan	2 tablespoons butter
1 tablespoon cake flour, for the pan	2 tablespoons raspberry jam
½ cup cake flour	½ cup toasted, ground hazelnuts
¼ cup unsweetened Dutch-processed cocoa powder	

1 Preheat the oven to 350 degrees. Cut a round of parchment to fit the bottom of a 9½- or 10-inch round springform pan. Use the tablespoon of butter to grease the inside of the pan and the top of the parchment paper round. Dust the inside of the pan with the flour and shake out the excess. Place a parchment paper round in the bottom of the pan, butter side up.

2 Over a medium piece of wax paper, sift together the cake flour and cocoa powder. In a large mixing bowl, using an electric mixer, beat the eggs with the sugar until they are very pale colored, thick, and hold a slowly dissolving ribbon as the beater is lifted, about 8 minutes. Fold the dry ingredients into the mixture in 3 stages, blending well.

3 Melt the butter over low heat or in a microwave oven on low power. Add ½ cup of the batter to the butter and blend together well. Then return the mixture to the mixing bowl and fold into the batter. Transfer the batter to the prepared pan and bake for 25 to 28 minutes, until a tester inserted in the center comes out clean.

4 Remove from the oven and cool on a rack for 15 minutes. Carefully remove the side ring of the pan. When the cake is completely cool, invert it onto another rack and peel off the parchment paper. Then re-invert onto a cardboard cake round or a plate.

5 To assemble the cake, slice it in half horizontally. Place the bottom layer on a cardboard cake round or a plate. Spread the raspberry jam evenly over the layer. Spread about one-third of the Truffle Cream over the raspberry jam, smoothly and evenly. Place the top layer of cake over the Truffle Cream. Frost the top and sides of the cake with the remaining Truffle Cream, smoothly and evenly. Press the ground hazelnuts into the sides of the cake up to the top edge.

6 Refrigerate the cake, well covered with aluminum foil, until 20 minutes before serving. Serve slices of the cake in a pool of Raspberry Sauce. Store the cake well covered in the refrigerator for up to 4 days.

Truffle Cream

12 ounces bittersweet or semisweet chocolate, finely chopped

1 cup heavy whipping cream
¾ cup (1½ sticks) butter, softened

1 Melt the chocolate in the top of a double boiler over hot water, stirring often with a rubber spatula or in a microwave oven on low power for 30 second bursts. In a small saucepan, scald the cream over medium. Remove the top pan of the double boiler, and wipe the bottom and sides very dry. Pour the cream into the chocolate and stir together until completely blended. Transfer the mixture to a bowl or other container, cover tightly, and cool to room temperature. Refrigerate until the consistency of thick pudding, about an hour.

2 In a large mixing bowl, using an electric mixer, beat the butter until very fluffy. Add the chocolate-cream mixture and beat together on medium speed, until the mixture is well blended, about 2 minutes.

Per serving: Calories 363 (From Fat 238); Fat 26g (Saturated 15g); Cholesterol 104mg; Sodium 25mg; Carbohydrate 29g (Dietary Fiber 3g); Protein 5g.

Devil's Food Cake with Vanilla Buttercream

This cake takes a bit of work and is not for beginners, but it's worth the effort. You'll have a much easier time preparing it if you have a stand mixer. For the best chocolate flavor in this classic cake be sure to use natural, not Dutch-processed or European-style, cocoa powder. It provides deeper flavor and darker color to the cake. The Vanilla Buttercream is a great contrast to the deep chocolate flavor.

Tools: Candy thermometer

Preparation time: 1 hour

Baking time: 30 minutes

Yield: 12 to 14 servings

Vanilla Buttercream (see the following recipe)

1 tablespoon butter, for the pans

1 tablespoon cake flour, for the pans

2 cups cake flour

1 teaspoon baking soda

¼ teaspoon salt

½ cup unsweetened natural cocoa powder, sifted

½ cup hot water

1 cup buttermilk

2 teaspoons pure vanilla extract

½ cup (1 stick) butter, softened

1½ cups light brown sugar

½ cup sugar

2 eggs

1 cup toasted and finely ground hazelnuts (for assembly)

1 Preheat the oven to 350 degrees. Cut two rounds of parchment to fit the bottom of two 9-x-2-inch round cake pans. Use the tablespoon of butter to grease the inside of two 9-x-2-inch cake pans and the tops of the parchment paper rounds. Dust the inside of the pans with the flour and shake out the excess. Place a parchment paper round in the bottom of each cake pan, butter side up.

2 Over a large piece of wax paper, sift together the cake flour, baking soda, and salt. Place the cocoa powder in a small mixing bowl and add the hot water. Stir until smooth. In a measuring cup, combine the buttermilk and vanilla.

3 In a large mixing bowl, using an electric mixer, beat the butter until fluffy. Add the brown sugar and sugar, and cream together well. Stop and scrape down the sides of the bowl with a rubber spatula occasionally.

4 In a small bowl, beat the eggs lightly with a fork, then add to the mixture. Blend well. Add the dry ingredients and buttermilk alternately in 3 stages, blending thoroughly after each addition.

5 Divide the batter between the two cake pans. Use the rubber spatula to smooth and even the top. Bake for 30 to 35 minutes, until a cake tester inserted in the center comes out clean. Remove from the oven and cool on racks. Invert the cake pans to remove the layers and peel the parchment paper off the back. Re-invert onto cardboard cake circles or plates. Store the cakes tightly wrapped in plastic at room temperature for up to 2 days. Freeze for longer storage.

6 To assemble the cake, slice each layer in half horizontally. Place one layer on a 9-inch cardboard circle. Reserve ½ cup of the Vanilla Buttercream for decoration. Spread a layer of buttercream, about ¼-inch thick, evenly on the cake. Then place another cake layer on top of the buttercream. Repeat with the remaining cake layers. Cover the top and sides with buttercream, smoothing it evenly.

7 Press the ground hazelnuts into the sides of the cake up to the top edge. Fit a 12– or 14-inch pastry bag with a large, open star tip and fill partway with frosting. Pipe a design of shells or rosettes around the top outer edge of the cake. If there are any remaining nuts, scatter them across the top of the cake.

8 Refrigerate the cake, well covered with aluminum foil, until 20 minutes before serving. Store the cake well covered in the refrigerator for up to 4 days.

Vanilla Buttercream

2 eggs	*¼ teaspoon cream of tartar*
2 egg yolks	*1¾ cups (3½ sticks) butter, softened*
1 cup plus 2 tablespoons sugar	*4 tablespoons pure vanilla extract*
½ cup water	

1 Combine the eggs and egg yolks in a large mixing bowl. Using an electric mixer, beat them until they are very pale colored and hold a slowly dissolving ribbon when the beater is lifted, about 8 minutes.

2 Combine the sugar, water, and cream of tartar in a 2-quart heavy-duty saucepan. Heat the mixture, without stirring, until it reaches 242 degrees on a candy thermometer. Wash down the sides of the pan with a damp pastry brush twice as the mixture is cooking to prevent the formation of sugar crystals.

3 Turn the mixer speed to low and pour the sugar syrup into the eggs in a slow stream. Turn the mixer speed to high and beat until the bowl is cool to the touch, about 8 minutes. Beat in the butter a couple of tablespoons at a time, then continue to beat until the buttercream is fluffy and well blended, about 3 minutes. (It may look curdled, but keep beating and it will smooth out.) Add the vanilla extract and beat until smooth. You can prepare the buttercream in advance and keep it in a tightly covered container in the refrigerator for 3 to 4 days or in the freezer for up to 4 months. To re-beat the buttercream, place chunks of it in a large mixing bowl and place the bowl in a saucepan with 1 inch of warm water. When the buttercream begins to melt around the bottom, remove the bowl from the water and wipe it very dry. Use an electric mixer to beat the buttercream until it is fluffy, about 2 minutes.

Per serving: Calories 619 (From Fat 352); Fat 39g (Saturated 20g); Cholesterol 174mg; Sodium 183mg; Carbohydrate 63g (Dietary Fiber 2g); Protein 6g.

White-Chocolate Layer Cake with White-Chocolate Frosting

White chocolate flavors both the cake and the frosting. This beautiful cake is delectable enough to be the centerpiece at any special occasion. But don't wait for something special to make this — it's too yummy!

Preparation time: *45 minutes (includes melting)*

Baking time: *40 minutes*

Yield: *12 to 14 servings*

1 tablespoon butter, for the pans	*1½ cups plus ⅓ cup sugar*
1 tablespoon flour, for the pans	*4 eggs*
8 ounces white chocolate, finely chopped	*1 teaspoon pure vanilla extract*
2¼ cups flour	*1¼ cups milk*
2½ teaspoons baking powder	*⅔ cup water*
¼ teaspoon salt	*¼ cup raspberry jam*
¾ cup (1½ sticks) butter, softened	*¾ cup sliced almonds, lightly toasted*

1 Preheat the oven to 350 degrees. Cut two rounds of parchment to fit the bottom of two 9-x-2-inch round cake pans. Use the tablespoon of butter to grease the inside of the two cake pans and the tops of the parchment paper rounds. Dust the inside of the pans with the flour and shake out the excess. Place a parchment paper round in the bottom of each cake pan, butter side up.

2 Melt the white chocolate in the top of a double boiler over hot water, stirring often with a rubber spatula or in a microwave oven on low power for 30-second bursts.

3 Over a large piece of wax paper, sift together the flour, baking powder, and salt. In a large mixing bowl, using an electric mixer beat the butter until fluffy. Add 1½ cups of the sugar, and cream together well.

4 Add the eggs one at a time, blending well after each addition. Blend in the vanilla. Add the dry ingredients in 3 stages, alternating with the milk. Beat well after each addition, and use a rubber spatula to scrape down the sides of the bowl often. Remove the top pan of the double boiler and wipe the bottom and sides very dry. Add the melted chocolate and blend together well.

5 Divide the batter evenly between the two prepared cake pans. Use a rubber spatula to smooth and even the tops. Bake the layers for 40 minutes, until a cake tester inserted in the center comes out clean and the cakes spring back when touched on top. Remove from the oven and cool on a rack for 15 minutes. Invert the cake pans to remove the layers and peel the parchment paper off the back. Re-invert onto cardboard cake circles or plates and cool completely. Store the cakes tightly wrapped in plastic at room temperature for up to 2 days. Freeze for longer storage.

6 Boil together the remaining ⅓ cup of sugar and the water until the sugar is dissolved, about 5 minutes. Cool.

7 To assemble the cakes, slice each layer in half horizontally. Place one layer on a 9-inch cardboard circle. Use a wide pastry brush to soak the layer with the sugar syrup. Spread the raspberry jam evenly over this layer. Reserve ½ cup of White-Chocolate Frosting for the top decoration. Spread a layer of frosting about ¼-inch thick, evenly on the cake, then place another cake layer on top of the frosting. Repeat with the remaining cake layers, sugar syrup, and frosting. Cover the top and sides with frosting, smoothing it evenly.

8 Press the toasted sliced almonds into the sides of the cake up to the top edge. Fit a 12– or 14-inch pastry bag with a large, open star tip and fill partway with the remaining frosting. Pipe a design of shells or rosettes around the top outer edge of the cake. Center a sliced almond on each serving piece.

9 Refrigerate the cake, well covered with aluminum foil, until 20 minutes before serving. Store the cake well covered in the refrigerator for up to 4 days.

White-Chocolate Frosting

1 pound 2 ounces white chocolate, finely chopped

1½ cups (3 sticks) butter, softened

1½ cups confectioners' sugar, sifted

2 teaspoons pure vanilla extract

1 Melt the chocolate in the top of a double boiler over hot water, stirring often with a rubber spatula or in a microwave oven on low power for 30-second bursts. Remove the top pan of the double boiler and wipe the bottom and sides very dry. Cool the chocolate for 10 minutes, stirring often to prevent a skin from forming on top.

2 In a large mixing bowl, using an electric mixer, beat the butter until fluffy. Add the melted white chocolate and blend together well. Add the confectioners' sugar and the vanilla and beat together until well blended.

Per serving: Calories 873 (From Fat 492); Fat 55g (Saturated 31g); Cholesterol 157mg; Sodium 203mg; Carbohydrate 89g (Dietary Fiber 1g); Protein 10g.

Taking cakes off the beating path

Looking for a cake that's a little different but a guaranteed winner? You've come to the right place. The cakes in this section are meant to excite and bedazzle those who eat them. One thing that makes them a little different is their texture. Most of them are creamy and soft and have a melt-in-the-mouth quality. Most of these cakes also need to be made at least a day before serving, to allow them to cool and chill.

Any of these cakes would be outstanding by themselves, but they're equally good as part of a dessert buffet. They even go nicely alongside other chocolate desserts — for people who can handle two chocolate desserts (and who can't?). Also, because these cakes are usually served cool, they go very well *alfresco* (outdoors). Next time you have an outdoor gathering make and serve one of these. Your guests will be delighted and will look forward to their next invitation.

White-Chocolate Cheesecake

This is the best cheesecake I've ever eaten! The white chocolate gives added richness to a creamy, yet dense cake. Try it with Raspberry Sauce (see Chapter 15) and fresh raspberries for outstanding color and flavor contrast.

Tools: *9½- or 10-inch round springform pan*

Preparation time: *30 minutes (including melting)*

Baking time: *1½ hours*

Yield: *12 to 14 servings*

Raspberry Sauce (see Chapter 15) (optional)	1 tablespoon butter, softened, for the pan

Crust:

8½ ounces (about 24) butter biscuit cookies	1 teaspoon ground cinnamon
2 tablespoons sugar	6 tablespoons (¾ stick) butter, melted

Filling:

1 pound white chocolate, finely chopped	4 eggs
2 pounds cream cheese at room temperature	1 egg yolk
¼ cup sugar	1 tablespoon pure vanilla extract

1 Preheat the oven to 300 degrees. Use the tablespoon of butter to grease the inside of a 9½-inch springform pan. Wrap the outside of the pan with a double layer of heavy-duty foil. Place the butter biscuit cookies in the work bowl of a food processor fitted with a steel blade and pulse until finely ground. The cookies can also be ground in a blender in small batches, or put them in a plastic bag and crush them with a rolling pin. Add the sugar and cinnamon and pulse to blend well. Transfer the ground cookies to a large mixing bowl. Pour the melted butter over them and use a rubber spatula to mix together well. Transfer the mixture to the prepared pan and press them evenly over the bottom and partway up the sides of the pan. Chill while preparing the filling.

2 For the filling, melt the white chocolate in the top of a double boiler over hot water, stirring often with a rubber spatula, or melt in a microwave oven on low power for 30-second bursts. In a large mixing bowl, using an electric mixer beat the cream cheese until fluffy. Add the sugar and blend together well. Add the eggs and egg yolk one at a time, beating well after each addition. Add the vanilla and blend well. Remove the top pan of the double boiler and wipe the bottom and sides very dry. Add the white chocolate to the batter and blend well.

3 Transfer the filling to the pan. Place the springform pan in a larger pan and pour hot water halfway up the sides of the springform pan. Bake about 1½ hours, until the cheesecake puffs over the top of the pan and the edges look slightly cracked. Remove the pan from the oven and cool the cheesecake on a rack. Cover the cake tightly and refrigerate for at least 6 hours.

4 The cake will keep well covered in the refrigerator for up to 5 days. Remove the sides of the pan. Serve slices of the cheesecake with Raspberry Sauce, if desired.

Per serving: Calories 571 (From Fat 403); Fat 45g (Saturated 26g); Cholesterol 172mg; Sodium 301mg; Carbohydrate 34g (Dietary Fiber 0g); Protein 10g.

To achieve a smooth, creamy texture when making cheesecake, have all ingredients at room temperature.

Baking cheesecake in a water bath helps prevent cracks by adding moisture in the form of steam to the heat of the oven.

Bake cheesecake at least a day before serving so it has time to cool and chill.

Using the right serving plates

When it comes to plates, there are really two different types to keep in mind: the plate on which the completed dessert is served and individual serving plates. As a general rule, you want plates to be attractive but not overly elaborate, because that will draw people's attention away from the dessert.

Make sure there's enough space on the serving plate and the individual plate so the dessert doesn't look crowded. If the dessert has been pre-sliced, take a little time to arrange them in a decorative fashion.

Triple-Chocolate Ricotta Cheesecake

Chocolate cookie crust, chocolate filling, and chocolate decoration make this cake a standout. It's soft and creamy texture is an added bonus.

Tools: *9½- or 10-inch round springform pan*

Preparation time: *4½ hours, includes chilling*

Baking time: *1 hour and 10 minutes*

Yield: *12 to 14 servings*

1 tablespoon butter, for the pan

Crust:

20 chocolate wafer cookies

4 tablespoons (½ stick) butter, melted

Filling:

1½ cups sugar

¼ cup unsweetened natural cocoa powder, sifted

30 ounces ricotta cheese

½ cup half-and-half

¼ cup flour

2 teaspoons pure vanilla extract

¼ teaspoon salt

3 eggs

1½ ounces (¼ cup) white chocolate, finely chopped, for garnish

1 Preheat the oven to 350 degrees. Use the tablespoon of butter to grease the bottom and sides of a 9½- or 10-inch round springform pan. Place the chocolate wafers in the work bowl of a food processor fitted with a steel blade and pulse until finely ground. The wafers can also be ground in a blender in small batches, or put them in a plastic bag and crush them with a rolling pin. Transfer the ground wafers to a large mixing bowl. Pour the melted butter over them and use a rubber spatula to mix together well. Transfer the mixture to the prepared pan and press them evenly over the bottom. Bake for 10 minutes. Remove the pan from the oven and cool while preparing the filling.

2 In a small mixing bowl, combine the sugar and cocoa powder. Toss to blend well. In a large mixing bowl, combine the ricotta cheese and half-and-half. Use an electric mixer to blend together well. Add the sugar and cocoa powder mixture and blend well. Add the flour, vanilla extract, and salt, and blend well. One at a time, add the eggs, beating well after each addition. Pour the filling over the crust.

3 Bake for 1 hour, until the center is set. Turn off the oven and cool the cake in the oven with the door propped open for 30 minutes. Remove the cake and cool completely on a rack. Run a thin metal spatula between the cake pan and the sides of the cake. Remove the sides of the springform pan. Cool the cake completely, then chill for at least 4 hours.

4 Prepare a small parchment paper pastry cone. Melt the white chocolate in a small bowl in a microwave oven on low power or in the top of a double boiler over hot water. Remove the top pan of the double boiler and wipe the bottom and sides very dry. Pour the melted white chocolate into the paper pastry cone. Fold in the sides and fold the top down, then snip off a small opening at the pointed end. Pipe lines of white chocolate or other designs across the top of the cheesecake. Chill briefly to set the chocolate.

5 Chill the cake until ready to serve. The cake will keep tightly covered in the refrigerator for up to 5 days.

Per serving: *Calories 352 (From Fat 150); Fat 17g (Saturated 10g); Cholesterol 91mg; Sodium 164mg; Carbohydrate 41g (Dietary Fiber 1g); Protein 11g.*

Be sure to chill the cheesecake thoroughly before cutting so it is firm and won't fall apart.

To cut a cheesecake cleanly, run the blade of the knife under hot water, then dry it between each cut. You can also use a piece of dental floss to cut cheesecake. If you do this, use a long piece that you can grasp with both hands tightly. Pull it straight down through the cake from top to bottom, then pull it out of the cake from the side.

Finding the right serving utensils

Having the right serving utensils can make your chocolate delivery go smoothly. For chocolate cakes and pies, there is a triangular shaped server that scoops the portion out in one perfect piece. Some of these servers have a serrated edge that also makes them good for cutting the pieces.

Use a sharp serrated knife to cut dessert so it doesn't get smashed in the process.

Some serving forks and knives are very elaborate with crystal handles or scrollwork on the handle. Use these to serve your most elegant desserts.

Individual Bittersweet Chocolate Cakes with Ganache Frosting

These little cakes may look like cupcakes, but they're definitely for adults. Try using different nuts in place of the hazelnuts to make a variation.

Preparation time: *15 minutes*

Baking time: *15 minutes*

Yield: *8 servings*

1½ tablespoons butter, softened, for the pan

2 tablespoons sugar, for the pan

Cakes:

¼ cup heavy whipping cream

1 tablespoon unsweetened natural cocoa powder

2 tablespoons butter

5 ounces bittersweet chocolate, finely chopped

2 eggs

¼ cup sugar

¼ cup toasted and ground hazelnuts

1 teaspoon vanilla extract

1 Preheat the oven to 350 degrees. Use the butter to grease the inside of 8 cavities of a muffin pan, then sprinkle with sugar.

2 For the cakes, combine the cream, cocoa powder, and butter in a medium heavy-duty saucepan. Bring to a boil over medium heat. Remove from the heat and stir in the chopped chocolate until smooth and completely melted.

3 In a large mixing bowl, using an electric mixer, whip the eggs with the sugar until very pale colored and the mixture holds a slowly dissolving ribbon as the beater is lifted. Pour in the chocolate mixture; blend thoroughly. Add the ground hazelnuts and vanilla; mix well. Divide the batter among the cavities of the muffin pan; halfway fill the remaining cavities with water. Bake 15 to 17 minutes, until a toothpick inserted in the center comes out clean. Remove from the oven. Pour out the water so the cakes don't get wet. Let the pan cool on a rack for 10 minutes. Turn the cakes out and let them cool.

4 Dip the top of each cake in the warm Ganache Frosting. Serve the cakes with fresh fruit, if desired. Store the cakes in a tightly sealed container in the refrigerator for up to 3 days. Bring to room temperature before serving.

Ganache Frosting

¼ cup heavy whipping cream

2 ounces bittersweet chocolate, finely chopped

Heat the cream in a small saucepan until it boils. Remove from the heat and stir in the chopped chocolate until completely melted and smooth. Let the ganache cool about 15 minutes, stirring frequently to prevent a skin from forming on the top.

Per serving: Calories 309 (From Fat 195); Fat 22g (Saturated 12g); Cholesterol 88mg; Sodium 24mg; Carbohydrate 25g (Dietary Fiber 2g); Protein 4g.

Bittersweet Chocolate Mousse Cake

The creamy, soft texture of this cake is similar to a mousse. It's one of my very favorite cakes because of its delicate texture and deep chocolate flavor.

Tools: *9½- or 10-inch round springform pan*

Preparation time: *20 minutes*

Baking time: *1 hour*

Yield: *12 to 14 servings*

1 tablespoon butter, softened, for the pan

2 cups heavy whipping cream

2 teaspoons pure vanilla extract

1 pound bittersweet chocolate, finely chopped

2 tablespoons instant espresso powder dissolved in ¼ cup warm water

6 eggs

½ cup sugar

1 Preheat the oven to 350 degrees. Use the tablespoon of butter to grease the inside of a 9½- or 10-inch round springform pan. Wrap the bottom of the cake pan with a double layer of heavy-duty foil.

2 In a large chilled mixing bowl, using an electric mixer, whip 1 cup of the cream until fluffy. Add 1 teaspoon of the vanilla and whip the cream until it holds soft peaks. Chill until needed.

3 Melt the chopped chocolate with the espresso in the top of a double boiler over hot water, stirring often with a rubber spatula or in a microwave oven on low power for 30-second bursts. In a large mixing bowl, using an electric mixer, whip the eggs until frothy. Add the sugar gradually and whip until the mixture is pale colored and holds a slowly dissolving ribbon as the beater is lifted, about 5 minutes. Remove the top pan of the double boiler and wipe the bottom and sides very dry. Stir the chocolate mixture until it is shiny, about a minute. Add the chocolate mixture to the whipped eggs and blend together thoroughly. Fold in the chilled whipped cream in 3 stages.

4 Transfer the batter to the prepared pan. Place the cake pan in a larger baking pan and fill halfway with hot water. Bake the cake for 1 hour. Turn off the oven and let the cake stand in the oven for 15 minutes. Remove from the oven and cool the cake on a rack.

5 Carefully remove the sides of the springform pan. In a large mixing bowl, using an electric mixer, whip the remaining cup of cream until frothy. Add the remaining vanilla, and whip until the cream holds soft peaks. Serve slices of the cake with a large dollop of whipped cream.

6 The cake is best eaten within 6 hours of preparation. It can be stored well covered in the refrigerator for up to 3 days. If refrigerated, the texture becomes dense and firm.

Per serving: Calories 368 (From Fat 238); Fat 27g (Saturated 16g); Cholesterol 141mg; Sodium 42mg; Carbohydrate 27g (Dietary Fiber 3g); Protein 6g.

Raspberry and White-Chocolate Mousse Cake

Eating this cake is like eating a cloud. It's light and delicate and full of wonderful flavor. The raspberry is a perfect counterpoint to the white chocolate. This is a beautiful dessert to serve in the springtime, but you don't have to wait for spring to enjoy it.

Tools: *9½- or 10-inch springform pan*

Preparation time: *6½ hours, includes chilling*

Yield: *12 to 14 servings*

20 to 24 butter biscuit cookies	*1¾ cup heavy whipping cream*
8 tablespoons (1 stick) butter, melted	*2 tablespoons orange liqueur or 2 teaspoons orange extract*
½ cup raspberry jam	
9 ounces white chocolate, finely chopped	*½ cup fresh raspberries, optional*

1 Place the cookies in the work bowl of a food processor fitted with a steel blade. Pulse until finely ground, about 1 minute. The cookies can also be crushed in a blender or clean coffee grinder, or place them in a plastic bag and crush with a rolling pin. Transfer the cookie crumbs to a large mixing bowl. Add the melted butter and toss together until the crumbs are completely coated. Press the mixture evenly into the bottom of a 9½- or 10-inch round springform pan. Chill for 15 to 30 minutes, until firm. Spread the jam evenly over the crust.

2 Melt the white chocolate in the top of a double boiler over hot water, stirring often with a rubber spatula or in a microwave oven on low power for 30 second bursts. In a separate small saucepan, scald ¼ cup of the cream over medium heat. Remove the top pan of the double boiler and wipe the bottom and sides very dry. Pour the cream into the white chocolate and stir together well. Add the orange liqueur or extract and stir until smooth.

3 In a large mixing bowl, using an electric mixer, whip the remaining 1½ cups cream until it holds soft peaks, about 2 minutes. Fold the whipped cream into the white-chocolate mixture in 3 stages, blending well after each addition. Spread the mixture evenly over the jam layer. Cover the pan tightly with plastic wrap and chill at least 6 hours.

4 To remove the sides of the pan, carefully run a thin metal spatula blade around the sides of the cake. Garnish the top of the cake with fresh raspberries, if desired. The cake will keep, well covered, in the refrigerator for up to 3 days.

Per serving: Calories 348 (From Fat 240); Fat 27g (Saturated 15g); Cholesterol 64mg; Sodium 82mg; Carbohydrate 26g (Dietary Fiber 0g); Protein 3g.

Chapter 11

Pies and Tarts

*W*hen people think of desserts, pies and tarts are two of the first things that come to mind — though *chocolate* pies and tarts may not. But I'm here to tell you that pies and tarts are some of the best ways you'll find to consume chocolate.

There's something a little intriguing about chocolate pies and tarts. When you mention to someone that you're serving them, you often get a peculiar glance of curiosity. Chocolate pies and tarts are not as common as many other chocolate desserts, because people mistakenly think they're too difficult to make. This is *definitely* not the case. Actually, these desserts are a great way to bedazzle your friends and family. Try any of the recipes in this chapter, and you'll see what I mean.

Perfect Pies

Pies are part of the American culture. You probably grew up eating pies for dessert, especially on holidays and special occasions. And nothing beats that wonderful smell of a pie baking in the oven. It makes the house feel cozy and lets you know that you're in for a treat before too long. Chocolate pies are at the top of the pie pyramid, at least in my book. They're the best of the best.

What I like about chocolate pies is that you get a nice crust along with a delicious chocolate filling. The crunchiness of the pie crust and the smoothness of the filling are a perfect textural combination for the palate.

One of the great things about pies is that they're made in component parts. In many cases, you can make these parts separately and assemble them at a later time. For example, you can make up the pie dough one day, the filling the next, and combine them the third day, just before serving. You can also make up component parts and store them for later use. One thing I like to do is make up an extra pie shell and store it in the freezer. That way I can pop it into the oven whenever I'm in the mood to bake a pie.

Chocolate Cream Pie

In this pie, a very rich and creamy chocolate filling is enclosed in a chocolate crumb crust. I love the contrast of smooth and crunchy textures this pie offers. If you want, you can make the crumb crust and the filling a day or two in advance, and then assemble it with the topping shortly before serving.

Tools: 9-inch round pie dish

Preparation time: 20 minutes, plus cooling time

Baking time: 6 minutes

Yield: 12 servings

Crust:

1½ cups chocolate wafer cookie crumbs

2 tablespoons sugar

5 tablespoons butter, melted

Filling:

⅔ cup sugar

¼ cup cornstarch, sifted

2 tablespoons unsweetened Dutch-processed cocoa powder, sifted

⅛ teaspoon salt

2⅔ cup milk

4 egg yolks

5 ounces unsweetened chocolate, finely chopped

2 tablespoons butter, melted

1 teaspoon pure vanilla extract

Topping:

1 cup heavy whipping cream

1 tablespoon confectioners' sugar, sifted

1 teaspoon pure vanilla extract

1 Preheat the oven to 325 degrees. For the crust, place the chocolate wafers in the work bowl of a food processor fitted with a steel blade. Pulse until they are finely ground, about 1 minute. Or place the wafers in a plastic bag and crush with a rolling pin.

Transfer the crumbs to a large mixing bowl and toss with the sugar. Pour in the melted butter, and use a rubber spatula or fork to mix completely.

2 Transfer the mixture to the pie dish and use your fingers to press it evenly against the bottom and sides of the dish, making sure not to leave any holes. Place the pie dish on a baking sheet and bake for 6 minutes. Remove from the oven and cool completely on a rack.

3 For the filling, combine the sugar, cornstarch, cocoa powder, and salt in a large heavy-duty saucepan. Stir to blend well. Add the milk and cook the mixture over medium heat until it is smooth, about 5 minutes.

4 In a small mixing bowl, whisk the yolks lightly. Add ½ cup of the warm milk mixture and blend well, then pour this mixture back into the saucepan. Cook the mixture, stirring constantly, over medium heat until it thickens and begins to bubble around the edges, about 5 minutes. Remove the pan from the heat and stir in the chocolate until completely smooth and melted. Stir in the butter and vanilla and blend well. Transfer the mixture to a mixing bowl and let cool for 15 minutes, stirring frequently to prevent a skin from forming on top.

5 Transfer the filling to the cooled crumb crust, mounding slightly in the center. For the topping, place the cream in a large mixing bowl. Using an electric mixer whip the cream until frothy. Add the confectioners' sugar and vanilla and whip the cream until it holds soft peaks. Spread the whipped cream over the chocolate filling. Refrigerate the pie until ready to cut into slices to serve.

Per serving: Calories 375 (From Fat 237); Fat 26g (Saturated 15g); Cholesterol 124mg; Sodium 151mg; Carbohydrate 34g (Dietary Fiber 3g); Protein 6g.

Making pie crust

Pie dough is really easy to make! Too often people shy away from making a pie because they think it's too tricky or involved. Here are several pointers that will ensure success when making pie dough:

✔ **Mix the dough quickly, and cut the butter in so that it stays in small pieces.** One of the important steps in making great pie dough is keeping the butter in tiny pieces that stay separate from the flour and melt when baked, leaving behind little air pockets. This is what creates a flaky crust.

✔ **Don't overmix or -knead the dough.** If you do, it will become tough because the gluten (protein) in the dough is activated when kneaded. Use all-purpose flour or cake flour, not bread flour, which has too much gluten, for pie dough. Or use a combination of half of both of these flours.

(continued)

(continued)

✔ **If you have time, chill the dough before rolling it out.** This allows the dough to relax so it won't be tough or sticky. However, if the dough is *too* cold, it will be difficult to roll out. Let it stand at room temperature for 15 to 30 minutes, until it becomes pliable.

✔ **To roll out pie dough, be sure to work on a flat, smooth surface.** Dust the surface lightly with flour or roll the pie dough between sheets of lightly floured wax paper. Roll from the center of the dough outward and away from you in all directions. Give the dough a quarter turn and continue to roll. This makes it easier to roll the dough evenly. As you work, lift the wax paper occasionally to be sure it's not sticking. Sprinkle on a little more flour as needed, but don't use too much, or the dough will become tough. Roll the dough a few inches larger than your pie pan so you won't have to stretch it to fit.

✔ **To transfer the pie dough to the pan, peel off the top layer of wax paper, if used.** Gently lift up one edge and loosely roll the dough around the rolling pin. Place the pie pan underneath the rolling pin and unroll the dough into the pan. Then gently lift up the sides of the dough to make sure they fit snugly against the bottom and sides of the pan.

✔ **To make a tidy top edge, trim off excess dough, leaving a border of about ½ inch.** Turn this to the inside, which helps strengthen the sides. Crimp the top edge with your fingers or use a fork to imprint an attractive design around the edge.

✔ **To freeze a crust, roll out the pie dough, fit it into the pan, and wrap it well.** It will keep for several months. And when you're ready to use it, you don't need to defrost the frozen crust. You can take it directly from the freezer and bake it, extending the baking time a few minutes longer than the recipe calls for.

Basic Pie Dough

Although classic pie dough is made with shortening or a mixture of shortening and butter to produce a light flaky crust, I prefer to use all butter because it makes a much tastier pie dough. A small amount of flakiness may be sacrificed for flavor, but I think it's worth it. And I think you will, too, when you taste this crust. Use this pie crust for White Chocolate Banana Cream Pie and Chocolate Pecan Pie.

Preparation time: *5 minutes*

Yield: *Dough for a 10-inch round single crust pie*

1¼ cups flour	7 tablespoons butter, cold
1 teaspoon sugar	3 to 4 tablespoons ice water
⅛ teaspoon salt	

1 Combine the flour, sugar, and salt in the work bowl of a food processor fitted with a steel blade. Pulse briefly to blend. Cut the butter into small pieces and add. Pulse until the butter is cut into tiny pieces. Add the cold water and process until the mixture forms a ball, about 30 seconds. (If not using a food processor, combine the flour, sugar, and salt in a large mixing bowl. Cut the butter into small pieces and add. Use two knives, a pastry blender, or a fork to cut the butter into tiny pieces. Add the ice water and blend just until the dough comes together.) Wrap the dough in plastic and chill for 30 minutes.

2 Roll the dough out on a lightly floured flat work surface or between sheets of lightly floured wax paper.

3 The dough can be tightly wrapped in plastic and kept in the refrigerator for up to 3 days before using, or it can be frozen for up to 4 months. If the dough is very cold, let it stand at room temperature for 15 to 30 minutes before rolling, so it becomes pliable.

Per serving: Calories 162 (From Fat 92); Fat 10g (Saturated 6g); Cholesterol 27mg; Sodium 38mg; Carbohydrate 15g (Dietary Fiber 1g); Protein 2g.

Don't overprocess pie dough when making it in the food processor. If it becomes too well blended, the little fat particles won't remain separate from the flour to make a flaky texture when the dough is baked.

If your pie dough develops any splits or holes while *baking blind* (without the filling), you can easily patch them. Use any scraps of dough left over from the rolling process. Lightly moisten one side of the dough scrap with water and press it over the area to be patched. Return the pie crust to the oven to bake for a few minutes to set the patch, then continue to prepare the pie.

Save any scraps of pie dough and keep them in the freezer. You can use these to make individual pies or tarts.

Rolling the pie crust is only part of the puzzle. Transferring and fitting it into the pie pan is the next step (see Figure 11-1). To do this run an offset spatula under the pie dough to make sure it's not sticking to the surface. Gently roll the pie dough up around the rolling pin, place the pie pan directly underneath the rolling pin, and carefully unroll into the pan.

Figure 11-1:
Transferring
pie dough to
the pie pan.

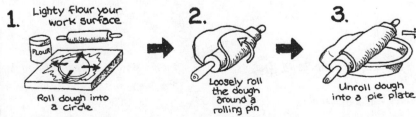

Carefully lift up the pie dough and press it gently against the bottom and sides of the pie pan (see Figure 11-2). This helps prevent shrinkage as the pie dough bakes. Trim the excess dough at the top and crimp or press the edges to form a decorative design.

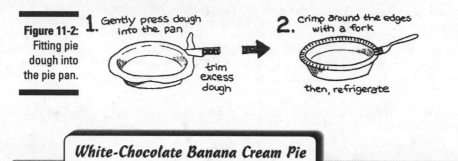

Figure 11-2: Fitting pie dough into the pie pan.

White-Chocolate Banana Cream Pie

This pie is a showstopper. It always elicits *oohs* and *aahs* from those who see and eat it. A delicate pie crust holds layers of fresh bananas, white-chocolate cream filling, and white-chocolate whipped-cream topping. For a final flourish, it's sprinkled with shaved white chocolate. If someone in your life is a white-chocolate lover, this is the perfect dessert to make.

Tools: *9-inch deep pie dish*

Preparation time: *45 minutes, plus cooling and chilling time*

Baking time: *30 minutes*

Yield: *12 servings*

Basic Pie Crust (see the recipe earlier in this chapter)

Filling:

2 cups milk

⅔ cup sugar

Pinch of salt

1 egg

2 egg yolks

¼ cup cornstarch, sifted

⅓ cup (1½ ounces) white chocolate, finely chopped

1 teaspoon pure vanilla extract

2 medium ripe bananas, peeled and cut into ¼-inch-thick slices

Topping:

¼ cup (1 ounce) white chocolate, finely chopped

1 cup heavy whipping cream

1 tablespoon confectioners' sugar, sifted

2 tablespoons shaved white chocolate

1 Preheat the oven to 350 degrees. On a flat work surface, roll out the pie dough between sheets of lightly floured wax paper to a large circle about 11 inches in diameter. Carefully roll the pie dough around the rolling pin and unroll into a 9-inch-round deep pie dish. Fit the dough against the bottom and sides of the pan. Trim off any excess pastry dough at the top edge, then crimp the edges or use a fork to make a decorative pattern. Pierce the bottom of the pie shell in a few places with a fork. Place the pie pan on a baking sheet, line the pan with a large piece of aluminum foil that fits against the bottom and sides of the dough. Fill the foil with tart or pie weights and bake for 10 minutes. Remove the foil and weights and bake another 20 to 25 minutes, until light golden brown. Remove from the oven and cool completely on a rack.

2 For the filling, combine 1½ cups of the milk, ⅓ cup of the sugar, and the salt in a medium heavy-duty saucepan. Stir the mixture and bring to a boil over medium-high heat. Remove the pan from the heat. In a large heavy-duty saucepan, combine the egg and egg yolks with the remaining ½ cup milk, the remaining ⅓ cup sugar, and the cornstarch. Whisk until smooth over low heat. Add the hot milk in a stream, stirring constantly. Cook, stirring continuously, on medium-high heat until the mixture thickens and bubbles around the edges, about 5 minutes.

3 Remove the pan from the heat and add the chopped white chocolate. Stir until it is completely melted and smooth, then stir in the vanilla. Transfer the custard to a bowl. Place a large piece of wax paper directly on top of the custard and let cool at room temperature. Refrigerate the custard until it is chilled, about 1 hour.

4 For the topping, melt the white chocolate in the top of a double boiler over hot water or in a microwave oven on low power. Stir often to ensure even melting. In a large mixing bowl, using an electric mixer, whip the cream with the confectioners' sugar to soft peaks. Add the melted white chocolate and blend well.

5 To assemble, whisk the chilled custard and mix one-third of it with the sliced bananas. Spread this over the bottom of the pie shell, then spread the remaining custard evenly over the bananas. Spread the whipped cream evenly over the custard, then sprinkle with the shaved chocolate. Chill the pie until ready to serve.

Per serving: *Calories 325 (From Fat 171); Fat 19g (Saturated 11g); Cholesterol 105mg; Sodium 78mg; Carbohydrate 35g (Dietary Fiber 1g); Protein 5g.*

If you're in a hurry to make a pie for dessert, use a store-bought pie shell instead of making your own. Be sure to follow the directions on the package for baking the crust.

Pies and tarts: What's the difference?

Both pies and tarts consist of a pastry crust that holds a filling. Pies are baked in pie pans, also called pie plates and pie dishes. These pans have sloped sides that range from 1 to 2 inches deep. Those that are 2 inches deep are called *deep-dish pie pans.* Pie crusts can be made from a variety of items, including dough, cookie crumbs, and ground nuts, to name a few. Pies can have a single bottom crust, or both a bottom and top crust. Pies are served from the pans in which they are baked.

Tarts are always *open face* (that is, they have only a bottom crust that encloses the filling).

They are shallow, usually only 1 inch high. Tarts are generally baked in pans with removable bottoms, making them easy to remove from the pan for serving. The flat surface of the pan makes a flat bottom for the tart. The sides of the pans are fluted, which makes an attractive design in the pastry dough. Tart pastry dough is usually richer than and not as flaky as pie dough, because it's made with eggs or egg yolks. Tarts can be made in many shapes and sizes, including individual and mini, which are called *tartlets.*

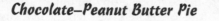

Chocolate–Peanut Butter Pie

Although this pie has a few components, it's very quick and easy to make. It's a delicious combination of cream cheese, peanut butter, dark chocolate, and cream in a graham cracker crust. If you're in a hurry, you can always use a ready-made crust. And this is a great dessert to make ahead and have on hand in the refrigerator or freezer.

Tools: *10-inch-round deep pie dish*

Preparation time: *20 minutes*

Baking time: *8 minutes*

Yield: *12 to 14 servings*

Crust:

1½ cups crushed graham cracker crumbs

½ teaspoon ground cinnamon

5 tablespoons butter, melted

Filling:

6 ounces bittersweet or semisweet chocolate

8 ounces cream cheese, softened

1 cup peanut butter (creamy or chunky)

1 cup confectioners' sugar, sifted

1 cup heavy whipping cream

1 teaspoon pure vanilla extract

Garnish:

1 cup heavy whipping cream

1 tablespoon confectioners' sugar, sifted

1 teaspoon pure vanilla extract

1 Preheat the oven to 350 degrees. For the crust, place the graham crackers in the work bowl of a food processor fitted with a steel blade. Pulse until they are finely ground, about 1 minute. Or place the graham crackers in a plastic bag and crush with a rolling pin. Transfer the crumbs to a large mixing bowl and toss with the cinnamon. Pour in the melted butter and use a rubber spatula or fork to mix completely.

2 Transfer the mixture to the pie dish and use your fingers to press it evenly against the bottom and sides of the dish, making sure not to leave any holes. Place the pie dish on a baking sheet and bake for 8 minutes. Remove from the oven and cool completely on a rack.

3 Melt the chocolate in the top of a double boiler over hot water or in a microwave oven on low power, stirring occasionally to ensure even melting. For the filling, combine the cream cheese and peanut butter in a large mixing bowl. Using an electric mixer beat together until smooth. Add the confectioners' sugar and blend well. In a separate large mixing bowl whip the cream until frothy. Add the vanilla and whip until the cream holds soft peaks. Fold the cream into the mixture in 3 stages

4 Remove the top pan of the double boiler and wipe the bottom and sides very dry. Cool for 5 minutes, stirring often to prevent a skin from forming on top. Add the chocolate and using a rubber spatula swirl it through the mixture. Transfer the filling to the cooled crust and spread it smoothly and evenly. Chill for 30 minutes. The pie can be frozen, well wrapped, at this point.

5 For the garnish, place the cream in a large mixing bowl. Using an electric mixer whip the cream until frothy. Add the confectioners' sugar and vanilla and whip until the cream holds soft peaks. Spread the cream evenly over the top of the pie. Keep the pie refrigeratred until ready to serve.

Per serving: Calories 500 (From Fat 334); Fat X37g (Saturated 19g); Cholesterol 76mg; Sodium 252mg; Carbohydrate 37g (Dietary Fiber 2g); Protein 8g.

You can easily make variations of the Chocolate–Peanut Butter Pie by adding an ingredient or changing the garnish:

- **Double-Chocolate–Peanut Butter Pie:** Use a chocolate crumb crust (see Chocolate Cream Pie earlier in this chapter for the recipe).

- **Chocolate Chip–Peanut Butter Pie:** Stir in ½ cup chocolate chips before folding in the whipped cream.

- **Cacao Nib–Chocolate–Peanut Butter Pie:** Stir in ½ cup cacao nibs before folding in the whipped cream.

- **Drizzled Chocolate Decoration:** Melt 1 ounce bittersweet or semisweet chocolate and drizzle over the top of the whipped cream.

- **Shaved Chocolate Decoration:** Sprinkle 2 tablespoons shaved bittersweet or semisweet chocolate over the top of the whipped cream.

Chocolate Pecan Pie

This is a chocolate and nut lover's dream pie. Although it has a sweet edge, it's not cloying. The crispness of the pie crust is a great contrast to the chewy, soft filling. Try this for your next Thanksgiving feast and watch your guests' eyes light up when it's served.

Tools: *10-inch deep pie dish*

Preparation time: *15 minutes*

Baking time: *30 minutes*

Yield: *12 to 14 servings*

Basic Pie Crust (see the recipe earlier in this chapter)

Filling:

1½ cups pecans	*1 tablespoon butter, melted*
3 eggs	*1 teaspoon pure vanilla extract*
1 cup light brown sugar	*¼ teaspoon salt*
½ cup dark corn syrup	*6 ounces bittersweet or semisweet chocolate*

Garnish:

1 cup heavy whipping cream	*1 teaspoon pure vanilla extract*
1 tablespoon confectioners' sugar, sifted	*1 pint vanilla ice cream*

1 Preheat the oven to 350 degrees. Place the pecans in a single layer in a cake or pie pan and toast in the oven for 6 minutes. Remove the pan from the oven and cool while preparing the crust. Raise the oven temperature to 400 degrees.

2 On a flat work surface, roll out the pie dough between sheets of lightly floured wax paper to a large circle about 11 inches in diameter. Carefully roll the pie dough around the rolling pin and unroll into a 9-inch round deep pie dish. Fit the dough against the bottom and sides of the pan. Trim off any excess pastry dough at the top edge, then crimp the edges or use a fork to make a decorative pattern. Pierce the bottom of the pie shell in a few places with a fork. Place the pie pan on a baking sheet, line the pan with a large piece of aluminum foil that fits against the bottom and sides of the dough. Fill the foil with tart or pie weights and bake for 10 minutes. Remove the foil and weights and bake another 6 to 8 minutes, until set. Remove from the oven and cool on a rack while preparing the filling.

3 Melt the chocolate in the top of a double boiler over hot water or in a microwave oven on low power, stirring occasionally to ensure even melting. For the filling, whisk the eggs in a large mixing bowl. Add the brown sugar, corn syrup, melted butter, vanilla, and salt, and whisk to combine. Remove the top pan of the double boiler and wipe the bottom and sides very dry. Add the melted chocolate and blend well. Stir in the toasted pecans. Pour the filling into the partially baked pie crust. Bake for 30 to 35 minutes, until the filling is set and a tester inserted in the center comes out clean. Remove from the oven and cool on a rack. Store the pie tightly covered with aluminum foil at room temperature for up to 2 days.

4 For the garnish, place the cream in a large mixing bowl. Using an electric mixer, whip the cream until frothy. Add the confectioners' sugar and vanilla and whip until the cream holds soft peaks. Serve a slice of the pie with a large dollop of whipped cream and a scoop of vanilla ice cream.

Per serving: Calories 418 (From Fat 238); Fat 27g (Saturated 12g); Cholesterol 87mg; Sodium 108mg; Carbohydrate 43g (Dietary Fiber 2g); Protein 5g.

Be sure to allow the pie to cool or set enough before cutting or it will fall apart.

Turning pie into tart

You can make Individual Chocolate Pecan Tarts instead of one large Chocolate Pecan Pie. Just refer to the Chocolate Pecan Pie recipe in this chapter and follow these steps:

1. Preheat the oven to 350 degrees. Roll out the pie dough and cut into eight to ten 4-inch rounds. Fit each circle of dough into a 3-inch round, 1-inch deep tartlet pan, pinching off any excess dough at the top.

2. Place the tartlet pans on a baking sheet. Fit another tartlet pan gently on top of each pan. This acts as a weight while the tartlet shells bake.

3. Bake the shells for 10 minutes, then remove the top tartlet pans, and bake another 6 to 8 minutes, until set and pale colored. Pour the filling into each tartlet shell up to three-fourths full. Bake 25 to 30 minutes, until the filling is set and a tester inserted in the center comes out clean. Remove from the oven and cool completely on a rack. Gently shake the tartlets from their pans to serve.

Tantalizing Tarts

In Europe, tarts have a starring role and pies are practically nonexistent. But tarts are starting to catch on in America. They take on a more sophisticated edge than pies and are usually more delicate in their appearance, which gives the illusion that they're difficult to make. Actually, tarts are just as simple to make as pies are. Like pies, tarts have component parts that often can be made in advance and assembled before baking or serving.

I love to make tarts because I can make the same recipes in a variety of shapes, such as square and rectangle, and they look like a completely different dessert. Also, tarts can be made in individual sizes, which makes them great to serve for buffets or picnics, as well as to pack for a surprise treat in someone's lunch bag.

Chocolate Hazelnut Tart

A dense, chewy chocolate and hazelnut filling is enclosed in a flaky tart pastry shell. This tart is great to make in advance and it travels well, so it's perfect to take the next time you're invited to a gathering. It's one of my very favorite tarts.

Tools: 11-inch round fluted-edge tart pan with removable bottom

Preparation time: 1 hour (includes chilling)

Baking time: 30 minutes

Yield: 16 to 18 servings

Pastry dough:

1¾ cups flour

½ teaspoon baking powder

⅛ teaspoon salt

⅓ cup sugar

1¼ sticks butter, chilled

1 teaspoon pure vanilla extract

Filling:

¾ stick butter

¾ cup sugar

2 eggs

1 tablespoon flour

1½ cups toasted and ground hazelnuts

6 ounces dark (bittersweet or semisweet) or milk chocolate, finely chopped

1 teaspoon pure vanilla extract

1 teaspoon chocolate extract (optional)

Garnish:

1 cup heavy cream

1 teaspoon pure vanilla extract

1 teaspoon chocolate extract (optional)

1 For the pastry dough, combine the flour, baking powder, salt, and sugar in the work bowl of a food processor fitted with the steel blade. Pulse briefly to blend. Cut the butter into small pieces and add. Pulse until the butter is cut into tiny pieces. Add the vanilla and process until the dough forms a ball, about a minute. (If not using a food processor, soften the butter and, using a mixer, beat the butter until light in a large mixing bowl. Add the sugar and cream together. Mix the salt and baking powder with the flour and add to the butter mixture in 2 stages, blending well after each addition. Shape the dough into a flat disk and proceed.)

2 Roll out the pastry dough on a lightly floured flat work surface to a 14-inch circle. Gently roll the pastry dough around the rolling pin and unroll into an 11-inch fluted-edge tart pan with removable bottom. Trim off the excess pastry dough, leaving a ½-inch border. Turn this to the inside, doubling the edge of the pastry. Pierce the bottom of the pastry shell in several places and chill for 30 minutes.

3 Preheat the oven to 375 degrees. For the filling, place the butter in a large mixing bowl. Using an electric mixer, beat the butter until fluffy, about 1 minute. Add the sugar and cream together. Lightly beat the eggs and add to the mixture. Stop and scrape down the sides of the bowl with a rubber spatula. Add the flour, ground hazelnuts, and chopped chocolate, and blend thoroughly. Stir in the vanilla and chocolate extract, if using.

4 Remove the tart pan from the refrigerator and place on a jelly roll pan. Pour the filling into the pastry shell. Bake until the filling is puffed, golden, and set, about 30 minutes. Remove from the oven and cool on a rack. Carefully remove the sides of the tart pan. Store the tart tightly covered with aluminum foil at room temperature for up to 3 days.

5 For the garnish, whip the cream in a medium mixing bowl using an electric mixer until frothy. Add the vanilla and chocolate extracts, if using, and whip until the cream holds soft peaks. Serve slices of the tart with a big dollop of whipped cream.

Per serving: Calories 329 (From Fat 232); Fat 26g (Saturated 12g); Cholesterol 70mg; Sodium 41mg; Carbohydrate 21g (Dietary Fiber 2g); Protein 5g.

When rolling out dough for a pie or tart, an easy way to tell if it's rolled out large enough to fit the pie or tart pan is to hold the pan over the dough. This allows you to see if you need to roll the dough more or if it's going to fit the pan.

Marble Two-Chocolate Tart

Two separate chocolate fillings are swirled together in this tart to make a striking visual pattern. Although it looks like it may have taken all day to prepare, it's really easy to make. Delight your guests with this tart at your next party.

Tools: *11-inch round fluted-edge tart pan with removable bottom*

Preparation time: *4 hours (includes chilling)*

Baking time: *22 minutes*

Yield: *16 servings*

Pastry dough:

2 cups flour

⅔ cup confectioners' sugar, sifted

Pinch of salt

1¼ sticks (½ cup plus 2 tablespoons) butter, chilled

2 egg yolks

2 tablespoons cold water

Dark chocolate ganache:

⅔ cup heavy cream

10 ounces bittersweet or semisweet chocolate, finely chopped

1 teaspoon pure vanilla extract

White chocolate ganache:

2 tablespoons heavy cream

2 ounces white chocolate, finely chopped

1 For the pastry dough, combine the flour, confectioners' sugar, and salt in the work bowl of a food processor fitted with a steel blade. Pulse for 5 seconds to blend. Cut the butter into small pieces and add. Pulse until the butter is cut into tiny pieces, about 1 minute. Lightly beat the egg yolks and add with 1 tablespoon of the water. Process until the dough forms a ball. If necessary, add the remaining tablespoon of water. Turn the dough out onto a large piece of plastic wrap. Form into a flat disc, wrap tightly, and chill until firm, about 2 hours. The dough can be prepared up to 2 days in advance and kept tightly covered in the refrigerator. It will need to be softened at room temperature before using. Knead the dough slightly before using to make sure it is pliable. (If not using a food processor, soften the butter and, using a mixer, beat the butter until light in a large mixing bowl. Add the confectioners' sugar and cream together. Add the egg yolks and water and blend well. Mix the salt with the flour and add to the butter mixture. Blend well, stopping to scrape down the sides of the bowl with a rubber spatula. Gather the dough into a ball, shape into a flat disk, and cover with plastic wrap. Chill the dough until firm enough to roll, about 2 hours.)

2 Preheat the oven to 375 degrees. On a flat work surface, roll out the pastry dough between 2 sheets of lightly floured wax paper to a large circle, about 13 inches round and ¼-inch thick. Gently roll the pastry dough around the rolling pin and unroll into an 11-inch fluted-edge tart pan with removable bottom. Carefully lift up the sides of the dough and fit against the bottom and sides of the pan. Trim off any excess dough at the top. Transfer the tart pan to a jelly-roll pan and chill in the freezer for 15 minutes.

3 Line the pastry shell with a large piece of aluminum foil, fitting it into the bottom and sides, and fill with tart weights. Bake for 10 minutes, then remove the foil and weights and bake another 12 to 14 minutes, until light golden colored and set. Remove from the oven and cool completely on a rack.

4 For the dark chocolate ganache layer, heat the cream to a boil in a medium saucepan. Remove the saucepan from the heat and stir in the chocolate until completely melted and smooth. Stir in the vanilla and blend well. Stir the mixture to cool for a few minutes.

5 While the dark chocolate mixture is cooling, heat the cream and white chocolate together in a small saucepan for the white chocolate ganache, just until the chocolate is melted. Remove the pan from the heat and stir until the mixture is smooth.

6 Pour the dark chocolate mixture into the tart shell. Working quickly, drizzle the white chocolate mixture over the dark chocolate mixture. Use a toothpick or the point of a sharp knife to pull through the white chocolate layer to create a marbelized look. Chill the tart until the filling is firm, about 2 hours. Store the tart tightly covered in the refrigerator for up to 2 days. Let the tart stand at room temperature for 30 minutes before serving.Cut into slices to serve.

Per serving: *Calories 305 (From Fat 177); Fat 20g (Saturated 12g); Cholesterol 64mg; Sodium 20mg; Carbohydrate 29g (Dietary Fiber 2g); Protein 4g.*

Cocoa Almond Tart

I was inspired to create this tart by the almond tarts that abound in all the pastry shop windows in Venice, Italy. A rich, almond cream filling is topped by whole almonds and, as the filling bakes, it puffs up and surrounds the almonds. This is one of my very favorite tarts.

Tools: *9½-inch round fluted-edge tart pan with removable bottom*

Preparation time: *50 minutes, includes chilling time*

Baking time: *55 minutes*

Yield: *16 servings*

Tart dough:

1¼ cups flour

2 teaspoons sugar

¼ teaspoon salt

½ cup (1 stick) butter, cold, cut into small pieces

¼ cup whipping cream

Filling:

⅓ cup almond paste

½ cup sugar

½ cup (1 stick) butter, softened

¼ cup unsweetened Dutch-processed cocoa powder

3 eggs

½ teaspoon vanilla extract

½ teaspoon almond extract

½ cup whole blanched almonds

Garnish:

2 tablespoons confectioners' sugar

1 For the tart dough, place the flour, sugar, and salt in the work bowl of a food processor fitted with a steel blade. Pulse to blend briefly. Cut the butter into small pieces and add. Pulse until the butter is cut into tiny pieces, about 1 minute. Pour the cream through the feed tube and pulse a few times until the dough forms a ball.

(If not using a food processor, soften the butter and, using a mixer, beat the butter until light in a large mixing bowl. Add the sugar and cream together. Blend the salt into the flour and add to the butter mixture. Blend well, stopping to scrape down the sides of the bowl with a rubber spatula. Add the cream and mix thoroughly. Gather the dough into a ball, shape into a flat disk, and cover with plastic wrap. Chill the dough until firm enough to roll, about 30 minutes.)

2 Turn the dough out onto a lightly floured flat work surface and roll out into a large circle, about 12 inches in diameter. Gently roll the dough up around the rolling pin and unroll into the tart pan. Carefully lift up the sides of the dough and fit them to the side of the pan. Trim the edge of the dough, leaving a 1-inch rim. Turn the rim in to double the sides. Chill the tart shell for 30 minutes.

3 For the filling, combine the almond paste and sugar in a large mixing bowl. Using a mixer blend together until the almond paste is broken into very small pieces. Add the butter and blend together well. Add the cocoa powder and blend thoroughly. Stop and scrape down the sides of the bowl with a rubber spatula. Beat the eggs lightly in a small bowl and add. Mix well and blend in the vanilla and almond extracts.

4 Remove the tart pan from the refrigerator and place on a jelly-roll pan. Pour the filling into the tart shell. Use a rubber spatula to spread the filling evenly. Arrange the almonds on the top of the filling in close circles, covering it completely.

5 Bake the tart for 35 minutes, until the top is set and a tester inserted in the center comes out with moist crumbs clinging to it. Remove from the oven and cool on a rack.

6 Dust the top of the tart lightly with confectioners' sugar. Store the tart at room temperature tightly wrapped with aluminum foil for up to 3 days.

Per serving: Calories 245 (From Fat 159); Fat 18g (Saturated 9g); Cholesterol 76mg; Sodium 53mg; Carbohydrate 19g (Dietary Fiber 1g); Protein 4g.

White-Chocolate Berry Pizza

This looks just like a pizza, but it sure doesn't taste like one! It's a delicious tart with a delicate cookie crust and a creamy white chocolate ganache filling, topped with fresh berries. It's a perfect summertime dessert.

Tools: *14-inch round pizza pan*

Preparation time: *45 minutes, plus chilling time*

Baking time: *20 minutes*

Yield: *16 to 18 servings*

Pastry dough:

2¼ cups flour	1¾ sticks butter, softened
¾ cup confectioners' sugar, sifted	2 egg yolks
⅛ teaspoon salt	½ teaspoon pure vanilla extract

Filling:

12 ounces white chocolate, finely chopped	¾ stick (6 tablespoons) butter
½ cup heavy whipping cream	

Garnish:

2 cups fresh raspberries	1 cup fresh blackberries or strawberries
1 cup fresh blueberries	2 tablespoons shaved white chocolate

1 For the pastry dough, combine the flour, confectioners' sugar, and salt in the work bowl of a food processor fitted with a steel blade. Pulse briefly to blend. Cut the butter into small pieces and add. Pulse until the butter is cut into tiny pieces, about 1 minute. In a small bowl, lightly beat the egg yolks with the vanilla and add. Process until the pastry forms a ball. Shape the pastry into a flat disc and wrap tightly in plastic. Chill until firm, about 3 hours.

2 Roll out the pastry dough between sheets of lightly floured wax paper on a flat work surface to a large circle, about 15 inches round. Gently roll the pastry dough around the rolling pin and unroll into the pan. Carefully fit the dough against the bottom and sides of the pan. Trim off any excess dough at the edges, then use a fork to imprint a design around the outer edge of the pastry. Chill for 15 minutes.

3 Preheat the oven to 375 degrees. Line the pastry dough with a large piece of aluminum foil, fitting it against the bottom and sides, then fill the foil with tart weights. Bake for 10 minutes, then remove the foil and weights, and bake another 10 to 12 minutes, until light golden in color and set. Remove from the oven and cool on a rack. The pastry shell can be prepared 2 days in advance and stored at room temperature tightly wrapped with aluminum foil.

4 For the filling, melt the white chocolate in the top of a double boiler over hot water. Stir often with a rubber spatula. In a separate small saucepan, scald the cream. Remove the top pan of the double boiler and wipe the bottom and sides very dry. Pour the cream into the chocolate and stir together until very smooth. Transfer the ganache to a bowl or other container, cover tightly and chill until thick, but not stiff, about 2 hours.

5 In a large mixing bowl, using an electric mixer beat the butter until very fluffy. Add the white chocolate ganache and beat together until the mixture forms light peaks, about 1 minute. Don't beat the mixture too long or it will curdle.

6 Using a small metal spatula or rubber spatula, spread the white chocolate filling over the pastry shell leaving a 1-inch border around the edges. Cover the top of the filling with tight circles of alternating colors of the berries. Sprinkle the top of the berries with the shaved white chocolate. Refrigerate the tart but serve at room temperature within 3 hours of preparation.

Per serving: Calories 344 (From Fat 209); Fat 23g (Saturated 14g); Cholesterol 71mg; Sodium 43mg; Carbohydrate 31g (Dietary Fiber 2g); Protein 4g.

TIP

What to drink with chocolate

Having something to drink with almost everything that you eat is customary. Chocolate is no exception — unless, of course, you're drinking chocolate, which is fine by itself. With chocolate the first rule is not to overpower its wonderful flavor with what you're drinking. The second rule is that you want to complement the flavor of chocolate. You don't want to have a conflict going on between your taste buds.

Milk goes well with all chocolate desserts and for some people it's a requirement. The colder the milk, the better. I don't think it makes too much difference whether it's whole milk or reduced-fat milk, as long as it's cold. Milk and chocolate is not just for kids. Grown-ups love it, too.

Coffee and tea are also natural partners for chocolate. Europeans love to eat chocolate accompanied by coffee and tea. It's not uncommon to be served coffee or tea with a small piece of chocolate on the side. These days you'll find this in many restaurants and even on airplanes. Regular, decaf, espresso, or just about any other coffee goes great with chocolate. It's always best if the coffee is freshly made

right before it's served. Also, adding a little sugar or milk to your coffee won't hurt the flavor of the chocolate. There are a lot of different teas on the market; black teas, green teas, and herbal teas to name a few. They all go well with chocolate, but the most common ones are English Breakfast, Darjeeling, and Earl Grey. These are full-bodied teas that complement the flavor of chocolate without overpowering it. Of course, it's important that the tea is freshly brewed right before it's served. Your favorite tea may not be the best accompaniment for chocolate. Some spiced teas may clash with the flavor of chocolate. It's best to test them before serving them with chocolate.

Chocolate and spirits go quite well together, too. Table wines that are dry and full-bodied are one of the best choices to match with chocolate. Cabernet Sauvignon or Merlot are good choices for pairing with chocolate. You can even go with Zinfandel or Pinot Noir. Keep in mind that chocolate and wine should complement each other, with the wine being slightly dominant. You'll find that the chocolate will enhance the flavor of the wine.

Part IV
Chocolate Treats with Minimal Baking

In this part . . .

Some of my favorite desserts are found in this part. Many are desserts that you can eat with a spoon or by hand. Here you'll find some wonderful chocolate mousses and puddings. A variety of especially easy recipes for chocolate candies, as well as some wonderful ice creams and sorbets are in this part as well. And, if you want to drink your chocolate, you'll find several recipes here. Chocolate sauces and sauces to complement chocolate desserts are here, too. Just make sure you make enough to go around, especially when it comes to ice cream — everyone will want second helpings.

Chapter 12

Mousses and Puddings

. . . .

In This Chapter

▶ Understanding the difference between mousses and puddings

▶ Stirring to create the correct consistency

▶ Using a water bath to cook puddings

. . . .

*W*elcome to the comfort zone. All the desserts in this chapter are eaten with a spoon and are usually served in a bowl — many of them in the bowl in which they are made. A characteristic shared by all of these desserts is their smooth and creamy texture. You'll find absolutely nothing intimidating about these recipes. As a matter of fact, mousses and puddings are so easy to devour that a second helping is a requirement.

Marvelous Mousses

When you tell people you're serving chocolate mousse, they come running. That's because they think you've been laboring in the kitchen for hours to make this dessert. Nothing could be farther from the truth. Mousses are very easy to make, involving only a few steps. And it's practically impossible to make a mistake.

Because mousses require time to chill and set, they need to be made at least a few hours in advance of serving. They can be served directly from a large bowl or from individual bowls or glasses. Personally, I like to let my guests serve themselves. However, for a more sophisticated look, serve mousses in a fluted glass. A dollop of whipped cream with a little bit of shaved chocolate on top makes a nice effect.

Dark-Chocolate Mousse

This is a light, soft, creamy mousse with lots of deep chocolate flavor. It's a wonderful dessert on its own, but it can be jazzed up when accompanied by fresh raspberries or strawberries. Other good accompaniments are some delicate wafer cookies or chocolate truffles.

Preparation time: *15 minutes, plus chilling time*

Yield: *1½ quarts, 6 to 8 servings*

8 ounces bittersweet or semisweet chocolate, finely chopped

2 cups heavy whipping cream

3 tablespoons orange-flavored liqueur or 2 teaspoons pure vanilla extract

3 egg whites, at room temperature

½ cup sugar

1 teaspoon pure vanilla extract

2 tablespoons shaved bittersweet or semisweet chocolate (for garnish)

1 Melt the chopped chocolate in the top of a double boiler over hot water. Stir often with a rubber spatula. Or melt the chocolate in a microwave oven on low power at 30-second intervals. Stir with a rubber spatula between intervals.

2 In a ½-quart saucepan, scald 1 cup of the cream. Remove the top pan of the double boiler and wipe the bottom and sides very dry. Pour the cream into the chocolate and stir together until thoroughly blended and shiny.

3 Transfer the chocolate mixture to a large mixing bowl. Add the orange-liqueur or vanilla and blend well.

4 In a large mixing bowl, using an electric mixer, whip 1 cup of the cream to soft peaks. Fold the cream into the chocolate mixture in three stages.

5 In a large mixing bowl, using an electric mixer, whip the egg whites until frothy. Slowly add the sugar and whip the egg whites until they hold firm peaks. Fold the whipped egg whites into the chocolate mixture in three stages, blending thoroughly. Pour the mousse into a 1½-quart serving bowl or into individual bowls or glasses. Cover the mousse with plastic wrap and refrigerate for at least 2 hours, until set.

6 In a large mixing bowl, using an electric mixer, whip the remaining ½ cup of cream until frothy. Add the vanilla and whip until the cream holds soft peaks. Fit a 12-inch pastry bag with a large star tip and fill partway with the whipped cream. Decorate the top of the mousse with rosettes, stars, or shells, then sprinkle the shaved chocolate over the cream. Serve the mousse within 6 hours of preparation.

Vary it! *You can easily make flavor variations of this mousse by adding an ingredient. To make spiced chocolate mousse, blend together ½ teaspoon cinnamon and ¼ teaspoon freshly ground nutmeg. Eliminate the orange-flavored liqueur and use vanilla extract. Add the spices and vanilla after blending together the melted chocolate and scalded cream. To make mocha mousse, add 1 tablespoon instant espresso powder to the scaled cream and stir until dissolved.*

Per serving: *Calories 453 (From Fat 292); Fat 33g (Saturated 20g); Cholesterol 83mg; Sodium 45mg; Carbohydrate 34g (Dietary Fiber 2g); Protein 5g.*

White-Chocolate Mousse

Eating this mousse is like eating a sweet cloud. It's soft, light, and airy. Try serving this with Raspberry Sauce (see Chapter 15) and fresh raspberries.

Preparation time: *15 minutes, plus chilling time*

Yield: *1½ quarts, 6 to 8 servings*

12 ounces white chocolate, finely chopped	4 egg whites
1½ cups heavy whipping cream	¼ cup sugar
2 teaspoons pure vanilla extract	

1 Melt the chopped chocolate in the top of a double boiler over hot water. Stir often with a rubber spatula. Or melt the chocolate in a microwave oven on low power at 30-second intervals. Stir with a rubber spatula between intervals.

2 In a ½-quart saucepan, scald ½ cup of the cream. Remove the top pan of the double boiler and wipe the bottom and sides very dry. Pour the cream into the chocolate and stir together until thoroughly blended and smooth. Add the vanilla and stir to blend well.

3 Place the egg whites and sugar in a large mixing bowl. Place the bowl over hot water until the mixture is warm. Using an electric mixer, whip the mixture until the egg whites hold soft peaks. Fold the egg whites into the chocolate mixture in three stages.

4 In a separate large mixing bowl, using an electric mixer, whip the remaining cup of cream until it holds soft peaks. Fold the whipped cream into the chocolate mixture in three stages. Divide the mousse among individual serving bowls. Cover the bowls tightly with plastic wrap and chill at least 2 hours before serving. The mousse will keep tightly covered in the refrigerator for 2 days.

Vary it! *You can easily make flavor variations of this mousse by adding an ingredient. To make white-chocolate orange mousse, replace the vanilla extract with 2 tablespoons orange liqueur. Garnish the mousse with orange zest. To make white-chocolate ginger mousse, fold in ⅓ cup finely chopped crystallized ginger to the mousse after folding in the whipped cream. Garnish the mousse with strips of crystallized ginger.*

Per serving: *Calories 432 (From Fat 286); Fat 32g (Saturated 19g); Cholesterol 70mg; Sodium 90mg; Carbohydrate 32g (Dietary Fiber 0g); Protein 6g.*

Tasty Puddings

You always know you're in for a treat when someone offers you a bowl of pudding. Puddings are one of the most common desserts and probably one of the first things you ate — I think that's the reason why almost people like puddings so much. And not only are puddings delicious to eat, they're simple to make.

Puddings work well just about anytime. Many people like to eat pudding as a snack, but it's fine as a main dessert as well. Pudding can even be a good substitute for ice cream during the cold winter months.

Stirred puddings

The recipes in this section require you to stir them while they cook. You need to stir until they thicken, which takes a few minutes. By stirring you prevent the mixture from forming lumps and help to distribute the heat evenly. Use a consistent stirring motion, kind of like making a figure-8, that gets into the corners of the pan.

The Best Deep-Chocolate Pudding

This is a very rich, smooth, creamy pudding with intense deep-chocolate flavor. It's wonderful on it's own and is also great as the filling in either a chocolate crumb or a graham cracker crust (see Chapter 11 for recipes).

Preparation time: 10 minutes, plus chilling time

Cooking time: 8 minutes

Yield: 6 to 8 servings

5 ounces bittersweet or semisweet chocolate, finely chopped	*2 cups milk*
	4 egg yolks
½ cup sugar	*2 cups heavy whipping cream*
¼ cup Dutch-processed cocoa powder, sifted	*2 tablespoons butter, softened*
3 tablespoons cornstarch, sifted	*3 teaspoons pure vanilla extract*
⅛ teaspoon salt	

1 Melt the chocolate in the top of a double boiler over hot water or in a microwave oven on low power in 30-second intervals. Stir often with a rubber spatula.

2 In a large mixing bowl, combine the sugar, cocoa, cornstarch, and salt. Add ½ cup of the milk and stir together until smooth. In a separate small bowl, lightly beat the egg yolks and stir into the mixture.

3 In a large heavy-duty saucepan, combine the remaining milk and 1 cup of the cream and bring to a boil over medium-high heat. Remove the saucepan from the heat and slowly pour the hot mixture into the mixture in the bowl from Step 2. Whisk together until well blended, then pour the mixture back into the saucepan. Return the saucepan to medium heat and stir the mixture constantly until it thickens, about 5 minutes.

4 Remove the saucepan from the heat and strain the mixture into a large bowl. Add the butter and stir until melted. Stir in 2 teaspoons of the vanilla. Remove the top pan of the double boiler and wipe the bottom and sides very dry, then add the melted chocolate and stir until completely blended. Place a piece of plastic wrap on top of the pudding with plastic wrap to prevent a skin from forming. Chill the pudding for 4 hours. The pudding will keep in the refrigerator, tightly covered, for 2 days.

5 In a large mixing bowl, using an electric mixer, whip the remaining 1 cup of cream until frothy. Add the remaining 1 teaspoon of vanilla and continue to whip until the cream holds soft peaks. Spoon the pudding into individual serving cups or bowls and top each with a large dollop of the whipped cream.

Tip: Stir the mixture constantly as it cooks to prevent it from burning.

Per serving: Calories 621 (From Fat 430); Fat 48g (Saturated 29g); Cholesterol 273mg; Sodium 126mg; Carbohydrate 42g (Dietary Fiber 3g); Protein 9g.

Use a long handle wooden spoon or whisk to stir the mixture while it cooks. This will keep your hand away from the heat, so there's no chance of getting burned. Don't use a utensil with a metal handle, because metal conducts heat.

What's the difference anyway?

The word *mousse* means "froth" or "foam" in French. A mousse is a soft and creamy dessert that is made by combining whipped egg whites and whipped cream with the mousse's base mixture. This results in a light and airy texture. Mousses are served straight from the refrigerator.

Puddings are also creamy and soft, but they are denser than mousses. Puddings are either cooked on the stovetop or baked in the oven. Those that are made on the stovetop require constant stirring so they result in the right consistency and don't burn. Puddings are served cold or at room temperature.

When it comes to deciding which I like best, it's a toss-up. Both mousses and puddings are easy to make and neither requires much time.

Chocolate Panna Cotta

Panna Cotta is an Italian dessert whose name translates as "cooked cream," even though the cream is only heated. Panna Cotta is a smooth, light, and airy cream. The addition of chocolate is unusual, but delicious.

Tools: *Six ½-cup bowls or custard cups*

Preparation time: *15 minutes plus chilling time*

Cooking time: *8 minutes*

Yield: *6 servings*

⅔ cup milk

1 envelope unflavored gelatin

2⅔ cups cream

⅓ cup sugar

1 vanilla bean, split

8 ounces bittersweet or semisweet chocolate, finely chopped

1 Pour the milk into a small bowl. Sprinkle the gelatin over the top of the milk and let it stand for 5 minutes to soften.

2 In a large heavy-duty saucepan, combine the cream, sugar, and vanilla bean. Stir over medium heat to dissolve the sugar and bring to a boil. Remove the saucepan from the heat and remove the vanilla bean. Add the chocolate and stir until melted.

3 Replace the saucepan over medium heat. Add the softened gelatin and milk and cook for a couple of minutes to dissolve. Strain the mixture into a bowl, then divide evenly between the bowls or cups. Cover tightly with plastic wrap and chill for several hours or overnight until the cream sets. Store the cream tightly covered in the refrigerator up to 3 days.

4 To remove the cream from the bowl or cups, dip the bottom of each in hot water, then run a thin-bladed knife around the sides. Place a plate over the bowl or cup and invert to release the cream. Scatter a few fresh berries around the plate, if you choose.

Per serving: Calories 640 (From Fat 476); Fat 53g (Saturated 33g); Cholesterol 151mg; Sodium 58mg; Carbohydrate 37g (Dietary Fiber 3g); Protein 7g.

Cover puddings tightly with plastic wrap to prevent a skin from forming on top.

When traveling in the British Isles, note that the word *pudding* refers to all types of dessert, so when you ask for pudding, you'll most likely get get something other than pudding as Americans know it.

Chocolate Zabaglione

Zabaglione is a light and airy classic Italian dessert made by whisking egg yolks over hot water with sugar and sweet Sicilian Marsala wine. Adding chocolate to this dessert is definitely a new twist, but a delicious one. You can make this and serve it immediately, which is traditional, or you can chill it.

Preparation time: *20 minutes*

Cooking time: *4 minutes*

Yield: *6 servings*

3 ounces bittersweet or semisweet chocolate

6 egg yolks

½ cup sugar

¾ cup Marsala

¼ cup unsweetened Dutch-processed cocoa powder, sifted

1 tablespoon shaved bittersweet or semisweet chocolate (for garnish)

1 Place a large heavy-duty saucepan on the stovetop. Fill about one-third with water and bring it to a boil, then reduce the heat so it's at a simmer.

2 Melt the chocolate in the top of a double boiler over hot water or in a microwave oven on low power for 30-second intervals. Stir often with a rubber spatula. In a large mixing bowl, combine the egg yolks and sugar. Using an electric mixer, whisk them together. In a medium mixing bowl, combine the Marsala and cocoa powder and stir until the cocoa is completely dissolved. Add this mixture to the egg yolk and sugar mixture and stir to blend well.

3 Transfer the mixing bowl to the pan of simmering water. Whisk the mixture constantly until it thickens and becomes light, about 4 minutes. Remove from the heat and using the electric mixer, whip the mixture until it is cool, about 4 minutes. Remove the top pan of the double boiler and wipe the bottom and sides very dry. Stir in the melted chocolate and blend well.

4 Divide the zabaglione between six ½-cup glasses, cups, or bowls. Garnish the top of each with a sprinkle of shaved chocolate. Serve immediately or cover with plastic wrap and chill.

Per serving: Calories 266 (From Fat 99); Fat 11g (Saturated 5g); Cholesterol 213mg; Sodium 12mg; Carbohydrate 32g (Dietary Fiber 2g); Protein 5g.

Baked puddings

All the puddings in this section are baked in a water bath. This means they're set in a larger baking pan and hot or boiling water is poured into the bottom pan until it reaches halfway up the sides of the pudding pan. This insulates the pudding and creates a gentle but consistent source of heat. It also keeps the puddings from curdling as they bake. This is not as elaborate as it may sound. All you need is a baking pan that is larger than the pudding pan, so there's room for the water to surround the pudding pan.

There are two ways to set this up. Place the baking pan in the oven with the pudding pan in place and carefully add the hot water to the bottom pan. Or set up the pans on the kitchen counter, add the hot water to the bottom pan, and carefully transfer the pans to the oven (see Figure 12-1). When adding the water, make sure it doesn't splash into the pudding pan.

Baked Gianduia Pudding

If you like hazelnuts, this pudding is for you. The full flavor of toasted hazelnuts and chocolate make this a pudding to die for. This recipe uses an unusual technique of pouring boiling water on top of the pudding before it goes into the oven. The water is absorbed while the pudding bakes, and it creates a sauce underneath the top crust.

Preparation time: *10 minutes*

Baking time: *35 minutes*

Yield: *8 to 10 servings*

2 teaspoons butter, softened, for the pan

4 tablespoons butter, cut into small pieces

1 ounce milk chocolate, finely chopped

½ cup unsweetened Dutch-processed cocoa powder, sifted

¾ cup sugar

1 cup flour

¾ teaspoon baking powder

½ cup toasted and finely ground hazelnuts

1 egg

⅓ cup milk

1 cup boiling water

½ cup heavy whipping cream

1 tablespoon confectioners' sugar, sifted

1 teaspoon pure vanilla extract

1 Preheat the oven to 350 degrees. Use the 2 teaspoons of butter to generously grease the inside of an 8-inch-square baking pan.

2 In the top of a double boiler, melt the butter and milk chocolate together over hot water. Stir often with a rubber spatula. Remove the top pan of the double boiler and wipe the bottom and sides very dry. Add the cocoa powder and stir until the mixture is a thick paste.

3 In a medium bowl, combine ½ cup of the sugar, the flour, baking powder, and hazelnuts. Toss to blend.

4 In a medium mixing bowl, using an electric mixer, whip the egg until frothy. Add the milk and blend. Add the chocolate mixture in two stages, stopping to scrape the sides of the bowl with a rubber spatula. Blend well. Add the dry ingredients in three stages, blending well after each addition. Transfer the batter to the prepared pan. Use a rubber spatula to spread the batter evenly. Sprinkle the remaining ¼ cup sugar over the top of the batter and pour on the boiling water.

5 Place the baking pan in a larger baking pan and pour boiling water into the bottom pan until it reaches halfway up the sides of the square pan. Bake the pudding for 35 minutes, until a tester inserted in the center comes out clean. Remove from the oven and cool on a rack for about 20 minutes.

6 For the garnish, whip the cream in a medium mixing bowl using an electric mixer until it is frothy. Add the confectioners' sugar and vanilla and whip the cream until it holds soft peaks. Use a large spoon to scoop out servings of the pudding and top each with a dollop of whipped cream.

Per serving: Calories 236 (From Fat 146); Fat 16g (Saturated 8g); Cholesterol 54mg; Sodium 47mg; Carbohydrate 21g (Dietary Fiber 2g); Protein 5g.

Figure 12-1:
Custard
cups in a
water bath.

Mocha Pots de Crème

Pots de crème is the sophisticated French version of chocolate pudding. It's rich and creamy with a deep chocolate flavor. The custard is baked in individual cups in a water bath in the oven. This is a great dessert to make in advance because it needs time to cool and chill.

Tools: *Eight ½-cup custard cups*

Preparation time: *15 minutes, plus chilling time*

Baking time: *25 minutes*

Yield: *8 servings*

2½ cups heavy whipping cream

1 tablespoon instant espresso powder

5 ounces bittersweet or semisweet chocolate, finely chopped

6 egg yolks

2 tablespoons sugar

Pinch of salt

1 teaspoon pure vanilla extract

Candy coffee beans (optional)

1 Preheat the oven to 325 degrees. In a 1-quart heavy-duty saucepan, scald 2 cups of the cream. Add the espresso powder and stir to dissolve completely. Cover the pan and let the mixture steep for several minutes.

2 Melt the chopped chocolate in the top of a double boiler over hot water or in a microwave oven on low power in 30-second bursts. Stir often with a rubber spatula. Remove the top pan of the double boiler and wipe the bottom and sides very dry. Pour the cream into the chocolate and stir to blend completely.

3 In a medium mixing bowl, whisk together the egg yolks, sugar, salt, and vanilla until smooth. Gradually whisk in the chocolate mixture and blend well.

4 Place eight ¾-cup custard cups in a 3-quart baking dish. Strain the custard into a large measuring cup and divide the custard evenly between the cups. Cover the custard cups tightly with aluminum foil. Pour boiling water into the baking dish until it reaches halfway up the sides of the custard cups. Bake the custard for 25 minutes, until set around the edges but slightly soft in the center. Remove the cups from the water and cool on a rack, then chill at least 2 hours. Store the custard tightly covered in the refrigerator up to 2 days.

5 For the garnish, whip the remaining ½ cup cream in a medium mixing bowl using an electric mixer until it holds soft peaks. Fit a 12-inch pastry bag with a large star tip and pipe a large rosette in the center of each custard or place a large dollop of cream in the center of each custard. If using the candy coffee beans for decoration, place one in the center of the cream.

Per serving: Calories 415 (From Fat 336); Fat 37g (Saturated 22g); Cholesterol 262mg; Sodium 52mg; Carbohydrate 16g (Dietary Fiber 1g); Protein 5g.

Chocolate Crème Brûlée

This is a wonderfully rich and creamy chocolate version of a classic. I love the difference in texture between the crisp topping of sugar and the velvety custard underneath.

Tools: *Eight ½-cup custard dishes, blow torch (optional)*

Preparation time: *15 minutes plus chilling time*

Baking time: *1 hour*

Yield: *8 servings*

3 cups heavy cream	*6 egg yolks*
⅓ cup sugar	*½ cup sugar, for caramelizing the tops*
8 ounces bittersweet chocolate, finely chopped	

1 Preheat the oven to 300 degrees. In a medium heavy-duty saucepan, combine the cream and sugar. Bring to a boil over medium heat. Remove the pan from the heat and stir in the chocolate until completely melted and smooth.

2 In a medium mixing bowl, whisk the egg yolks. Slowly add the warm chocolate mixture, stirring until completely blended. Strain the mixture into a large measuring cup.

3 Divide the custard evenly among eight ½-cup custard cups. Place the cups in a large roasting pan and fill the pan halfway with hot water. Bake the custards for 1 hour, until a tester inserted in the center comes out with a few crumbs clinging to it. Remove the pan, remove the custard cups from the pan, and cool on a rack. Tightly cover the custard cups with plastic wrap and chill at least 4 hours. The custard can be prepared up to 2 days in advance of serving and kept tightly covered in the refrigerator.

4 Evenly sprinkle the top of each custard with 1 to 2 teaspoons of the remaining sugar. To caramelize the sugar, use a blow torch or place the custard cups in a roasting pan and caramelize under the broiler for about 3 minutes (see Figure 12-2). Serve the custard immediately or within an hour, holding it at room temperature.

Per serving: Calories 591 (From Fat 418); Fat 46g (Saturated 28g); Cholesterol 283mg; Sodium 41mg; Carbohydrate 40g (Dietary Fiber 2g); Protein 6g.

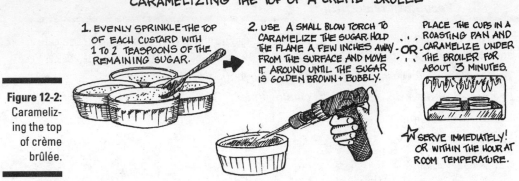

Figure 12-2:
Caramelizing the top of crème brûlée.

Chapter 13

Dandy Candies and Dipped Fruit

● ●

In This Chapter

▶ Understanding different types of candies

▶ Mastering truffles

▶ Making candies the easy way

● ●

I've asked the question before, "Who doesn't like chocolate?" Another good question is, "Who doesn't like candy?" The next logical question is, "Who doesn't like chocolate candy?" The answer: "Nobody." Okay, there may be *someone,* but I don't know that person. Chocolate candy may very well be at the tiptop of the most loved foods. And one of the neat things about chocolate candy is that there's something for everyone, because it comes in so many different varieties.

The difference between homemade candy and store-bought candy is like the difference between night and day. Store-bought candy is mass produced for mass consumption. And it has a tendency to sit around for a while before it's consumed. Homemade candy is produced on a limited basis for consumption by a select few, which means it tastes much, much better.

Making homemade candies is really not that big of a deal. Many people are scared off because they think they need special tools and equipment, as well as some secret ingredients. This isn't the case. Homemade candies are made using things you already have in your kitchen, including the ingredients.

The trick to making great homemade candies is in applying the necessary techniques. You may not be familiar with candy-making techniques, but I assure you they can be mastered in a short time — and in this chapter, I show you how!

Terrific Truffles

Truffles have a big reputation as being some of the tastiest yet trickiest candies. But they're actually some of the easiest candies to make. Truffles are made from *ganache,* which is a mixture of chocolate and cream. The proportions of chocolate and cream can be varied to create ganache textures that are soft or firm. Also, the ganache can be flavored in myriad ways with nuts, extracts, and liqueurs to make numerous different truffles. And truffles can have a variety of different coatings, which also makes them unique. But the best feature about truffles is their taste. Only a few ingredients go into making truffles, so it's important that they be the very best-quality ingredients you can afford. Eating truffles is pretty close to eating pure chocolate.

You may think that making truffles is a big deal, but they're really no trouble to prepare. One of the great things about making truffles is that you can do many of the steps in advance of when you want to serve them. Actually, it takes some time between the steps for the truffle cream and the truffles themselves to cool. This makes spreading the process out over a few days easier — so it fits into busy lives. And truffles keep very well in tightly covered and well wrapped containers in the refrigerator for up to a month, or they can be frozen for up to two months. This makes them perfect to have on hand for unexpected guests or for when you have a truffle craving.

Truffles go well in many settings. They're the crown jewel of an assortment of candies. They're perfect served with after-dinner coffee and can also be the dessert, or they can be an addition to dessert. Truffles go well at picnics, potluck gatherings, and as a delightful surprise in a lunch bag.

When you get into making truffles you'll find it hard to stop, because it's so much fun. Truffle making is a perfect way to spend quality family time together. Having extra hands to help roll them is always appreciated. And if a few truffles disappear into someone's mouth along the way, the smiles of appreciation are well worth it!

Use *couverture* chocolate to achieve a uniform, thin coating on the outside of truffles. This is chocolate that has at least 32 percent cocoa butter, which is a higher percentage than regular eating and baking chocolate. This makes the chocolate the correct consistency to create thin, smooth, and shiny coatings on dipped truffles and candies. Because of its high cocoa butter content, *couverture* must be tempered before use. It's the chocolate used by professionals for dipping, molding, and decorating and is also used for baking. All types of chocolate — dark, milk, and white — are available as *couverture* and are sold in cookware shops and through many online and mail-order sources.

The Best Dark-Chocolate Truffles

Customizing these scrumptious truffles is easy. You can vary the flavor depending on the brand of chocolate used. You can also choose to leave out the rum or cognac and add up to a tablespoon more vanilla extract. However you choose to tailor your truffles, they will be delicious. Before you get started, just be sure to read about tempering chocolate in Chapter 5.

Preparation time: *4½ hours (includes chilling)*

Yield: *36 truffles*

9 ounces bittersweet or semisweet chocolate, finely chopped

⅔ cup heavy whipping cream

1 teaspoon vanilla extract

1½ tablespoons dark rum or cognac (optional)

2 to 3 tablespoons unsweetened Dutch-processed cocoa powder

1 pound bittersweet or semisweet couverture chocolate, finely chopped, for tempering (see Chapter 5 for information on tempering chocolate)

1 Melt the 9 ounces of chocolate in the top of a double boiler over hot water or in a microwave oven on low power for 30-second intervals. Stir often with a rubber spatula to ensure even melting. In a separate small saucepan, scald the cream over medium heat.

2 Remove the top pan of the double boiler and wipe the bottom and sides very dry. Pour the cream into the chocolate and stir to blend until the mixture is smooth. Stir in the vanilla and rum or cognac, if using. Pour the truffle cream into a bowl or other container, cover tightly with plastic wrap, and cool to room temperature. Refrigerate until the consistency of thick pudding, 1 to 2 hours.

3 Line a baking sheet with wax paper. Using a 14-inch pastry bag fitted with a ½-inch plain round tip, pipe out 1-inch mounds of the truffle cream. Or use a small ice cream scoop or melon baller to scoop out truffle mounds. Cover with plastic wrap and chill in the freezer about an hour, until firm enough to roll into balls.

4 To form the truffle centers dust your hands with cocoa powder and shape the mounds into balls. Cover and chill again while melting and tempering the chocolate.

5 Line another baking sheet with wax paper. Melt and temper the chocolate. Using a fork or dipping tool, dip each truffle center in the chocolate and gently shake off the excess as it is lifted out. Place the truffles on the baking sheet and chill for 15 minutes, to set the chocolate.

6 Place each truffle in a paper candy cup and serve at room temperature. Store the truffles between layers of wax paper in an airtight container wrapped with aluminum foil in the refrigerator for up to 3 weeks or in the freezer for up to 2 months. If frozen, defrost in the refrigerator for a day before bringing to room temperature.

Per serving: Calories 126 (From Fat 75); Fat 8g (Saturated 5g); Cholesterol 7mg; Sodium 3mg; Carbohydrate 12g (Dietary Fiber 2g); Protein 2g.

White Chocolate–Apricot Truffles

Plump dried apricots are the perfect counterpart for white chocolate in these delicious truffles.

Preparation time: *3 hours (includes chilling)*

Yield: *4 dozen truffles*

2 tablespoons water

2 tablespoons apricot brandy or orange liqueur

⅔ cup dried apricots, finely chopped

12 ounces white chocolate, finely chopped

½ cup heavy whipping cream

4 tablespoons confectioners' sugar

1 pound white couverture chocolate, finely chopped, for tempering (see Chapter 5 for information on tempering chocolate)

48 slivers dried apricot

1 Place the water and orange liqueur in a 1-quart saucepan. Bring to a boil over medium heat. Stir in the chopped apricots, cover, remove from the heat, and let stand for 30 minutes. Strain the apricots and pat dry on paper towels.

2 Melt the white chocolate in the top of a double boiler over hot water or in a microwave oven on low power for 30-second intervals. Stir often with a rubber spatula to ensure even melting. In a separate small saucepan, scald the cream over medium heat.

3 Remove the top pan of the double boiler and wipe the bottom and sides very dry. Pour the cream into the chocolate and stir to blend until the mixture is smooth. Stir in the chopped apricots. Pour the truffle cream into a bowl or other container, cover tightly with plastic wrap, and cool to room temperature. Refrigerate until the consistency of thick pudding, 2 to 3 hours.

4 Line a baking sheet with wax paper. Using a 14-inch pastry bag fitted with a ½-inch plain round tip, pipe out 1-inch mounds of the truffle cream. Or use a small ice cream scoop or melon baller to scoop out truffle mounds. Cover with plastic wrap and chill in the freezer about an hour, until firm enough to roll into balls.

5 To form the truffle centers, dust your hands with confectioners' sugar and shape the mounds into balls. Cover and chill again while melting and tempering the chocolate.

6 Line another baking sheet with wax paper. Melt and temper the chocolate. Using a fork or dipping tool, dip each truffle center in the chocolate and gently shake off the excess as it is lifted out. Place the truffles on the baking sheet. After dipping 4 truffles, center a sliver of dried apricot on top of each. When all the truffles are dipped, chill them for 15 minutes, to set the chocolate.

7 Place each truffle in a paper candy cup and serve at room temperature. Store the truffles between layers of wax paper in an airtight container wrapped with aluminum foil in the refrigerator for up to 3 weeks or in the freezer for up to 2 months. If frozen, defrost in the refrigerator for a day before bringing to room temperature.

Per serving: Calories 111 (From Fat 62); Fat 7g (Saturated 4g); Cholesterol 7mg; Sodium 19mg; Carbohydrate 12g (Dietary Fiber 0g); Protein 1g.

Malted Milk Chocolate Truffles

Malted milk powder gives these truffles their distinctive flavor. They remind me of drinking malted milk as a child.

Preparation time: *2 hours (includes chilling)*

Yield: *4½ dozen truffles*

8 ounces milk chocolate, finely chopped	1 cup heavy whipping cream
8 ounces semisweet chocolate, finely chopped	½ cup malted milk powder
	½ cup cocoa powder

1 Melt the milk chocolate and semisweet chocolate together in the top of a double boiler over hot water or in a microwave oven on low power for 30-second intervals. Stir often with a rubber spatula to ensure even melting.

2 In a separate small saucepan, scald the cream over medium heat. Add the malted milk powder and stir to dissolve any lumps. Cover the pan and steep for 15 minutes, then strain the mixture.

3 Remove the top pan of the double boiler and wipe the bottom and sides very dry. Pour the cream into the chocolate and stir to blend until the mixture is smooth. Pour the truffle cream into a bowl or other container, cover tightly with plastic wrap, and cool to room temperature. Refrigerate until the consistency of thick pudding, 1 to 2 hours.

4 Line a baking sheet with wax paper. Using a 14-inch pastry bag fitted with a ½-inch plain round tip, pipe out 1-inch mounds of the truffle cream. Or use a small ice cream scoop or melon baller to scoop out truffle mounds. Cover with plastic wrap and chill in the freezer about an hour, until firm enough to roll into balls.

5 To form the truffle centers dust your hands with cocoa powder and shape the mounds into balls. Line another baking sheet with wax paper. Roll the balls in cocoa powder to coat completely, then place on the baking sheet. Place each truffle in a paper candy cup and serve at room temperature. Store the truffles between layers of wax paper in an airtight container wrapped with aluminum foil in the refrigerator for up to 3 weeks or in the freezer for up to 2 months. If frozen, defrost in the refrigerator for a day before bringing to room temperature.

Per serving: Calories 63 (From Fat 43); Fat 5g (Saturated 3g); Cholesterol 7mg; Sodium 10mg; Carbohydrate 6g (Dietary Fiber 1g); Protein 1g.

When rolling truffles in your hands, you need to move fairly quickly because the heat from your hands will warm the truffle and may start it melting. If you have naturally warm hands, run them under cold water and dry before starting to roll your truffles.

Cracking the secret truffle code

How can you tell what's inside a truffle just by looking? It's not easy, because most truffles tend to look alike, or at least similar. The way to tell truffles apart is by their outer decoration. Apricot truffles have a sliver of apricot on top.

Hazelnut truffles have a sprinkling of ground hazelnuts on top. The predominant flavor of the truffle can be used in the top decoration, as a code to what's inside.

Milk Chocolate–Peanut Butter Balls

Chocolate and peanut butter are a perfect flavor combination. Use a natural style or freshly ground peanut butter in chunky texture for the most flavor and texture. For a variation, use almond or hazelnut butter, which you can buy in specialty markets.

Preparation time: 4½ *hours (includes chilling)*

Yield: 5 *dozen truffles*

8 ounces semisweet chocolate, finely chopped

4 ounces milk chocolate, finely chopped

⅔ cup heavy whipping cream

⅔ cup chunky, natural style peanut butter

3 to 4 tablespoons unsweetened cocoa powder

1 pound milk chocolate couverture, finely chopped, for tempering (see Chapter 5 for information about tempering chocolate)

2 to 3 tablespoons finely chopped, toasted peanuts

1 Melt the semisweet and milk chocolates together in the top of a double boiler over hot water or in a microwave oven on low power for 30-second intervals. Stir often with a rubber spatula to ensure even melting. In a separate small saucepan, scald the cream over medium heat.

2 Remove the top pan of the double boiler and wipe the bottom and sides very dry. Pour the cream into the chocolate and stir to blend until the mixture is smooth. Add the peanut butter and stir until the mixture is smooth. Pour the truffle cream into a bowl or other container, cover tightly with plastic wrap, and cool to room temperature. Refrigerate until the consistency of thick pudding, 1 to 2 hours.

3 Line a baking sheet with wax paper. Using a 14-inch pastry bag fitted with a ½-inch plain round tip, pipe out 1-inch mounds of the truffle cream. Or use a small ice cream scoop or melon baller to scoop out truffle mounds. Cover with plastic wrap and chill in the freezer about an hour, until firm enough to roll into balls.

4 To form the truffle centers, dust your hands with cocoa powder and shape the mounds into balls. Cover and chill again while melting and tempering the chocolate.

5 Line another baking sheet with wax paper. Melt and temper the chocolate. Using a fork or dipping tool, dip each truffle center in the chocolate and shake off the excess as it is lifted out. Place the truffles on the baking sheet. After dipping 4 truffles, sprinkle a bit of chopped peanuts on top of each. When all the truffles are dipped, chill them for 15 minutes, to set the chocolate.

6 Place each truffle in a paper candy cup and serve at room temperature. Store the truffles between layers of wax paper in an airtight container wrapped with aluminum foil in the refrigerator for up to 3 weeks or in the freezer for up to 2 months. If frozen, defrost in the refrigerator for a day before bringing to room temperature.

Per serving: Calories 95 (From Fat 63); Fat 7g (Saturated 4g); Cholesterol 6mg; Sodium 23mg; Carbohydrate 8g (Dietary Fiber 1g); Protein 2g.

Truffle cream can be kept in a tightly covered container in the refrigerator for up to a month or in the freezer for up to two months. If frozen, defrost for at least 24 hours. Bring the truffle cream to room temperature before piping or scooping it into balls.

Chocolate is sensitive to rapid temperature changes, which causes the outer coating of truffles to crack. To avoid this, allow frozen truffles to defrost in the refrigerator for at least 24 hours before serving.

Chocolate picks up other flavors like a sponge. Be sure to keep containers of chocolate truffles and other candies tightly wrapped. Also, be careful about the other foods that are near containers of chocolate in the refrigerator. You wouldn't want your chocolate to taste like pickles or onions.

How chocolate truffles got their name

Truffle may seem like a funny name for such a delectable confection. Actually, chocolate truffles are a whimsical interpretation of the highly prized fungi delicacy that grows on the roots of oak trees in France and Italy. Chocolate truffles are equally treasured, making their name fit them perfectly.

Putting finishing touches on truffles

If dipping truffles in tempered chocolate seems like too much work, don't let that stand in your way. Finish truffles by rolling them in sifted cocoa powder, confectioners' sugar, or toasted ground nuts or toasted coconut. It's a good idea to match the outer coating to the inner flavor.

Molded Candies

Did you ever wonder how chocolate is made in a heart shape or how it's shaped into bunnies? The trick is that it's made in a mold of those particular shapes. Molded candies are some of the easiest candies to make because the mold does the work of shaping the chocolate.

Collecting chocolate molds and using them for different seasons and occasions is fun. Solid chocolate hearts wrapped in red foil are the perfect gift for all your valentines. Other solid molded chocolates are nice remembrances to give your guests after a dinner party or other gathering. All kinds of events can be celebrated with specialty molded chocolates. You can find molds at party stores, at cookware shops, and through many online and catalog sources.

Solid Molded Chocolates

Use the best-quality *couverture* chocolate you can afford when molding. Because it's the only ingredient, it stands out. You can mold different shapes to celebrate the seasons and special occasions.

Tools: *2 large paper pastry cones, two 12-cavity 1-inch chocolate molds*

Preparation time: *30 minutes (includes chilling)*

Yield: *24 pieces*

1 pound couverture chocolate, finely chopped, for tempering (see Chapter 5 for information on tempering)

1 Prepare two large paper pastry cones (see Chapter 4 for information on how to make a paper pastry cone). Place the chocolate molds on a flat work surface. Melt and temper the chocolate.

2 Pour half of the chocolate into one of the paper pastry cones. Fold down the top and snip off a ¼-inch opening at the pointed end. Pipe the chocolate into the cavities of one of the molds, filling each to the top. Repeat with the remaining paper pastry cone and mold.

3 Tap the molds lightly on the countertop to remove any air bubbles, then place them on a baking sheet. Chill in the freezer on a flat surface for 15 to 20 minutes to set the chocolate.

4 Remove the molds from the freezer and invert over a large piece of wax paper. Holding the mold by opposite corners, twist it carefully in opposite directions to dislodge the chocolates. If they don't drop out quickly, chill the molds again for another 10 minutes and try to unmold them again.

5 Store the molded chocolates between layers of wax paper in an airtight container, tightly wrapped with aluminum foil, in the refrigerator for up to a month. Freeze for longer storage.

Per serving: Calories 106 (From Fat 57); Fat 6g (Saturated 4g); Cholesterol 1mg; Sodium 1mg; Carbohydrate 11g (Dietary Fiber 2g); Protein 1g.

Tap the filled chocolate molds on the countertop gently to eliminate air bubbles before chilling. Air bubbles will make holes in the chocolate when it is set.

You can add texture to molded chocolates by adding an ingredient to the main recipe. Here are some of my favorite variations:

- **Ground Nut:** Stir ¼ cup finely ground toasted nuts into the chocolate before molding.

- **Toasted Coconut:** Stir ¼ cup toasted, shredded coconut into the chocolate before molding.

- **Dried Fruit:** Stir ¼ cup finely chopped dried fruit into the chocolate before molding.

- **Ginger:** Stir ¼ cup finely chopped crystallized ginger into the chocolate before molding.

- **Candied Orange Peel:** Stir ¼ cup finely chopped candied orange peel into the chocolate before molding.

Milk Chocolate–Peanut Butter Cups

These are some of my favorite candies. I love the combination of chocolate and peanut butter. For best results use a natural-style or freshly ground peanut butter. Although the recipe calls for smooth peanut butter, you can use crunchy if you want more texture in your candies.

Tools: *2 chocolate molds with twelve 1½-inch diameter fluted-edge cavities, 3 large paper pastry cones*

Preparation time: *1 hour*

Yield: *2 dozen 1½-inch cups*

1 pound milk chocolate, finely chopped, for tempering (see Chapter 5 for information on tempering chocolate)

¾ cup smooth peanut butter

1 Line the cavities of the chocolate molds with fluted-edge candy papers. Have 3 large parchment paper pastry cones ready.

2 Melt and temper the chocolate. Transfer half of the chocolate to one of the paper pastry cones. Fold down the top and snip off the pointed end. Pipe chocolate into each mold cavity, filling it one-third full. Soften the peanut butter in a microwave oven for 30 seconds on low power, then fill another paper pastry bag partway with the peanut butter. Fold down the top and snip off the end. Pipe peanut butter into the center of the chocolate in each cavity.

3 Fill the remaining paper pastry bag with chocolate. Fold down the top and snip off the end. Pipe chocolate into each cup, filling it to the top and covering the peanut butter. Gently tap the molds against the countertop to eliminate any air bubbles. Carefully transfer the molds to a baking sheet and chill on a flat surface in the freezer for about 20 minutes.

4 Remove the cups from the molds and serve at room temperature. Store between layers of wax paper in an airtight container wrapped with aluminum foil in the refrigerator for up to 3 weeks. Freeze for longer storage.

Per serving: Calories 144 (From Fat 89); Fat 10g (Saturated 4g); Cholesterol 4mg; Sodium 53mg; Carbohydrate 13g (Dietary Fiber 1g); Protein 3g.

Types of chocolate molds

There are two types of chocolate molds: shallow molds used for solid molding and two-part hinged molds used for both hollow and filled chocolate.

The shallow molds are usually made of plastic and are very flexible. They are available in a huge variety of shapes and designs with 12 or 18 cavities per mold, depending on the design. This type of mold is used to shape hearts, trees, and leaves, to name a few.

Two-part molds are made of either strong plastic or metal. These are also available in many shapes and sizes. This type of mold is used to make three-dimensional candies, such as bunnies.

Some chocolate molds are antiques and are highly prized. It is possible to find reproductions of many older chocolate molds.

Instead of using parchment paper pastry cones, you can use a plastic bag that zips shut. Cut off a tiny bit at one of the pointed ends and squeeze the chocolate and/or peanut butter out of that end.

Dipped Delights

Dipping in chocolate is a delectable way to embellish an already good thing. Just about anything can be dipped in chocolate. You can use any type of chocolate — dark, milk, or white — for dipping. But for best results, use *couverture* chocolate, which has more cocoa butter than baking and eating chocolate. *Couverture* chocolate makes a thinner, smoother coating, which leaves your dipped goodies looking great.

Chocolate-Dipped Fruit

Chocolate enhances everything, so why not dip excellent tasting fruit in chocolate? You can dip large fresh strawberries, apple slices, and orange sections or any dried fruit, such as apricot, peach, and pear halves. Make sure the fruit is very dry before dipping or the chocolate may not adhere to it.

Preparation time: *30 minutes (includes cooling)*

Yield: *2 cups*

2 cups fruit

½ to ¾ pound couverture chocolate, finely chopped, for tempering (see Chapter 5 for information on tempering chocolate)

1 Line 2 baking sheets with wax paper. If using fresh strawberries, rinse them and pat completely dry with paper towels.

2 Melt and temper the chocolate.

3 Holding a piece of fruit between your thumb and forefinger, dip it halfway into the chocolate. Lift the fruit from the chocolate and let the excess drip off, then place the fruit on the wax paper. Repeat with all the fruit.

4 Chill the fruit to set the chocolate for 15 minutes. Serve the fresh strawberries within 4 hours. Keep them refrigerated until 15 minutes before serving. Store dipped dried fruit between layers of wax paper in an airtight container in the refrigerator for up to a month.

Per serving: *Calories 43 (From Fat 22); Fat 2g (Saturated 2g); Cholesterol 0mg; Sodium 1mg; Carbohydrate 5g (Dietary Fiber 1g); Protein 1g.*

Nut and Chocolate Candies

I don't know who first came up with it, but nuts and chocolate are one of the world's best combinations. All nuts go well with chocolate. You can easily make lots of variations with these candies by changing the chocolate from one type to another and by using different nuts.

Toasting enhances the flavor of all nuts, so I highly recommend toasting any nuts you plan to use in your candies. You can toast nuts in advance and have them on hand in the freezer.

Dark-Chocolate Nut Clusters

The combination of hazelnuts, almonds, and dried cranberries creates a candy with lots of crunchy texture that's not too sweet. You can vary these by using milk or white chocolate and any combination of nuts and dried fruit you choose.

Preparation time: *40 minutes (includes chilling)*

Yield: *3 to 3½ dozen*

12 ounces (¾ pound) bittersweet or semisweet chocolate, finely chopped

1 cup toasted hazelnuts, coarsely chopped

1 cup slivered almonds, toasted

1 cup dried cranberries

1 Melt three-fourths of the chopped chocolate (9 ounces) in the top of a double boiler over hot water or in a microwave oven on low power for 30-second intervals. Stir often with a rubber spatula. Remove the top of the double boiler and wipe the bottom and sides very dry. In three stages, stir in the remaining chopped chocolate, making sure each batch is melted before adding the next. This cools the chocolate. When all the chopped chocolate has been added, check the temperature of the chocolate by placing a dab just below your lower lip. It should feel comfortable, slightly less than body temperature. If it's too hot, stir in more chopped chocolate to bring down the temperature. If it's too cold, place the top pan of the double boiler back over the hot water for a couple of minutes and stir to bring up the temperature.

2 In a large mixing bowl, combine the nuts and dried cranberries. Toss to mix well. Add to the chocolate and stir to coat completely with chocolate.

3 Line a baking sheet with wax paper. Spoon out clusters about an inch in diameter onto the baking sheet. When all the clusters have been scooped out, chill the baking sheet to set the chocolate for about 15 minutes.

4 Place each cluster in a paper candy cup and serve at room temperature. Store the clusters between layers of wax paper in a tightly sealed container in the refrigerator for up to a month. Freeze for longer storage.

Per serving: Calories 89 (From Fat 54); Fat 6g (Saturated 2g); Cholesterol 0mg; Sodium 1mg; Carbohydrate 8g (Dietary Fiber 1g); Protein 2g.

Chocolate Marzipan Rolls

Chocolate is on both the inside and outside of these yummy candies. A layer of *marzipan* (a confection made from almonds) encloses a rich chocolate cream filling and chocolate is painted on the outside of the marzipan. These are cut into bite-size pieces. You may want to make a double batch, because they disappear so quickly. Marzipan is readily available in many supermarkets and cookware shops. It keeps for months, so you can also have this ingredient on hand.

Preparation time: *3 hours (includes chilling)*

Yield: *About 4 dozen ½-inch rolls*

12 ounces semisweet chocolate, finely chopped

½ cup heavy whipping cream

¼ cup confectioners' sugar, sifted

1 roll (7 ounces) marzipan

1 Melt half of the chopped chocolate in the top of a double boiler over warm water or in a microwave oven on low power for 30-second intervals. Stir often with a rubber spatula. In a separate small saucepan, scald the cream. Remove the top pan of the double boiler and wipe the bottom and sides very dry. Pour the cream into the chocolate and stir together until smooth. Transfer the mixture to a bowl or other container, cover tightly, and cool to room temperature. Refrigerate until the consistency of thick pudding, 1 to 2 hours.

2 Dust a flat work surface and the marzipan with confectioners' sugar and roll the marzipan out to a large rectangle, about 6 by 12 inches. Trim the edges and cut the marzipan in half to make two rectangles, 3 by 12 inches. Line a baking sheet with wax paper and carefully transfer the rectangles to the sheet.

3 Fit a 14-inch pastry bag with a ½-inch plain round tip and fill partway with the chocolate cream. Pipe a line of the mixture lengthwise down one edge of each rectangle, leaving a ¼-inch border at each end. Use a damp pastry brush to moisten the opposite long end of each rectangle, then roll the marzipan around the line of chocolate, enclosing it. Press gently with your fingertips to seal the marzipan. Wrap the rolls tightly in plastic wrap and chill in the freezer until firm, about 45 minutes.

4 Melt the rest of the chocolate in the top of a double boiler over hot water or in a microwave oven on low power for 30-second intervals. Remove the top pan of the double boiler and wipe the bottom and sides very dry. Remove the marzipan rolls from the freezer and unwrap. Using a dry pastry brush, paint the chocolate over the rolls. It will firm up quickly. Use a sharp knife to cut each roll into ½-inch-thick slices.

5 Serve the rolls at room temperature. Store the rolls between layers of wax paper in an airtight container tightly wrapped with aluminum foil in the refrigerator for up to 2 weeks. Freeze for longer storage.

Per serving: Calories 61 (From Fat 40); Fat 5g (Saturated 2g); Cholesterol 3mg; Sodium 2mg; Carbohydrate 6g (Dietary Fiber 0g); Protein 1g.

White Chocolate–
Peppermint Candy Bark

This candy is on the sweet side. It appeals to kids of all ages who have a sweet tooth. Although this recipe doesn't call for nuts, any nut and/or dried fruit can replace the peppermint candy.

Preparation time: *1 hour (includes chilling)*

Yield: *1 pound, 2 ounces*

2 cups (14 ounces) peppermint candy

1 pound white chocolate couverture, finely chopped, for tempering (see Chapter 5 for information on tempering chocolate)

1 Crush the peppermint candy into pieces by pulsing it in a work bowl fitted with a steel blade for about 1 minute. Or place the candy in a plastic bag, twist and tie the top of the bag, and crush with a rolling pin.

2 Melt three-fourths of the chopped chocolate (12 ounces) in the top of a double boiler over hot water or in a microwave oven on low power for 30-second intervals. Stir often with a rubber spatula. Remove the top of the double boiler and wipe the bottom and sides very dry. In three stages, stir in the remaining chopped chocolate, making sure each batch is melted before adding the next. This cools the chocolate. When all the chopped chocolate has been added, check the temperature of the chocolate by placing a dab just below your lower lip. It should feel comfortable, slightly less than body temperature. If it's too hot, stir in more chopped chocolate to bring down the temperature. If it's too cold, place the top pan of the double boiler back over the hot water for a couple of minutes and stir to bring up the temperature.

3 Line a baking sheet with wax paper. Stir the crushed peppermint candy into the chocolate, coating completely. Pour the mixture out onto the lined baking sheet and spread it out to evenly cover most of the baking sheet. Lightly tap the baking sheet on the countertop to eliminate any air bubbles.

4 Chill the bark in the refrigerator for about 30 minutes, until it's firm enough to break. If chilled longer than 30 minutes, let it stand at room temperature for 10 to 15 minutes, so it's not too cold.

5 Gently peel the wax paper off the back of the bark, then break into pieces by hand.

6 Store the bark between layers of wax paper in an airtight container, wrapped with aluminum foil, in the refrigerator for up to 2 weeks. Freeze for longer storage.

Per serving: Calories 115 (From Fat 41); Fat 5g (Saturated 26g); Cholesterol 3mg; Sodium 18mg; Carbohydrate 18g (Dietary Fiber 0g); Protein 1g.

Cooked Candies

This category of candies is probably the trickiest to make, but it yields some of the tastiest results. These candies aren't difficult, but they do require that you pay close attention while making them. Most of the candies in this section involve cooking sugar to a particular temperature. The easiest way to know when you've reached that temperature is to use a candy thermometer. It's important that the thermometer is accurate so you don't over– or under-cook the candy mixture. You also have to move quickly when the mixture reaches the correct temperature, because the mixture retains a lot of heat and the temperature will continue to rise until it is removed from the pan.

Using a heavy-duty saucepan that won't warp is another key to success with cooked candies. They're cooked to high temperatures that will cause light-weight pans to buckle. Trying to clean up a mess of spilled hot sugar is not my idea of fun! Also, be sure to use a long-handled wooden spoon when stirring these candies. This will keep your hands far from the hot mixture, so burns won't be a problem.

Cooked candies are the most vulnerable to humidity. They tend to pick up on moisture in the air and quickly become soggy. Avoid making these on rainy or very humid days. But if you can't resist, a trick to help them stay crisp is to cook them a couple of degrees higher than the temperature called for in the recipes. Some of my favorite candies are in this category — fudge, peanut brittle, and toffee. Yum!

An easy way to test the accuracy of a candy thermometer is to place it in a pan of boiling water. If it reads 212 degrees, it's correct. If the thermometer reads over or under 212 degrees, take note of the difference and add or subtract that amount when taking the temperature of cooked candies.

Sugar crystallization occurs when sugar particles lump together because the liquid they're mixed with is saturated to its fullest point and has no more room to absorb sugar. Crystallization can be set off by stirring a sugar syrup while it's cooking. Brushing down the sides of the pan with a damp pastry brush while sugar is cooking pushes any crystals back into the solution, thereby preventing crystallization.

The Best Chocolate Walnut Fudge

This is the kind of fudge you dream about. It's creamy, chewy, and delicious.

Tools: *Candy thermometer*

Preparation time: *2 hours (includes resting)*

Yield: *Sixty-four 1-inch squares*

2 tablespoons butter, softened	¾ cup whipping cream
1 cup sugar	6 ounces semisweet chocolate, finely chopped
1 cup light brown sugar	
⅛ teaspoon salt	1 teaspoon vanilla extract
¼ cup light corn syrup	1¼ cups coarsely chopped walnuts

1 Line an 8-inch square baking pan with a large piece of aluminum foil, letting it extend over the edges about 2 inches. Butter the foil lightly with ½ tablespoon of the butter. Cut the rest of the butter into small pieces and set aside.

2 Combine the sugar, brown sugar, salt, corn syrup, and cream in a 3-quart heavy duty saucepan. Cook over medium heat, stirring continuously with a wooden spoon until the sugar is dissolved, about 5 minutes. Using a damp pastry brush, wash down the sides of the pan to prevent the sugar from crystallizing.

3 Remove the pan from the heat and stir in the chocolate until it is melted and smooth. Return the pan to medium heat and cook without stirring until it registers 238 degrees on a sugar thermometer, 15 to 20 minutes.

4 Remove the pan from the heat and stir in the remaining butter and vanilla extract. Stir quickly to blend well. Sprinkle the back of a baking sheet with cold water and pour the hot mixture onto the pan. Don't scrape out the bottom of the pan. Let the mixture cool on the baking sheet to 110 degrees, about 15 minutes.

5 Use a pastry scraper to transfer the mixer to a mixing bowl. Using a mixer, beat the fudge on low speed until it thickens, loses its shine, and holds soft peaks, 5 to 10 minutes. Stop occasionally and scrape down the sides of the bowl with a pastry scraper. Add the chopped walnuts and beat to blend, about 1 minute.

6 Turn the fudge into the prepared pan. Use your fingertips to smooth the top and push the fudge into the corners. Let the fudge stand on a rack until it's set, about 2 hours.

7 Lift the fudge from the pan by holding onto the edges of the aluminum foil. Peel the foil from the fudge. Cut into 6 rows in each direction. Place each piece of fudge in a paper candy cup and serve at room temperature.

8 Store the fudge between layers of wax paper in an airtight container tightly wrapped with aluminum foil at room temperature for up to 10 days or in the refrigerator for 3 weeks.

Per serving: Calories 70 (From Fat 36); Fat 4g (Saturated 2g); Cholesterol 5mg; Sodium 9mg; Carbohydrate 9g (Dietary Fiber 0g); Protein 1g.

Chocolate-Covered Peanut Brittle

This peanut brittle is my favorite. It's very crunchy and loaded with peanuts. It's a bit different than many nut brittles because it's clear, not cloudy. You can use other nuts in place of the peanuts and still have a delicious brittle. I prefer to coat my peanut brittle with bittersweet or semisweet chocolate, but you can use any chocolate you prefer, including milk or white chocolate.

Preparation time: *1 hour (includes cooling)*

Yield: *2¾ pounds*

2 tablespoons unflavored vegetable oil	*½ teaspoon cream of tartar*
2 cups sugar	*2 cups peanuts, toasted and salted*
½ cup water	*4 ounces chocolate, finely chopped*

1 Use the vegetable oil to grease a 12-x-17-x-1-inch jelly roll pan. Combine the sugar, water, and cream of tartar in a 3-quart heavy-duty saucepan. Cook over medium heat without stirring until the mixture bubbles around the sides of the pan. Use a damp pastry brush to wash down the sides of the pan to prevent crystallization. Continue cooking the mixture until it turns a medium caramel color, about 8 minutes.

2 Add the peanuts and use a wooden spoon to coat them quickly with the caramel. Remove the pan from the heat and immediately turn the mixture out onto the greased baking pan. Working quickly, use the wooden spoon to spread the brittle out evenly.

3 Immediately sprinkle the chopped chocolate on top of the brittle. Wait about 3 minutes for it to melt, then use a small offset spatula to spread the chocolate over the brittle. Let the brittle stand at room temperature until completely set and firm, about 30 minutes, then chill for 30 minutes to set the chocolate. Break the brittle into pieces with your hands.

4 Store the brittle between layers of wax paper in an airtight container at room temperature for up to 3 weeks.

Per serving: Calories 111 (From Fat 54); Fat 6g (Saturated 1g); Cholesterol 0mg; Sodium 35mg; Carbohydrate 14g (Dietary Fiber 1g); Protein 2g.

Almond Toffee

Crispy, crunchy, and *buttery* are the best words to describe this toffee. It's scrumptious! You can substitute any nuts for the almonds. I love to use toasted, ground hazelnuts. As with the peanut brittle, you can also use any chocolate you prefer.

Tools: *Candy thermometer*

Preparation time: *1½ hours, includes cooling*

Yield: *2⅔ pounds*

2 tablespoons unflavored vegetable oil

1¼ cups (2½ sticks) butter

1 cup sugar

4 tablespoons water

½ teaspoon salt

2 cups sliced almonds, lightly toasted, finely chopped

7 ounces bittersweet, semisweet, or milk chocolate, finely chopped

1 Use the vegetable oil to grease a 12-x-17-x-1-inch jelly roll pan. Cut the butter into small pieces and melt in a 3-quart heavy-duty saucepan on low heat. Add the sugar, water, and salt. Raise the heat to medium and stir continuously with a wooden spoon until the mixture registers 260 degrees on a candy thermometer, about 20 minutes.

2 Add ½ cup of the chopped almonds and continue to cook the mixture, stirring continuously, until it registers 305 degrees on the candy thermometer, about 12 more minutes.

3 Remove the pan from the heat and immediately pour the toffee out onto the prepared pan. If necessary, use the wooden spoon to help spread the toffee over the pan.

4 Immediately sprinkle the chopped chocolate on top of the toffee. Wait about 3 minutes for it to melt, then use a small offset spatula to spread the chocolate over the toffee. Sprinkle the remaining chopped almonds over the chocolate. Let the toffee stand at room temperature until completely set and firm, about 15 minutes, then chill for 30 minutes to set the chocolate.

5 Use a small flexible-blade spatula to help lift the toffee from the pan. Break the toffee into irregular pieces with your hands. Store the toffee between layers of wax paper in an airtight container at room temperature for up to 3 weeks.

Per serving: Calories 149 (From Fat 108); Fat 12g (Saturated 5g); Cholesterol 18mg; Sodium 35mg; Carbohydrate 10g (Dietary Fiber 1g); Protein 2g.

Chocolate Divinity

Divinity is aptly named — it's divine. This treat is very light. It's like eating air that melts in your mouth.

Tools: *Candy thermometer*

Preparation time: *1 hour and 10 minutes (includes cooling)*

Yield: *4 dozen 1½-inch pieces*

2½ cups sugar

½ cup water

½ cup light corn syrup

2 egg whites at room temperature

Pinch cream of tartar

6 ounces semisweet or bittersweet chocolate, melted

1 cup finely chopped pecans

1½ teaspoons vanilla extract

1 Combine the sugar, water, and corn syrup in a medium heavy-duty saucepan. Cook over medium heat, stirring with a wooden spoon, until the sugar is dissolved, about 5 minutes. Using a damp pastry brush, wash down the sides of the pan to prevent the sugar from crystallizing. Increase the heat and cook without stirring until the mixture registers 256 degrees on a candy thermometer.

2 At the same time the mixture is cooking, use a mixer to whip the egg whites in a mixing bowl until they are frothy. Add the cream of tartar and whip on high speed until the whites hold firm peaks, about 4 minutes.

3 Remove the pan from Step 1 from the heat. Turn the mixer speed to low and slowly pour the sugar syrup into the egg whites. Turn the mixer speed to high and beat the mixture until it is firm, about 12 minutes. Stir in the melted chocolate, chopped pecans, and vanilla and blend well.

4 Line 2 baking sheets with wax paper. Spoon out mounds about 1½ inches in diameter. Leave at least 1 inch of space between the mounds. Let the candy stand at room temperature to set, about 45 minutes. Store the candy between layers of wax paper in an airtight container at room temperature for up to 4 days.

Per serving: Calories 85 (From Fat 29); Fat 3g (Saturated 1g); Cholesterol 0mg; Sodium 7mg; Carbohydrate 15g (Dietary Fiber 0g); Protein 1g.

Finger food

Candy is usually made to be eaten in two or three bites. Small pieces can be eaten with one bite. Occasionally, you'll run into bigger pieces of candy, like candy bars. But when most people think of candy, they usually have in mind individual pieces that come in boxes. Serve an assortment of candy, and people can select what they like and try several different candies. Plus, you can pace yourself when you're eating candy. Take a piece or two and then come back later for another piece. Candy can be set out for serving just about anywhere, or you can offer it from a nice serving tray. A small napkin is all that's required.

You can easily make variations of Chocolate Divinity by adding another ingredient. Here are some of my favorites:

- **Chocolate-Hazelnut Divinity:** Replace the pecans with toasted, ground hazelnuts.

- **Chocolate-Almond Divinity:** Replace the pecans with toasted, finely chopped almonds.

- **Chocolate-Orange Divinity:** Add the finely grated zest of 1 large orange when adding the nuts.

- **Chocolate-Lemon Divinity:** Add the finely grated zest of 1 large lemon when adding the nuts.

- **Chocolate-Ginger Divinity:** Replace the nuts with ⅓ cup finely chopped crystallized ginger and replace the vanilla extract with 1 teaspoon ground ginger.

- **Chocolate-Cinnamon Divinity:** Replace the vanilla extract with 1½ teaspoons ground cinnamon.

- **Chocolate-Coconut Divinity:** Replace the nuts with ⅔ cup lightly toasted shredded coconut.

- **Double-Chocolate Divinity:** Replace the nuts with 1 cup dark-chocolate chunks or chocolate chips.

Finding ways to use your leftover chocolate

Chocolate that has been used for dipping truffles and candies or for decorating can be saved and used again. Be sure that nothing has mixed with the chocolate to contaminate it. If you've been dipping truffles, you want to be sure that none of the truffle centers have disintegrated into the chocolate. Transfer the chocolate to a clean, dry container, cover it tightly, and store at room temperature. This chocolate can be chopped and used again. It will need to be tempered again if it is to be used for dipping, molding, or decorating, because as it sets, it goes out of temper.

Chapter 14

Ice Cream and Sorbet

When it comes to ice cream and sorbet, you don't have to worry about anyone saying no. As a matter of fact, your biggest concern will be making enough to meet the demand. I truly don't know anyone who doesn't like ice cream and sorbet. They're the type of dessert that's hard to stop eating.

Most people were raised on ice cream. Among children, it's probably the single most requested dessert. As you grew up, you probably kept up with your ice cream habit and started to eat sorbets, too. You may have been lucky enough to be able to make and eat homemade ice cream, which beats store-bought ice cream hands-down. Making homemade ice cream or sorbets is no longer a big chore, because of the large number of easy-to-use ice cream makers available in the marketplace. In this chapter, I show you how to bring this favorite dessert into your kitchen . . . and the mouths of those you love.

I Scream, You Scream, We All Scream for Ice Cream!

Just the thought of a bowl of chocolate ice cream makes my mouth water — and I don't believe I'm alone on this. It's a cool, refreshing, and very satisfying dessert. Homemade ice cream is definitely the best. Despite what you may have heard, I can assure you that ice cream is very easy to make in your home kitchen and you won't need much time to do it. It does, of course, have to cool and chill, so it's a good idea to make your ice cream several hours before serving. But it will keep for a few months in the freezer, so you can make more than you need and store the rest.

TIP

Choosing an ice cream maker

There are several types of ice cream makers (shown here). All ice cream makers have a canister that is surrounded by a freezing agent. The freezing agent depends on the type of machine used — it's ice mixed with rock or table salt, a liquid chemical coolant, or a self-contained refrigeration unit. Inside the canister, a paddle, called a *dasher,* stirs the ice cream mixture while it chills. This stirring action keeps the ice cream mixture from forming ice crystals, creating a smooth texture.

Hand-operated ice cream makers come in two forms. The traditional machine is a wooden or plastic bucket that holds a canister in the center. Ice and salt are placed between the bucket and the canister. The dasher and canister are turned by a hand crank at the side of the bucket. This type of ice cream maker produces up to a gallon of ice cream. The other type has

a hollow metal canister that contains a liquid coolant. This canister must be chilled in the freezer for 24 hours before use. It's placed in the plastic housing and the dasher is inserted in the center. A hand crank is attached to the dasher through a hole in the lid and is turned every 2 to 3 minutes for about 20 minutes to freeze the ice cream or sorbet mixture. Both of these ice cream makers are very reasonably priced. They also come in electric versions.

The most elaborate and expensive electric ice cream maker is a countertop model with a self-contained refrigeration unit. It is the easiest to use. Simply pour the ice cream base into the canister, cover it with the lid, and turn on the machine. It works rapidly and produces very smooth ice cream. The only drawback to this type of ice cream maker is the price, which can be several hundred dollars.

ICE CREAM MACHINES

Keep the canister of your ice cream maker in your freezer so you're always ready to churn a batch of ice cream.

Semisweet Chocolate Ice Cream

This smooth and creamy ice cream has deep chocolate flavor. It's one of my all-time favorites.

Tools: *Ice cream freezer*

Preparation time: *10 minutes, plus cooling and chilling time*

Cooking time: *10 minutes*

Yield: *1 quart, 8 servings*

10 ounces semisweet chocolate, finely chopped	1 vanilla bean
	8 egg yolks
2 cups milk	¾ cup sugar
2 cups heavy cream	

1 Place the chopped chocolate in a large mixing bowl.

2 Place the milk and cream in a large heavy-duty saucepan. Use a sharp knife to split the vanilla bean in half lengthwise. Scrape out the seeds and add the seeds and vanilla bean to the liquid. Bring the mixture to a simmer over medium heat.

3 In a large mixing bowl, using an electric mixer, whip the egg yolks and sugar together until they're very thick and pale colored and hold a slowly dissolving ribbon as the beater is lifted, about 5 minutes.

4 Slowly pour a cup of the hot liquid into the egg and sugar mixture. Blend well, then return the mixture to the saucepan. Cook over low heat, stirring constantly to prevent curdling, until the mixture is thick enough to coat the back of a wooden spoon, about 10 minutes.

5 Remove the saucepan from the heat, and strain the mixture into the bowl of chopped chocolate. Stir to melt the chocolate and blend well. Cover the mixture tightly with plastic wrap and cool, then chill at least 4 hours or overnight. Process in an ice cream freezer following the manufacturer's directions. Store the ice cream in a tightly covered container in the freezer for up to 2 months. If frozen solid, soften in the refrigerator for 30 minutes before serving.

Per serving: Calories 544 (From Fat 389); Fat 43g (Saturated 24g); Cholesterol 303mg; Sodium 61mg; Carbohydrate 40g (Dietary Fiber 1g); Protein 9g.

You can easily create another flavor of ice cream by adding an ingredient:

- ✔ **Semisweet Chocolate–Chocolate Chip Ice Cream:** Add 1 cup chocolate chips halfway through churning the ice cream.

- ✔ **Semisweet Chocolate–Cacao Nib Ice Cream:** Add 1 cup cacao nibs halfway through churning the ice cream.

- ✔ **Semisweet Chocolate-Hazelnut Ice Cream:** Add 1 cup toasted and finely ground hazelnuts to the ice cream mixture before chilling.

- ✔ **Mocha Ice Cream:** Add 1 tablespoon instant espresso powder to the milk and cream after bringing them to a boil.

- ✔ **Semisweet Chocolate-Spice Ice Cream:** Eliminate the vanilla bean and add 2 teaspoons finely ground cinnamon to the milk and cream after boiling.

Gianduia Ice Cream

This is a delectable combination of chocolate and hazelnut. There's a nice surprise of texture from the ground hazelnut paste that's part of the ice cream mixture.

Tools: *Ice cream freezer*

Preparation time: *8 minutes, plus cooling and chilling time*

Cooking time: *8 minutes*

Yield: *1 quart, 8 servings*

1 cup raw hazelnuts	*2 cups milk*
2 to 3 tablespoons unflavored vegetable oil	*2 cups heavy cream*
5 ounces bittersweet or semisweet chocolate, finely chopped	*1 vanilla bean*
	8 egg yolks
3 ounces milk chocolate, finely chopped	*¾ cup sugar*

1 Preheat the oven to 350 degrees. Place the hazelnuts in a single layer in a cake or pie pan. Toast in the oven for 15 minutes, until the skins blister and the nuts turn light golden brown. Remove the nuts from the oven and wrap in a kitchen towel. Let them steam for 5 to 8 minutes, then rub the nuts in the towel to loosen the skins. Not all the skins will come off. Let the nuts cool completely, then place them in the work bowl of a food processor fitted with a steel blade. Add the vegetable oil and pulse until the mixture forms a paste, similar to the consistency of peanut butter. If not using a food processor, grind the nuts in a blender or clean coffee grinder.

2 Place the chopped chocolates and the hazelnut paste from Step 1 in the top of a double boiler over hot water. Stir with a rubber spatula until the chocolate is melted and the mixture is smooth.

3 Combine the milk and cream in a large heavy-duty saucepan. Use a sharp knife to split the vanilla bean in half lengthwise. Scrape out the seeds and add the seeds and vanilla bean to the liquid. Bring the mixture to a simmer over medium heat, then remove the pan from the heat.

4 In a large mixing bowl, using an electric mixer, whip the egg yolks and sugar together until they're very thick and pale colored and hold a slowly dissolving ribbon as the beater is lifted, about 5 minutes. Slowly add the hot cream mixture. Blend well, then return the mixture to the saucepan. Cook over low heat, stirring constantly, until the mixture is thick enough to coat the back of a wooden spoon, about 10 minutes.

5 Strain the mixture into a large bowl. Add the chocolate mixture from Step 1 and blend well. Cover the bowl tightly with plastic wrap and cool, then chill at least 4 hours or overnight. Process in an ice cream freezer following the manufacturer's directions. Store the ice cream in a tightly covered container in the freezer for up to 2 months. If frozen solid, soften in the refrigerator for 30 minutes before serving.

Per serving: *Calories 664 (From Fat 469); Fat 52g (Saturated 23g); Cholesterol 306mg; Sodium 69mg; Carbohydrate 43g (Dietary Fiber 3g); Protein 11g.*

Top tips for making great ice cream

Making ice cream is fun and easy, but it's even more so if you follow these simple tips:

✔ **Use the best-quality ingredients you can find.** There's no way to mask inferior ingredients.

✔ **Don't allow the ice cream custard to boil when cooking.** If you do, the eggs will curdle, creating an unpleasant texture. Straining the custard after cooking eliminates lumps.

✔ **Be sure to cool and chill the mixture thoroughly before processing in an ice cream maker.**

✔ **Chill the mixture in the refrigerator for at least 4 hours or over a bowl of ice cubes for a quicker chill.**

✔ **Leave a few inches of room in the top of the canister of the ice cream freezer when filling it with the ice cream mixture.** This mixture expands as it freezes because the churning incorporates air.

✔ **Always store ice cream in a tightly sealed container in the freezer.** If the container is not completely full, press a piece of plastic wrap on top of the ice cream to help seal it from air.

✔ **Use a metal ice cream scoop for serving the ice cream.** Dip the scoop in hot water and dry between servings.

Malted Milk Chocolate Ice Cream

This tastes just like a chocolate malt. It has a wonderful creamy texture. Try combining it with Semisweet Chocolate Ice Cream or Gianduia Ice Cream for a taste treat.

Tools: *Ice cream freezer*

Preparation time: *10 minutes, plus cooling and chilling time*

Cooking time: *10 minutes*

Yield: *1 quart, 8 servings*

1 ounce bittersweet or semisweet chocolate, finely chopped

2 ounces milk chocolate, finely chopped

1 cup milk

1 cup heavy cream

⅓ cup sugar

6 egg yolks

1 cup malted milk powder

1 Place the chopped chocolates in a large mixing bowl. Place the milk, cream, and 2 tablespoons of the sugar in a large heavy-duty saucepan. Stir over medium to dissolve the sugar, then bring the mixture to the simmering point. Remove from the heat.

2 At the same time, combine the egg yolks and the remaining sugar in a large mixing bowl. Using an electric mixer, whip them together until the mixture is very thick and pale colored. Stir about ½ cup of the hot milk mixture into the egg yolks. Blend well, then pour the egg mixture into the saucepan. Return the pan to the heat and, whisking constantly, cook until the mixture is thick enough to coat a wooden spoon, about 5 minutes.

3 Remove the saucepan from the heat and pour the mixture into the bowl of chopped chocolates. Stir to melt the chocolate, then stir in the malted milk powder until completely blended.

4 Strain the mixture into a large mixing bowl. Cover tightly with plastic wrap and cool, then chill thoroughly, at least 4 hours or overnight. Process in an ice cream freezer following the manufacturer's directions. Store the ice cream in a tightly covered container in the freezer for up to 2 months. If frozen solid, soften in the refrigerator for 30 minutes before serving.

Per serving: Calories 314 (From Fat 185); Fat 21g (Saturated 11g); Cholesterol 210mg; Sodium 94mg; Carbohydrate 27g (Dietary Fiber 1g); Protein 6g.

Chocolate Silk Ice Cream

This ice cream is named perfectly. It's smooth as silk and easy to eat. Whenever chocolate ice cream is called for, this fills the bill.

Tools: *Ice cream freezer*

Preparation time: *5 minutes, plus cooling and chilling time*

Cooking time: *8 minutes*

Yield: *1 quart, 8 servings*

1½ cups milk	2 cups heavy cream
3 egg yolks	1 teaspoon pure vanilla extract
1 cup sugar	
⅓ cup unsweetened natural cocoa powder, sifted	

1 Combine the milk and egg yolks in a large heavy-duty saucepan. Whisk together to break up the egg yolks. Add the sugar and stir. Cook the mixture over medium heat, stirring constantly, until it is thick enough to coat a wooden spoon, about 8 minutes.

2 Remove the saucepan from the heat. Stir the cocoa into the mixture until well blended. Transfer the mixture to a large mixing bowl, cover tightly with plastic wrap, and cool. Blend in the cream and vanilla, cover tightly, and chill thoroughly, at least 4 hours or overnight.

3 Process in an ice cream freezer following the manufacturer's directions. Store the ice cream in a tightly covered container in the freezer for up to 2 months. If frozen solid, soften in the refrigerator for 30 minutes before serving.

Per serving: Calories 362 (From Fat 234); Fat 26g (Saturated 16g); Cholesterol 168mg; Sodium 49mg; Carbohydrate 31g (Dietary Fiber 1g); Protein 5g.

Don't let ice cream stand at room temperature too long before serving or you'll have ice cream soup, especially in hot weather.

Ice Cream Desserts

How is it possible to make ice cream any better than it already is? By combining it with sauce, cake, or cookies to make a dessert. In this section, I give you the recipes for several yummy desserts that are super-easy to make by pairing ice cream with a few other ingredients. Let your imagination go wild and make different combinations than the ones I've included here. The only requirement is that it tastes delicious!

Have an ice cream sundae party. Get a group of friends together and have everyone bring one ingredient, so no one has to do too much work. You'll want to have a few different flavors of ice cream, a few sauces, and other things like whipped cream, chopped nuts, shaved chocolate . . . you get the idea. Set everything out along with glasses, bowls, and spoons, and let each person make his own sundae. Seeing what everyone puts together will be loads of fun — but the most fun will be in the eating. Bon appétit!

Hot Chocolate Sundae

This is a delicious way to combine your favorite ice cream with warm chocolate sauce. Yum!

Tools: *4 deep stemmed glasses, chilled*

Preparation time: *10 minutes*

Yield: *4 servings*

Warm Chocolate Sauce (see Chapter 15 for recipe)

1 quart Gianduia or Malted Milk Ice Cream (see the recipes early in this chapter)

½ cup heavy cream

2 tablespoons confectioners' sugar, sifted

1 teaspoon pure vanilla extract

4 tablespoons shaved semisweet chocolate, cacao nibs, or toasted, chopped nuts (peanuts, almonds, hazelnuts, and so on)

1 Pour 2 tablespoons of Warm Chocolate Sauce into the bottom of a deep stemmed glass. Place a scoop of ice cream on top of the sauce. Repeat this process until the glass is full, ending with sauce on top (see Figure 14-1). Repeat for each glass.

2 Place the cream in a large mixing bowl. Using an electric mixer, whip the cream until frothy. Add the confectioners' sugar and vanilla and whip until the cream holds soft peaks. Spoon a large dollop of whipped cream over the top of each glass and top with shaved chocolate, chopped cacao nibs, or chopped nuts. Serve immediately.

Per serving: Calories 1,878 (From Fat 1,302); Fat 145g (Saturated 71g); Cholesterol 710mg; Sodium 171mg; Carbohydrate 131g (Dietary Fiber 10g); Protein 25g.

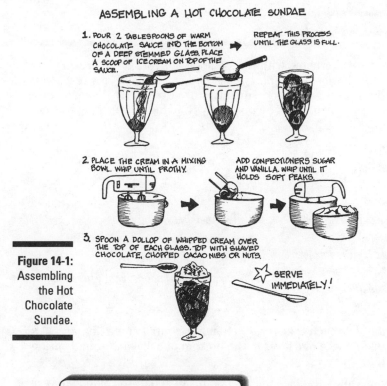

ASSEMBLING A HOT CHOCOLATE SUNDAE

1. POUR 2 TABLESPOONS OF WARM CHOCOLATE SAUCE INTO THE BOTTOM OF A DEEP STEMMED GLASS. PLACE A SCOOP OF ICE CREAM ON TOP OF THE SAUCE.

REPEAT THIS PROCESS UNTIL THE GLASS IS FULL.

2. PLACE THE CREAM IN A MIXING BOWL. WHIP UNTIL FROTHY.

ADD CONFECTIONERS SUGAR AND VANILLA. WHIP UNTIL IT HOLDS SOFT PEAKS.

3. SPOON A DOLLOP OF WHIPPED CREAM OVER THE TOP OF EACH GLASS. TOP WITH SHAVED CHOCOLATE, CHOPPED CACAO NIBS OR NUTS.

SERVE IMMEDIATELY!

Figure 14-1:
Assembling
the Hot
Chocolate
Sundae.

Double-Chocolate Parfait

A *parfait* is another name for a fancy sundae. Use your prettiest glasses for this dessert.

Preparation time: *10 minutes*

Yield: *4 servings*

Warm Chocolate Sauce (see Chapter 15 for recipe

Semisweet Chocolate Ice Cream (see the recipe earlier in this chapter)

Raspberry Sauce (see Chapter 15 for recipe)

½ cup fresh raspberries

2 tablespoons sliced almonds, lightly toasted

1 Pour 2 tablespoons of Warm Chocolate Sauce into the bottom of a deep stemmed glass. Place a scoop of Semisweet Chocolate Ice Cream on top of the sauce. Pour a tablespoon of Raspberry Sauce on top of the ice cream. Then place a scoop of ice cream on top of the sauce. Repeat this process until the glass is full, ending with raspberry sauce on top. Repeat for each glass.

2 Top each glass with a few fresh raspberries and sliced almonds. Serve immediately.

Per serving: *Calories 1,561 (From Fat 1,034); Fat 115g (Saturated 65g); Cholesterol 663mg; Sodium 143mg; Carbohydrate 134g (Dietary Fiber 10g); Protein 22g.*

Chocolate Ice Cream Cake

Dark chocolate cake layers are alternated with two delicious flavors of ice cream to create this outstanding cake. This is a great party cake and can serve a crowd. It's very rich, so cut thin slices. You can substitute good-quality store-bought ice cream if you aren't in the mood to make your own. Don't be put off by thinking that making this cake is difficult, because it's not.

Tools: *9½-inch round springform pan*

Preparation time: *30 minutes, plus chilling time*

Yield: *12 to 16 servings*

The Best Chocolate Layer Cake (see Chapter 10 for recipe)

1 quart Semisweet Chocolate Ice Cream (see the recipe earlier in this chapter)

1 pint Gianduia Ice Cream (see the recipe earlier in this chapter)

2 cups heavy whipping cream

1 tablespoon sugar

1 teaspoon pure vanilla extract

1¼ cups sliced almonds, lightly toasted

1 Using a long serrated knife, slice each cake layer in half horizontally (see Chapter 10 for instructions on slicing cakes). Place one layer in the bottom of a 9½-inch round spring-form pan.

2 Soften both of the ice creams slightly. Place the ice creams in separate chilled large mixing bowls. Using an electric mixer, beat each ice cream on medium speed until it holds soft peaks, about a minute.

3 Spread half of the Semisweet Chocolate Ice Cream evenly over the cake layer, using a small metal offset spatula or a rubber spatula. Place another cake layer over the ice cream and spread evenly with the Gianduia Ice Cream. Position another cake layer over the ice cream and spread with the remaining Semisweet Chocolate Ice Cream. Top with the final cake layer. Cover the cake tightly with plastic wrap and freeze until firm, several hours or overnight.

4 Place the cream in a large mixing bowl. Using an electric mixer, whip the cream until it's frothy. Add the sugar and vanilla and whip the cream until it holds soft peaks. Set aside 20 almond slices for garnish. Finely chop the remaining almonds. Remove the cake from the freezer. Dip the blade of a flexible-blade metal spatula in hot water and dry. Run the blade around the sides of the pan to help it release, then lift off the sides of the pan.

5 Set aside ½ cup of the whipped cream for the final decoration. Spread the sides and top of the cake with the remaining whipped cream, smoothly and evenly. Press the chopped almonds into the sides of the cake up to the top edge. Fit a pastry bag with a large open star tip and pipe a border of shells or rosettes around the top edge of the cake. Arrange the almond slices decoratively around the border.

6 Store the cake in the freezer until ready to serve, for up to 1 hour. Store the cake in a cake box, tightly wrapped with plastic wrap or in a plastic cake saver for up to 1 month. Transfer the cake to the refrigerator 1 hour before serving.

Per serving: Calories 916 (From Fat 630); Fat 70g (Saturated 34g); Cholesterol 319mg; Sodium 234mg; Carbohydrate 69g (Dietary Fiber 4g); Protein 14g.

Banana Split with Hot Fudge Sauce

This yummy ice cream dessert is a classic for a reason: It's hard to improve on perfection. You can vary the flavor of the ice cream and the topping, but make sure to use bananas and hot fudge sauce, a divine combination.

Preparation time: 10 minutes

Yield: 4 servings

4 ripe bananas

1 quart Semisweet Chocolate Ice Cream (see the recipe earlier in this chapter) or other ice cream

1 cup Hot Fudge Sauce (see Chapter 15 for recipe)

½ cup heavy cream

2 tablespoons confectioners' sugar, sifted

1 teaspoon pure vanilla extract

1 Peel each banana and slice in half lengthwise. Place 2 banana halves against the sides of an oval bowl or plate. Arrange 3 large scoops of ice cream inside the banana halves on each plate.

2 Spoon half of the Hot Fudge Sauce over the ice cream.

3 Place the cream in a large mixing bowl. Using an electric mixer, whip the cream until it's frothy. Add the confectioners' sugar and vanilla and whip until the cream holds soft peaks. Spoon the whipped cream over the Hot Fudge Sauce, then drizzle the remaining Hot Fudge Sauce over the whipped cream. Serve immediately.

Per serving: Calories 1,483 (From Fat 1,008); Fat 112g (Saturated 65g); Cholesterol 667mg; Sodium 158mg; Carbohydrate 121g (Dietary Fiber 6g); Protein 21g.

Ice Cream Sandwiches

These ice cream sandwiches are great to have on hand in the freezer for quick snacks. Kids love them and they're super-easy to prepare. All you need are cookies and ice cream to put these together. Use Chocolate-Cinnamon Coins, Chocolate Peanut Butter Coins, chocolate wafers from Double-Chocolate Sandwich Cookies (see Chapter 7 for recipes), or any cookie of your choice. In a pinch, you can always use store-bought cookies.

Preparation time: *10 minutes*

Yield: *About 2 dozen*

4 dozen cookies

1 quart ice cream flavor of your choice (see the recipes earlier in this chapter)

1 Soften the ice cream at room temperature for about 15 minutes, until pliable. Or soften the ice cream in the microwave oven on low power for 5-second bursts. Stir to make sure it is pliable. Be careful not to melt the ice cream.

2 For each sandwich, spread ⅛ to ¼ cup ice cream evenly over one cookie to a thickness of about 1 inch. Top with another cookie and press down lightly to make sure the ice cream is even and the top cookie will stay in place. Repeat with the remaining cookies and ice cream.

3 Place the ice cream sandwiches on a plate in the freezer to firm up the ice cream, about 30 minutes. Then tightly wrap each sandwich individually with plastic wrap. Store in the freezer for up to 2 months. If frozen solid, soften the ice cream sandwiches in the refrigerator for 20 minutes before serving.

Per serving: Calories 452 (From Fat 264); Fat 29g (Saturated 17g); Cholesterol 159mg; Sodium 39mg; Carbohydrate 45g (Dietary Fiber 2g); Protein 6g.

Scrumptious Sorbet

Sorbet is the French word for sherbet, which is made of fruit juice or puree, sugar, and water. It's also known as a water ice. No cream, milk, or eggs are used in sorbet. It has a smooth texture and is noticeably lighter than ice cream.

Bittersweet Chocolate Sorbet

This sorbet has a very intense chocolate flavor and smooth texture. It's delicious served with cookies or fresh fruit.

Tools: *Ice cream freezer*

Preparation time: *10 minutes, plus cooling and chilling time*

Cooking time: *8 minutes*

Yield: *1 quart, 8 servings*

2½ cups water

1½ cups sugar

⅔ cup unsweetened Dutch-processed cocoa powder, sifted

8 ounces bittersweet chocolate, finely chopped

1 Combine the water and sugar in a large heavy-duty saucepan and bring to a boil over medium heat. Stir briefly to dissolve the sugar.

2 Add the cocoa powder and whisk together until smooth. Remove the pan from the heat and add the chopped chocolate. Stir until it is completely melted and smooth.

3 Strain the mixture into a large bowl. Cover tightly with plastic wrap and cool, then chill at least 4 hours or overnight. Process in an ice cream maker following the manufacturer's directions.

4 Store the sorbet in a tightly covered container in the freezer for up to a month. If it is frozen solid, soften in the refrigerator for 30 minutes before serving.

Per serving: Calories 320 (From Fat 95); Fat 11g (Saturated 6g); Cholesterol 1mg; Sodium 3mg; Carbohydrate 58g (Dietary Fiber 4g); Protein 3g.

Chocolate-Mint Sorbet

Mint adds a burst of freshness to this delectable deep-chocolate sorbet. It's perfect for a springtime dessert.

Tools: *Ice cream freezer*

Preparation time: *10 minutes, plus cooling and chilling time*

Cooking time: *35 minutes*

Yield: *1 quart, 8 servings*

4 cups fresh mint leaves

3½ cups water

1¼ cups sugar

¾ cup unsweetened Dutch-processed cocoa powder, sifted

10 ounces bittersweet chocolate, finely chopped

Fresh mint leaves, for garnish

1 Wash the mint leaves and pat dry on paper towels. Combine the water and sugar in a large heavy-duty saucepan. Bring to a boil over medium heat. Turn off the heat, add the mint leaves, cover the pan, and leave to infuse for 15 minutes.

2 Strain the mixture to remove the mint leaves then return the mixture to the saucepan. Heat the sugar syrup, add the cocoa powder, and whisk together until smooth. Bring the mixture to a boil and simmer until it is slightly thickened, about 15 minutes.

3 Remove the saucepan from the heat. Add the chopped chocolate and stir until it is completely melted and smooth. Strain the mixture into a large bowl. Cover the bowl tightly with plastic wrap and cool, then chill at least 4 hours or overnight. Process in an ice cream maker following the manufacturer's directions.

4 Store the sorbet in a tightly covered container in the freezer for up to 1 month. If it is frozen solid, soften in the refrigerator for 30 minutes before serving. Garnish scoops of the sorbet with a sprig of fresh mint leaves.

Per serving: Calories 337 (From Fat 117); Fat 13g (Saturated 8g); Cholesterol 2mg; Sodium 4mg; Carbohydrate 56g (Dietary Fiber 5g); Protein 4g.

The Chinese introduced sorbet in the 18th century. The name derives from the Turkish word *chorbet,* which means "drink." The Italians called it *sorbetto.* Whatever the name, it's delicious.

Chapter 15

Liquid Chocolate: Potions and Sauces

About the easiest way to consume chocolate is to drink it. Other than raising the cup to your mouth, very little effort is required. And for pure chocoholics, that's good news. Plus, it's hard to beat the cozy feeling you get from a warm chocolate drink.

As with chocolate drinks, chocolate sauces and sauces that go well with chocolate desserts require very little effort to make. But that small amount of effort can double the pleasure of your dessert. Not only will it taste better, but the appearance of a pool of sauce surrounding, or poured over, a dessert is guaranteed to tantalize the taste buds.

Morning, Noon, and Night

As a child, I drank chocolate milk, which I still like. When I grew up I was introduced to drinking chocolate in a more pure form, commonly called hot chocolate. On a cold day or evening, hot chocolate is a great substitute for coffee or tea — and you can make it even faster.

Many people like to start their day with hot chocolate — others drink it throughout the day or as a nightcap. You don't have to consume chocolate drinks by themselves. What goes best with a chocolate drink? A chocolate dessert, of course. Maybe even one that you can dip into your hot chocolate. Now that's a chocolate lover's dream!

Heavenly Hot Chocolate

This very rich and creamy beverage is best sipped slowly and savored.

Preparation time: 5 minutes

Cooking time: 10 minutes

Yield: 4 servings

2 cups whole milk

1¼ cups heavy cream

¼ cup unsweetened Dutch-processed cocoa powder, sifted

6 ounces bittersweet or semisweet chocolate, finely chopped

1 teaspoon pure vanilla extract

2 teaspoons confectioners' sugar

1 Combine the milk, 1 cup of the cream, and the cocoa powder in a medium heavy-duty saucepan. Cook over medium heat and stir to dissolve the cocoa. Add the chopped chocolate, and stir until it is completely melted and smooth. Bring the mixture to a simmer. Do not boil. Cook for 5 minutes, stirring often.

2 Remove the saucepan from the heat and stir in the vanilla. Stir to cool the mixture slightly and blend well, then pour into the serving cups.

3 In a medium mixing bowl, using an electric mixer, whip the remaining ¼ cup cream until frothy. Add the confectioners' sugar and continue to whip until the cream holds soft peaks. Place a large dollop of whipped cream on top of each cup of chocolate. Serve immediately.

Per serving: Calories 587 (From Fat 420); Fat 47g (Saturated 29g); Cholesterol 120mg; Sodium 91mg; Carbohydrate 36g (Dietary Fiber 5g); Protein 9g.

Hot chocolate can be scorching hot. Let it cool slightly before drinking it so you don't burn your mouth. When you serve it to a group, caution everyone to sip the chocolate slowly at first.

If hot chocolate sits and cools too much before it's served, you can reheat it in a saucepan over low heat. Be sure to spoon off any skin that forms on top while it cools before reheating.

Spiced Hot Chocolate

Cinnamon, cloves, and nutmeg add warm spicy tones to this delicious, creamy hot chocolate.

Preparation time: *5 minutes*

Cooking time: *15 minutes*

Yield: *4½ cups*

8 ounces bittersweet chocolate, finely chopped

1 cup water

3 cups whole milk

4 cinnamon sticks

5 whole cloves

⅔ cup plus 1 tablespoon sugar

1 cup heavy whipping cream

1½ teaspoons pure vanilla extract

½ teaspoon freshly grated or ground nutmeg

1 Place the chopped chocolate and the water in the top of a double boiler over hot water. Stir often with a rubber spatula until the chocolate is completely melted.

2 In a medium heavy-duty saucepan, combine the milk, cinnamon sticks, and cloves. Warm over medium heat until the milk begins to boil. Stir the milk into the chocolate mixture. Remove the top of the double boiler and wipe the bottom and sides of the pan very dry. Pour the mixture into the saucepan, add ⅔ cup of the sugar, and bring to a boil over medium heat. Reduce the heat and simmer for 5 minutes.

3 Use a slotted spoon to remove the cinnamon sticks. Rinse the cinnamon sticks, dry with paper towels, and save to use for garnish. Add ½ cup of the cream to the mixture in the pan and bring the mixture to a simmer over low heat. Stir in 1 teaspoon of the vanilla and ¼ teaspoon of the nutmeg.

4 In a small mixing bowl, use an electric mixer to whip the remaining ½ cup of cream until frothy. Add the remaining 1 tablespoon of sugar and ½ teaspoon vanilla, and whip until the cream holds soft peaks.

5 Divide the hot chocolate among 4 mugs. Top each mug with a big scoop of the whipped cream. Sprinkle the remaining ¼ teaspoon nutmeg on top of the four mugs and garnish with the reserved cinnamon sticks.

Per serving: *Calories 575 (From Fat 227); Fat 25g (Saturated 16g); Cholesterol 27mg; Sodium 93mg; Carbohydrate 78g (Dietary Fiber 4g); Protein 10g.*

Hot White Chocolate

Chocolate Whipped Cream (see the recipe later in this chapter) is a perfect accompaniment to this creamy, sweet drink.

Preparation time: *5 minutes*

Cooking time: *10 minutes*

Yield: *4 servings*

Chocolate Whipped Cream (see the recipe later in this chapter)

2 cups whole milk

1 cup heavy cream

4 ounces white chocolate, finely chopped

1 Place the milk and cream together in a medium heavy-duty saucepan. Bring to a boil over medium heat. Remove from the heat and stir in the chocolate until melted and smooth. For frothy chocolate, place the mixture in a blender. Secure the top tightly, place a towel over the top, just in case it leaks, and blend for 30 to 45 seconds.

2 Divide the chocolate between serving cups. Top each with a dollop of Chocolate Whipped Cream.

Per serving: Calories 442 (From Fat 327); Fat 36g (Saturated 22g); Cholesterol 104mg; Sodium 113mg; Carbohydrate 24g (Dietary Fiber 0g); Protein 7g.

Chocolate wares

When chocolate first made its way to Spain in the early 16th century, it was consumed as a beverage. It was embraced enthusiastically by the rest of Europe about 100 years later and enjoyed great popularity in liquid form for nearly another 100 years. Many chocolate pots and chocolate cups for preparing and serving this delectable beverage were created by several well-known porcelain manufacturers. These items are known as *chocolate wares.* One of the most interesting new developments was the creation of a cup called a *trembleuse.* It was designed to fit into the deep hollow of a special saucer, which prevented the drinker from spilling the contents. Some of these also had two handles, which made them easier to hold while drinking. Many of these chocolate wares are so highly prized that today they are the highlights of collections in museums in Holland, England, France, and Germany.

Chocolate fit for a king

Louis XIV of France and his successor, Louis XV, set the stage for the refinement of what we know today as chocolate. In the lavish parties they had at the Chateau of Versailles, they entertained with music, theater, and chocolate. Maria-Theresa brought chocolate with her from the Spanish court in 1660 when she came to Versailles to marry Louis XIV. She also brought her own private maid to Versailles to mix her chocolate using a tool called the *molinillo*. This maid was called La Molina by the French court. It was Louis XIV who granted a license to David Chaillon to open one of the first chocolate-making shops in Paris.

Hot Cocoa

This rich and creamy drink is very satisfying on a cold winter's day. It's also a snap to prepare.

Preparation time: *5 minutes*

Cooking time: *5 minutes*

Yield: *4 cups*

4 cups whole milk

½ cup unsweetened Dutch-processed cocoa powder, sifted

¼ cup superfine sugar

1 Place the milk in a medium heavy-duty saucepan and bring to a boil over medium heat.

2 In a small mixing bowl, combine the cocoa powder and sugar. Toss to blend well. Add 4 tablespoons of the hot milk and stir until the mixture forms a paste.

3 Pour the cocoa paste into the hot milk and stir until the mixture is completely smooth. Divide the hot chocolate milk between 4 mugs and serve immediately.

Per serving: Calories 219 (From Fat 86); Fat 10g (Saturated 6g); Cholesterol 33mg; Sodium 122mg; Carbohydrate 29g (Dietary Fiber 3g); Protein 10g.

Enhancing Dessert with a Special Sauce

"Would you like chocolate sauce?" That question is music to my ears. And there's only one answer, "Yes, please." A chocolate sauce and other sauces that go well with chocolate provide that extra-special touch that makes the dessert pure ecstasy. They're so easy to make that there's no reason to overlook them. You can also make them in advance and use them on several different occasions.

Hot Fudge Sauce

What would a hot fudge sundae be without hot fudge sauce? Any ice cream and many other desserts benefit from this yummy sauce as well.

Preparation time: *5 minutes*

Cooking time: *15 minutes*

Yield: *1½ cups*

½ cup water

4 tablespoons (½ stick) butter, cut into small pieces

2 tablespoons unsweetened Dutch-processed cocoa powder

4 ounces bittersweet chocolate, finely chopped

¼ cup light corn syrup

¼ cup light brown sugar

¼ cup sugar

1 teaspoon pure vanilla extract

1 Combine the water and butter in a medium heavy-duty saucepan and bring to a simmer over medium heat. Add the cocoa powder and stir until it is completely blended.

2 Remove the saucepan from the heat. Add the chopped chocolate and stir until it is melted and smooth. Add the corn syrup, brown sugar, and sugar. Stir to blend, then return the saucepan to the heat and bring to a simmer over medium heat. Cook for 5 minutes, stirring often.

3 Remove the saucepan from the heat and stir to cool the mixture for about 2 minutes. Add the vanilla and stir to blend. Serve the sauce while warm or store in an airtight container in the refrigerator for up to 2 weeks. Warm the sauce in a double boiler or in a microwave oven before serving.

Per serving: Calories 133 (From Fat 64); Fat 7g (Saturated 4g); Cholesterol 11mg; Sodium 10mg; Carbohydrate 17g (Dietary Fiber 1g); Protein 1g.

Don't drown your dessert in too much sauce. It should be used to accent the dessert it accompanies.

Mocha Sauce

Use this sauce to enhance any cake. It goes especially well with the Individual Chocolate-Spice Cakes in Chapter 10.

Preparation time: *5 minutes*

Cooking time: *10 minutes*

Yield: *½ cup*

⅓ cup milk	1/4 teaspoon instant espresso powder
¼ cup sugar	4 ounces bittersweet or semisweet chocolate, finely chopped
1 teaspoon pure vanilla extract	

1 Combine the milk, sugar, vanilla, and espresso powder in a small saucepan. Cook over medium heat until bubbles form around the edges, about 5 minutes.

2 Remove the pan from the heat and stir in the chocolate until completely melted and smooth. The sauce can be stored in a tightly covered container in the refrigerator for up to a week. Warm the in the microwave oven on low power or in a small saucepan over low heat before serving.

Per serving: Calories 222 (From Fat 92); Fat 10g (Saturated 6g); Cholesterol 4mg; Sodium 12mg; Carbohydrate 30g (Dietary Fiber 2g); Protein 3g.

Warm Chocolate Sauce

This is another great chocolate sauce to enhance any cake.

Preparation time: *5 minutes*

Cooking time: *10 minutes*

Yield: *¾ cup*

⅓ cup light brown sugar	4 ounces bittersweet or semisweet chocolate, finely chopped
½ cup heavy cream	2 tablespoons butter, softened
1 teaspoon pure vanilla extract	

1 Combine the sugar, cream, and vanilla in a small saucepan. Stir to dissolve the sugar and cook over medium heat until bubbles form around the edges of the pan, about 5 minutes.

2 Remove the pan from the heat and stir in the chocolate until completely melted and smooth. Then stir in the butter until melted. The sauce can be stored in a tightly covered container in the refrigerator for up to a week. Warm in the microwave oven on low power or in a small saucepan over low heat before serving.

Per serving: Calories 255 (From Fat 158); Fat 18g (Saturated 11g); Cholesterol 38mg; Sodium 14mg; Carbohydrate 23g (Dietary Fiber 2g); Protein 2g.

Caramel Sauce

Caramel and chocolate are a match that must have been made in heaven. This sauce is wonderful served with ice cream (see Chapter 14), many chocolate cakes (see Chapter 10), and brownies (see Chapter 8). This sauce keeps well in the refrigerator, so you can make it up in advance and have it on hand.

Preparation time: *5 minutes*

Cooking time: *15 minutes*

Yield: *1¼ cups*

¾ cup heavy cream	4 tablespoons butter, softened, cut into small pieces
1 cup sugar	
½ cup water	1½ teaspoons pure vanilla extract
1 tablespoon light corn syrup	

1 Place the cream in a small saucepan. Warm over medium heat until the edges begin to bubble.

2 In a medium heavy-duty saucepan, combine the sugar, water, and corn syrup. Bring to a boil over medium heat, without stirring. Cook until the mixture turns a light amber color, about 10 minutes. Brush down the sides of the pan with a pastry brush dipped in warm water twice while the mixture is cooking to prevent crystallization.

3 Remove the saucepan from the heat and stir in the hot cream. This will bubble up dramatically. Be sure to use a long-handled wooden spoon to stir the mixture constantly. Return the pan to the heat and stir to dissolve any lumps.

4 Add the butter and stir until it is completely melted. Remove the pan from the heat and stir in the vanilla. Transfer the sauce to a bowl or other container. Cover tightly and let cool slightly. Use immediately or store in a tightly covered container in the refrigerator for up to a month. Warm the sauce in a double boiler or microwave oven before using.

Note: Caramel can go from the ideal amber color to burned in the blink of an eye, so keep your eyes on the pan of caramel as it cooks and take the pan off the heat the instant it reaches the color you want.

Per serving: *Calories 187 (From Fat 101); Fat 11g (Saturated 7g); Cholesterol 37mg; Sodium 10mg; Carbohydrate 22g (Dietary Fiber 0g); Protein 0g.*

Don't stir sugar syrup while it is cooking to caramel. This will cause crystallization, making the mixture unusable.

Orange-Ginger Caramel Sauce

Orange and ginger give extra flavor to a delicious classic caramel sauce.

Preparation time: 5 minutes

Cooking time: 15 minutes

Yield: 1 cup

Zest of 2 large oranges	*1 tablespoon light corn syrup*
½ cup crystallized ginger, finely chopped	*½ cup cream*
1 cup sugar	*2 tablespoons butter*
¼ cup water	*1 tablespoon orange extract*

1 Place the orange zest and chopped ginger in a small mixing bowl. Cover with boiling water and let steep for 10 minutes. Drain the mixture and pat dry on paper towels.

2 Combine the sugar, water, and corn syrup in a 1-quart heavy-duty saucepan. Cook over medium heat until the sugar dissolves, about 3 minutes. Then raise the heat to medium-high and cook the mixture until it turns a deep amber color, about 10 minutes. While the sugar mixture cooks, wash down the sides of the pan with a damp pastry brush 2 or 3 times to prevent crystallization.

3 Remove the pan from the heat and stir in the butter, orange zest, and ginger. Add the cream, return the pan to medium heat, and stir to dissolve any lumps. Store the sauce in a tightly covered container in the refrigerator for up to 2 weeks. Warm the sauce in a microwave oven on low power or in a small saucepan over low heat before serving.

Per serving: Calories 219 (From Fat 76); Fat 8g (Saturated 5g); Cholesterol 28mg; Sodium 13mg; Carbohydrate 37g (Dietary Fiber 0g); Protein 0g.

The best way to loosen hardened caramel from a saucepan is to fill it three-fourths of the way with water and bring it to a boil over high heat.

Raspberry Sauce

Raspberry and chocolate are a perfect combination. This sauce is a delicious accompaniment to many cakes (see Chapter 10), brownies (see Chapter 8), and ice cream (see Chapter 14).

Preparation time: *5 minutes*

Yield: *1½ cups*

2 cups fresh or fresh-frozen raspberries

2 tablespoons raspberry-flavored liqueur (Framboise, Chambord, or Kirsch) (optional)

3 tablespoons superfine sugar

2 teaspoons fresh lemon juice

1 Place the raspberries in the work bowl of a food processor fitted with a steel blade or in a blender. Pulse until the berries are liquid, 30 seconds to 1 minute. Strain the raspberries to remove the seeds.

2 Transfer the strained raspberry puree to a medium mixing bowl. Combine the remaining ingredients and mix well. Store in a tightly covered container in the refrigerator for up to a week.

Per serving: Calories 22 (From Fat 1); Fat 0g (Saturated 0g); Cholesterol 0mg; Sodium 0mg; Carbohydrate 5g (Dietary Fiber 1g); Protein 0g.

Chocolate Whipped Cream

This is a delicious accompaniment to Hot White Chocolate and many other recipes, such as cakes (see Chapter 10) and brownies (see Chapter 8).

Preparation time: *5 minutes*

Yield: *About 2 cups*

¼ cup unsweetened Dutch-processed cocoa powder

3 tablespoons confectioners' sugar

1 cup heavy cream

1 teaspoon pure vanilla extract

1 In a small bowl or over a piece of wax paper, sift together the cocoa powder and confectioners' sugar. In a large mixing bowl, using an electric mixer, whip the cream until frothy. Add the vanilla and whip until the cream holds soft peaks.

2 Fold the cocoa mixture into the whipped cream in 3 stages, blending well after each addition. Keep the whipped cream in an airtight container in the refrigerator for up to 3 days.

Per serving: Calories 59 (From Fat 51); Fat 6g (Saturated 4g); Cholesterol 20mg; Sodium 6mg; Carbohydrate 2g (Dietary Fiber 0g); Protein 1g.

Part V

Chocolate Desserts to Dazzle and Impress Your Friends

The 5th Wave   By Rich Tennant

TROUBLE AT THE CHOCOLATE PLANT

"Okay-there's been a meltdown in cooling tower 9!
Chocolate syrup's leaking everywhere! This is why
you signed up for this job. Now grab your sliced
fruit and your fondue forks and let's go to work!!"

In this part . . .

*I*f you want to be a little different or extravagant, you've arrived in the right place. In this part you'll find some unusual chocolate recipes that are eye-openers. I also include recipes for what can be called "fancy" chocolate desserts. These require a little extra effort, but they're oh-so worth it. You may want to get the camera out for these — the results will be snapshot-worthy.

Chapter 16

Desserts with a Difference

In This Chapter

▶ Trying your hand at unusual recipes

▶ Planning and preparing in advance

▶ Working with different components

Recipes in This Chapter

▶ Chocolate Tacos

▶ Chocolate Sushi

▶ Chocolate Soufflé

▶ Double-Chocolate Pavlova

▶ Chocolate Bread Pudding

▶ Chocolate Nut Purses

▶ Chocolate Fondue

*1*f you're looking for a way to dazzle your friends and family, you're in the right chapter. Here you'll find recipes that you may not have had before. But I can assure you they're all crowd pleasers. I love to make these desserts because not only do they always get rave reviews for the way they taste, but they have a very creative appearance. I'm sure you'll want to include these in your repertoire of chocolate desserts.

Out-of-the-Ordinary Chocolate Desserts

Inviting someone over for chocolate tacos and chocolate sushi, I have to admit, sounds a little odd. Actually, both of these desserts are made to look like their real food counterparts — but they definitely taste different! They both require component parts, which are easy to prepare in advance and can be put together quickly shortly before serving.

Soufflés have a bad reputation for being difficult to prepare, but nothing is farther from the truth. Most soufflé batters can be prepared up to 24 hours before baking and kept tightly covered in the refrigerator. All you have to do is pop them in the oven and — voila! — you have a fabulous dessert that is sure to please anyone.

Also in this section is Pavlova, one of my personal favorites. Making it with chocolate is unusual, but oh-so-yummy. Although tropical fruit is generally used in Pavlova, feel free to use any fruit you like best. This dessert is definitely an eye catcher, so you may want to bring out that beautiful platter you've been saving for special occasions.

Chocolate Tacos

Every time I make this recipe, I have a smile on my face. They're my whimsical version of tacos and they look *very* real — but they taste nothing like the tacos you're used to! Everyone who eats these loves them. A crisp almond cookie is formed into a curved shape while warm, then filled with a delectable chocolate ganache, and topped with shaved white chocolate. Serve these for your next gathering and watch the fun.

Tools: Two 2-inch diameter rolling pins or 1 rolling pin and an empty wine bottle

Preparation time: 20 minutes

Baking time: 7 minutes

Yield: 2 dozen

Taco shells:

2 tablespoons butter, softened for the pans	⅓ cup flour
3½ tablespoons butter, softened	⅓ cup finely ground almonds
½ cup sugar	½ teaspoon almond extract
2 egg whites	

Filling:

10 ounces semisweet chocolate, finely chopped	⅔ cup heavy cream
4 ounces milk chocolate, finely chopped	10 tablespoons (1 stick plus 2 tablespoons) butter, softened

Garnish:

1 ounce white chocolate, finely chopped

1 Preheat the oven to 425 degrees. Line 2 baking sheets with aluminum foil and generously butter the foil. Set the rolling pins on a flat work surface.

2 In a medium mixing bowl, using an electric mixer, beat the butter until fluffy. Add the sugar, and cream together well. Add the egg whites. Stop and scrape down the sides of the bowl with a rubber spatula, then blend well. Sprinkle on the flour and the ground almonds and blend quickly. Stir in the almond extract.

3 Drop teaspoonfuls of the batter onto the prepared baking sheets, leaving 3 inches of space between them. Dip the back of a spoon in cold water and flatten each mound of batter into a circle about 2 to 3 inches in diameter.

4 Bake the cookies for 7 to 8 minutes, until the outer edges are light golden brown and the centers are set. Remove the baking sheet from the oven. Work very quickly using a small offset spatula to lift the cookies from the baking pan. Drape the cookies over a rolling pin and let them cool in their curved shape, as shown in Figure 16-1. (If you don't have two rolling pins, you can use an empty wine bottle instead.) If the cookies are hard to remove from the baking pan, return the pan to the oven for 20 to 30 seconds. The cookies will keep in an airtight container at room temperature for up to 5 days.

5 For the filling, melt the chocolates together in the top of a double boiler over hot water or in a microwave oven on low power for 30-second bursts. Stir often with a rubber spatula. In a separate small saucepan, scald the cream. Remove the top pan of the double boiler (if using) and wipe the bottom and sides very dry. Pour the cream into the chocolate and stir until smooth and well blended. Transfer the mixture to a bowl or other container, cover tightly, and let stand at room temperature until the consistency of thick pudding, or refrigerate the mixture until it thickens. If too cold, the mixture will need to be softened before use.

6 In a large mixing bowl, using an electric mixer, whip the butter until very fluffy. Add the softened chocolate ganache and beat until the mixture holds soft peaks, about 1 minute. Fit a 12– or 14-inch pastry bag with a pastry tip with a ½-inch plain round opening. Pipe about 2 tablespoons of filling into each taco shell.

7 Sprinkle the top of each taco with some of the shaved white chocolate. Cover the tacos with wax paper and then wrap with foil. Hold the tacos at room temperature for up to 3 hours or refrigerate, but bring to room temperature before serving.

Vary it! Make a variation of Chocolate Tacos by changing the topping. For example, you can top the tacos with Warm Chocolate Sauce (see Chapter 15) and fresh sliced strawberries, then sprinkle with shaved white chocolate.

Per serving: Calories 224 (From Fat 167); Fat 19g (Saturated 10g); Cholesterol 31mg; Sodium 15mg; Carbohydrate 16g (Dietary Fiber 1g); Protein 3g.

SHAPING CHOCOLATE TACO SHELLS

Figure 16-1: Shaping chocolate taco shells over a rolling pin.

1. BAKE THE COOKIES FOR 7 to 8 MINUTES. THE OUTER EDGES ARE GOLDEN BROWN AND CENTERS ARE SET. REMOVE FROM THE OVEN.

2. USE AN OFFSET SPATULA TO REMOVE COOKIES FROM THE BAKING SHEET. WORK QUICKLY!

3. DRAPE WARM COOKIES OVER A ROLLING PIN AND LET COOL IN THEIR CURVED SHAPE.

☆ THE COOKIES WILL KEEP IN AN AIRTIGHT CONTAINER AT ROOM TEMPERATURE FOR UP TO 5 DAYS.

Chocolate Sushi

This is a yummy whimsical interpretation of sushi. You can make the components in stages and assemble the dessert not long before serving. Or you can assemble the sushi and have it on hand in the refrigerator to slice off pieces as needed.

Preparation time: _1 hour, plus cooling time_

Baking time: _12 minutes_

Yield: _Thirty-six ½-inch slices_

Cake:

1 tablespoon butter, softened for the pan

1 tablespoon flour, for the pan

3 ounces white chocolate, finely chopped

2 tablespoons hot water

5 eggs

½ cup sugar

½ cup plus 2 tablespoons flour

1 tablespoon cornstarch

Pinch of salt

1 teaspoon pure vanilla extract

Filling:

1½ cups hazelnuts, toasted

¼ cup unflavored vegetable oil

3 ounces milk chocolate, finely chopped

6 ounces bittersweet chocolate, finely chopped

¼ cup heavy cream

Chocolate plastic:

8 ounces semisweet chocolate, finely chopped

¼ cup light corn syrup

Assembly:

¼ cup Dutch-processed cocoa powder

1 Preheat the oven to 350 degrees. Line a jelly roll pan with parchment paper. Use the tablespoon of butter to grease the parchment paper, then dust with the tablespoon of flour.

2 Melt the white chocolate in the top of a double boiler over hot water or in a microwave oven on low power for 30-second bursts. Stir often with a rubber spatula. Remove the top pan of the double boiler, if using, and wipe the bottom and sides very dry. Add the hot water and stir until the mixture is smooth.

3 In a large mixing bowl, using an electric mixer, whip the eggs and sugar together until pale colored and the mixture holds a slowly dissolving ribbon as the beater is lifted, about 5 minutes.

4 Over a large piece of wax paper or in a mixing bowl, sift together the flour, cornstarch, and salt, then add to the beaten eggs and sugar mixture and blend quickly. Fold about a cup of this mixture into the white chocolate, blending well. Then fold the white chocolate mixture back into the eggs, blending well. Add the vanilla and blend well.

5 Transfer the batter to the prepared pan, spreading it smoothly and evenly into the corners. Bake for 12 to 15 minutes, until the cake is light golden brown and the top springs back when touched.

6 Lay a kitchen towel on a flat surface and place a piece of parchment paper over the towel. Remove the jelly roll pan from the oven. Immediately use a small sharp knife to release the edges of the cake from the pan. Carefully lift the cake from the pan by the parchment paper and turn it upside down onto the parchment paper and towel. Carefully peel the parchment paper off the back of the cake and discard. Roll the cake lengthwise tightly in the towel and parchment paper and leave to cool completely. The cake can be prepared up to a day in advance and stored at room temperature tightly wrapped in plastic wrap. (See Figure 16-2 for an illustration of how to roll and tighten the sushi.)

7 For the filling, place the toasted hazelnuts in the work bowl of a food processor fitted with a steel blade (use a blender or a clean coffee grinder if you don't have a food processor). Add the vegetable oil and pulse until the nuts are finely ground and the mixture forms a paste.

8 Melt the chocolates together in the top of a double boiler over hot water or in a microwave oven on low power for 30-second bursts. Stir often with a rubber spatula. In a separate small saucepan, scald the cream. Remove the top pan of the double boiler (if using) and wipe the bottom and sides very dry. Pour the cream into the chocolate and stir until smooth, then add the hazelnut paste and stir until well blended. Transfer the mixture to a bowl or other container, cover tightly, and let stand at room temperature until the consistency of thick pudding. Or refrigerate the mixture until it thickens. If too cold, the mixture will need to be softened before use.

9 For the chocolate plastic, melt the chocolate in the top of a double boiler over hot water or in a microwave oven on low power for 30-second bursts. Stir often with a rubber spatula. Remove the top pan of the double boiler (if using) and wipe the bottom and sides very dry. Add the corn syrup and stir together well. Pour the mixture out onto a large piece of plastic wrap, form it into a flat disc, cover tightly, and leave to set up at room temperature until firm but pliable, about 2 hours.

10 Unroll the cake and remove the towel. Spread the filling evenly over the cake. Carefully re-roll the cake. To make a tight roll, pull about a third of the parchment paper over the top of the cake. Position a ruler against the cake and parchment and push it against the cake while pulling the parchment from the bottom edge toward you. Cut the cake roll in half and wrap the rolls in plastic. Let them stand at room temperature while preparing the chocolate plastic.

11 Lightly dust a flat work surface with cocoa powder. Divide the chocolate plastic in half and roll out each half to a large rectangle about ⅛-inch thick. Run an offset spatula under the chocolate plastic occasionally to make sure it is not sticking, and brush off any excess cocoa powder.

12 Remove the parchment paper from the rolled cake. Carefully transfer one of the cake rolls to the chocolate plastic rectangle. Roll the cake up in the rectangle. Seal the edge by brushing lightly with water. Trim the ends so the chocolate plastic lines up exactly. Wrap the roll tightly in plastic wrap; chill at least 30 minutes. Repeat with the second half of the chocolate plastic and cake roll. Use a sharp serrated knife to cut the rolls into ½-inch-thick slices. Serve at room temperature. Store tightly wrapped in plastic wrap in the refrigerator for up to 3 days or in the freezer for up to 3 months.

Per serving: Calories 178 (From Fat 111); Fat 12g (Saturated 5g); Cholesterol 34mg; Sodium 21mg; Carbohydrate 16g (Dietary Fiber 1g); Protein 3g.

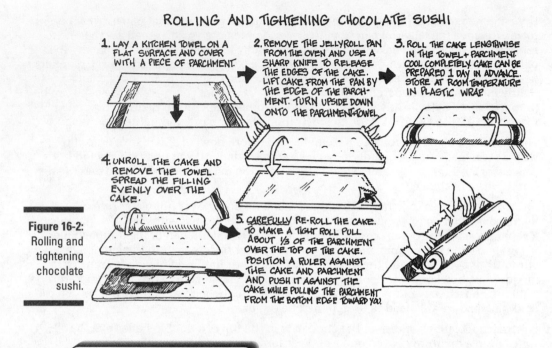

Figure 16-2:
Rolling and
tightening
chocolate
sushi.

ROLLING AND TIGHTENING CHOCOLATE SUSHI

1. LAY A KITCHEN TOWEL ON A FLAT SURFACE AND COVER WITH A PIECE OF PARCHMENT.

2. REMOVE THE JELLYROLL PAN FROM THE OVEN AND USE A SHARP KNIFE TO RELEASE THE EDGES OF THE CAKE. LIFT CAKE FROM THE PAN BY THE EDGE OF THE PARCHMENT. TURN UPSIDE DOWN ONTO THE PARCHMENT+TOWEL

3. ROLL THE CAKE LENGTHWISE IN THE TOWEL + PARCHMENT COOL COMPLETELY. CAKE CAN BE PREPARED 1 DAY IN ADVANCE. STORE AT ROOM TEMPERATURE IN PLASTIC WRAP

4. UNROLL THE CAKE AND REMOVE THE TOWEL. SPREAD THE FILLING EVENLY OVER THE CAKE.

5. CAREFULLY RE-ROLL THE CAKE. TO MAKE A TIGHT ROLL PULL ABOUT 1/3 OF THE PARCHMENT OVER THE TOP OF THE CAKE. POSITION A RULER AGAINST THE CAKE AND PARCHMENT AND PUSH IT AGAINST THE CAKE WHILE PULLING THE PARCHMENT FROM THE BOTTOM EDGE TOWARD YOU.

Chocolate Soufflé

This is a dense yet airy dessert that puffs up high as it bakes. It's very impressive, so save this one for those people you want to wow the most.

Tools: *2-quart soufflé dish or 8 individual soufflé dishes*

Preparation time: *10 minutes*

Baking time: *30 minutes*

Yield: *6 to 8 servings*

1 tablespoon butter, softened, for the pan	*2 teaspoons pure vanilla extract*
1 tablespoon sugar, for the pan	*4 eggs*
8 ounces bittersweet chocolate, finely chopped	*2 egg whites*
6 tablespoons butter, cut into small pieces	*1/4 teaspoon cream of tartar*
	1/3 cup sugar

Garnish:

2 tablespoons confectioners' sugar	*Whipped cream (optional)*
Warm Chocolate Sauce (see Chapter 15 for recipe)	

1 Use the tablespoon of butter to grease the inside of a 2-quart soufflé dish or 8 individual soufflé dishes. Then sprinkle with the tablespoon of sugar. Preheat the oven to 375 degrees.

2 Combine the chopped chocolate and butter in the top of a double boiler and melt over hot water or in a microwave oven on low power for 30-second intervals. Stir often with a rubber spatula. Remove the top pan of the double boiler and wipe the bottom and sides very dry. Stir in the vanilla. Cool the mixture for a few minutes, stirring often to prevent a skin from forming on top.

3 Separate the eggs and whisk the egg yolks into the chocolate and butter mixture. In a large mixing bowl, using an electric mixer whip the egg whites with the cream of tartar until frothy. Slowly add the sugar and whip the egg whites until they hold firm peaks. Fold into the chocolate mixture in 3 stages.

4 Pour the soufflé mixture into the prepared pans and smooth the tops. Bake for 30 minutes, until risen and baked through, but soft in the center if a tester is inserted.

5 Remove the soufflé from the oven and dust the top with confectioners' sugar. Use a large spoon to scoop out portions of souffle onto individual dishes or bowls. Serve immediately with Warm Chocolate Sauce or whipped cream.

Vary it! *To make Milk Chocolate Soufflé, substitute 12 ounces milk chocolate for the bittersweet chocolate. Reduce the sugar to 2 tablespoons. To make Gianduia Soufflé, reduce the bittersweet chocolate to 6 ounces and add 3 ounces milk chocolate. Fold ½ cup toasted and finely ground hazelnuts into the batter after folding in the whipped egg whites.*

Per serving: *Calories 527 (From Fat 318); Fat 35g (Saturated 21g); Cholesterol 163mg; Sodium 59mg; Carbohydrate 45g (Dietary Fiber 3g); Protein 7g.*

Make sure everyone is seated and ready for dessert because soufflé must be served immediately or else it will deflate.

You can prepare the soufflé base up to a day in advance and keep it in the refrigerator tightly covered with plastic wrap. Be sure to remove the plastic before baking.

Determining exactly when a soufflé is done baking can be a little tricky. When the least amount of time is up, look in the oven and see if the soufflé has risen well over the top of the pan. Insert a cake tester at an angle from the side into the center of the soufflé. It should come out with a few moist clumps clinging to it. If the tester is wetter than that, the soufflé will need to bake a few more minutes.

Double-Chocolate Pavlova

Pavlova is a dessert that was created in Australia by a pastry chef to honor the visit of the famed Russian ballerina, Anna Pavlova. The dessert is an airy, crisp, light meringue bowl filled with whipped cream and tropical fruit.

Preparation time: *20 minutes*

Baking time: *1½ hours*

Yield: *12 to 14 servings*

Meringue bowl:

4 egg whites

¼ teaspoon cream of tartar

1 cup superfine sugar

1 tablespoon cornstarch

¼ cup unsweetened Dutch-processed cocoa powder

1 teaspoon white vinegar

Filling:

2 cups heavy whipping cream

6 ounces bittersweet or semisweet chocolate

4 cups fresh fruit, such as strawberries, raspberries, kiwis, and sliced bananas

1 Preheat the oven to 400 degrees. Line a baking sheet with aluminum foil. Using a 9-inch cake cardboard or cake pan as a guide, trace a circle in the middle of the foil.

2 In a large mixing bowl, using an electric mixer, whip the egg whites and cream of tartar until frothy. Slowly sprinkle on the sugar and whip the egg whites until they hold firm peaks, about 3 minutes. Sift the cornstarch and cocoa powder together and add to the egg whites on low speed. Blend well, then add the vinegar and blend.

3 Using a rubber spatula, spread the meringue mixture onto the foil, using the circle as a guide. Mound the mixture around the outer edges so they're slightly thicker than the center, creating a shallow bowl.

4 Place the baking sheet in the oven; reduce the oven temperature to 250 degrees. Dry the meringue for 1½ hours. Turn the oven off and prop the door open with a wooden spoon. Leave the meringue in the oven until cool. You can prepare the meringue up to 2 days in advance and store it at room temperature tightly wrapped in aluminum foil.

5 For the filling, melt the chocolate in the top of a double boiler over hot water or in a microwave oven on low power for 30-second intervals. Place the cream in a large mixing bowl. Using an electric mixer, whip the cream until it holds soft peaks. Remove the top pan of the double boiler (if using) and wipe the bottom and sides very dry. Cool the chocolate slightly, then fold into the whipped cream.

6 Place the meringue bowl on a serving plate. Mound the cream in the center of the meringue and arrange the fruit on top in concentric circles. Assemble the dessert no more than 1 hour before serving. Refrigerate the dessert until ready to serve. Cut into wedges with a sharp serrated knife.

Per serving: Calories 274 (From Fat 154); Fat 17g (Saturated 11g); Cholesterol 47mg; Sodium 30mg; Carbohydrate 30g (Dietary Fiber 3g); Protein 3g.

Meringues can become soft and soggy if exposed to too much humidity. If it's raining or very humid, you probably want to wait for a drier day to make them.

Great Rewards for Minimal Effort

Very little work is required to make the recipes in this section. You'll have to be patient with the Chocolate Bread Pudding because it takes a little time to bake — but it's well worth it. The Chocolate Nut Purses almost make themselves. Puff pastry gives them a light, flaky texture. Of course, it's the chocolate that makes both of these recipes so delicious. Don't be shy about making an extra batch!

Fondue an intense liquid chocolate mixture into which you dip various pieces of fruit and cake. Exactly what you choose to dip and how many times you dip is up to you. I think of fondue as a very special dessert that is both easy to make and fun to eat. Chocolate fondue goes best as a dessert for a small, intimate party.

Chocolate Bread Pudding

When I think of comfort food, this recipe is the first thing that comes to mind. It's warm, creamy, and chocolate, of course! Although bread pudding is often made from leftover bread, you can dress this up by buying a good-quality fresh loaf.

Preparation time: *45 minutes (includes chilling)*

Baking time: *40 minutes*

Yield: *8 to 10 servings*

Half of a 1-pound loaf of fresh Filone, French, or egg bread

1 tablespoon butter, for the pan

1 tablespoon sugar for the pan

10 ounces bittersweet chocolate, finely chopped

½ cup dried sour cherries

5 large eggs

1 cup milk

2 cups heavy cream

2 teaspoons pure vanilla extract

½ cup sugar

½ cup light brown sugar

½ teaspoon ground cinnamon

¼ teaspoon freshly grated or ground nutmeg

¾ cup walnuts, finely chopped

1 Preheat the oven to 400 degrees. Cut the crusts off the bread, and cut the bread into 1-inch cubes. Place the cubes in a shallow layer in a baking pan and dry in the oven for 15 minutes. Reduce the oven temperature to 350 degrees. Use the tablespoon of butter to generously grease the inside of a 7-x-11-inch glass baking pan. Sprinkle the table-spoon of sugar over the butter.

2 Melt the chopped chocolate in the top of a double boiler over hot water or in a microwave oven on low power for 30-second bursts. Stir often with a rubber spatula. Place the dried cherries in a small bowl. Cover them with boiling water and steep for 10 minutes. Drain and pat dry on paper towels.

3 Transfer the bread cubes to the buttered baking pan and sprinkle the dried cherries over the bread.

4 In a large mixing bowl, whisk the eggs until smooth. Add the milk, cream, vanilla, sugar, brown sugar, cinnamon, and nutmeg. Blend well. Remove the top pan of the double boiler and wipe the bottom and sides dry. Pour the melted chocolate into the mixture and blend well. Stir in the chopped walnuts. Pour the mixture over the bread and dried cherries. Cover the pan tightly with plastic wrap and chill in the refrigerator for 30 minutes.

5 Remove the plastic from the baking pan and place the baking pan in a larger baking pan. Place the pan on the oven rack and pour boiling water into the bottom pan until it reaches halfway up the sides of the bread pudding pan. Bake the pudding 40 to 45 minutes, until it is puffed and a tester inserted in the center comes out clean. Remove the pudding from the water bath and cool on a rack.

6 Serve the pudding warm or at room temperature. Store the pudding tightly covered with plastic wrap in the refrigerator for up to 3 days.

Per serving: Calories 671 (From Fat 343); Fat 38g (Saturated 20g); Cholesterol 179mg; Sodium 345mg; Carbohydrate 72g (Dietary Fiber 4g); Protein 13g.

 Bake bread pudding in a water bath to ensure a smooth texture.

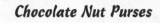

Chocolate Nut Purses

These look like they take a lot of time to prepare, but they're deceptively easy. You can use any type of chocolate and any type of nuts you like. By mixing and matching different chocolates and nuts, you can create endless variations.

Preparation time: 15 minutes

Baking time: 15 minutes

Yield: 8 servings

6 ounces bittersweet, semisweet, milk, or white chocolate, finely chopped	1 teaspoon ground cinnamon
⅓ cup walnuts, hazelnuts, or almonds, toasted and finely chopped	2 sheets frozen puff pastry, thawed
	Confectioners' sugar, for garnish

1 Preheat the oven to 425 degrees. Line a baking sheet with parchment paper.

2 In a medium mixing bowl, combine the chopped chocolate and nuts. Add the cinnamon and toss to mix well.

3 On a lightly floured flat work surface, roll out each sheet of puff pastry to a 12-inch square. Cut each square in half lengthwise and in half again horizontally, creating 4 smaller squares. Place about 2 tablespoons of chocolate filling in the center of each square. Bring the points of the square together in the center above the filling. Squeeze the pastry together just above the filling, then spread out the top edges. Place the purses on the lined baking sheet with a few inches of space between them.

4 Bake 15 minutes, until light golden brown. Remove the baking sheet from the oven and cool on a rack. Dust the pastries lightly with confectioners' sugar before serving. They are best served slightly warm.

5 Store the pastries tightly covered with aluminum foil at room temperature for up to 2 days. Warm them in a 325-degree oven for 10 minutes before serving.

Per serving: Calories 494 (From Fat 301); Fat 33g (Saturated 8g); Cholesterol 1mg; Sodium 156mg; Carbohydrate 43g (Dietary Fiber 3g); Protein 7g.

Chocolate Fondue

Chocolate and fruit are the perfect combination, and they're showcased in this dessert. All you have to do is prepare the chocolate mixture and the fruit. Then your guests serve themselves.

Tools: *Fondue pot and 6 forks*

Preparation time: *15 minutes*

Yield: *6 servings*

7 ounces bittersweet or semisweet chocolate, finely chopped

2 tablespoons water

4 tablespoons heavy cream

2 tablespoons orange liqueur or 2 teaspoons pure vanilla extract

1 tablespoon unsweetened Dutch-processed cocoa powder, sifted

¼ teaspoon ground cinnamon

Cubes of pound cake or angel food cake

Whole fresh strawberries

Thick slices of banana

Dried apricot halves

1 In the top of a double boiler, combine the chocolate and water. Stir over warm water until the chocolate melts and is smooth. Add the cream, orange liqueur or vanilla, cocoa powder, and cinnamon. Stir until the mixture is smooth.

2 Transfer the mixture to a fondue pan and keep it warm over a low flame. Arrange the cake and fruit on a serving platter.

3 Supply each guest with a fondue fork so they can spear the item of their choice and dip it in the fondue mixture (see Figure 16-3).

Per serving (for sauce, not for accompaniments): Calories 238 (From Fat 135); Fat 15g (Saturated 9g); Cholesterol 15mg; Sodium 6mg; Carbohydrate 22g (Dietary Fiber 3g); Protein 3g.

Your fondue mixture must be kept warm so that it will stay liquid. The best way to do this is to use a fondue pot that has room for a candle or a liquid heat source underneath.

FONDUE SETUP

Figure 16-3:
Dipping into
fondue.

Chapter 17

Distinctive Chocolate Desserts

These days, when you go to a restaurant, it's not unusual to be presented with a dessert that looks like it was made by an artist. After getting over the delightful surprise, I always take time to study the creation, saying to myself, "How did they make that?" and "I wonder if I could make something like that." Although these desserts look very complicated, they really aren't that difficult to make. All you need is some planning, attention to detail, and practice. But it's all well worth it — because you end up with a beautiful creation that tastes good, too.

The desserts in this chapter do require a bit more effort than those in the rest of this book. You may have eaten these desserts before — or maybe you've heard of them, because they all have world-class origins. But you probably haven't tried to make these, thinking that it would just be too involved and can only be done in a restaurant kitchen. Rest assured you *can* make them in your very own kitchen, and this chapter shows you how.

I truly love all of these desserts. I make them when I'm celebrating a special occasion or when I just want to show off! After you've mastered these desserts, you'll want to make them often. Actually, your family and friends will beg you to!

Chocolate Desserts to Die For

This section contains some of the world's most exquisite chocolate desserts. I've heard people say, "These are to die for," while eating them. Well, I wouldn't want anything *that* drastic to happen, but eating these should make you feel as though you're in heaven.

Rigó Jansci

Pronounced REE-go YON-she, this pastry takes its name from a legendary 19th-century Hungarian violinist who was reputed to break many women's hearts. Maybe that's why the pastry is chocolate through and through — to soothe those broken hearts. Two layers of chocolate cake enclose a rich whipped chocolate filling. A shiny chocolate glaze tops it all off.

Preparation time: *1 hour*

Baking time: *20 minutes*

Yield: *Twenty-four 2-inch squares*

Cake:

5½ ounces bittersweet or semisweet chocolate, finely chopped

5 eggs, separated

½ cup plus 2 tablespoons sugar

2 tablespoons instant espresso powder dissolved in 2 tablespoons water

1 teaspoon pure vanilla extract

¼ teaspoon cream of tartar

2 tablespoons unsweetened Dutch-processed cocoa powder, in a sifter

Filling:

3 cups heavy whipping cream

1¼ pounds bittersweet or semisweet chocolate, finely chopped

2 tablespoons orange liqueur (optional)

1 tablespoon pure vanilla extract

Glaze:

4 ounces bittersweet or semisweet chocolate, finely chopped

¼ cup heavy whipping cream

1 Preheat the oven to 375 degrees. Line a 12-x-17-x-1-inch jelly roll pan with a sheet of parchment paper. Cut a rectangle of sturdy cardboard that measures 6 x 16 inches to be used for the base when assembling the cake.

2 Melt the chocolate in the top of a double boiler over hot water or in a microwave oven on low power for 30-second bursts. Stir often with a rubber spatula.

3 In a large mixing bowl, using an electric mixer, whip the egg yolks with 2 tablespoons of the sugar until very pale colored and the mixture holds a slowly dissolving ribbon as the beater is lifted. Remove the top pan of the double boiler and wipe the bottom and sides very dry. Fold the melted chocolate into the mixture, then add the espresso and vanilla and blend well.

4 In a large mixing bowl, using an electric mixer, whip the egg whites with the cream of tartar until frothy. Slowly add the remaining ½ cup sugar and whip the egg whites until they are glossy and hold firm peaks.

5 Fold one quarter of the egg whites into the egg yolk mixture in Step 3. Then fold in the remaining egg whites until well blended.

6 Transfer the mixture to the baking pan and spread evenly and smoothly with a spatula. Bake for 10 minutes, then reduce the oven temperature to 350 degrees. Bake another 10 minutes, until the top of the cake cracks lightly when touched.

7 Remove the baking pan from the oven and cool on a rack. When cool, dust the top of the cake lightly with cocoa powder.

8 For the ganache filling, melt the chocolate in the top of a double boiler over hot water or in a microwave oven on low power for 30-second bursts. Stir often with a rubber spatula. In a separate small saucepan, scald the cream. Remove the top pan of the double boiler and wipe the bottom and sides very dry. Pour the cream into the chocolate and stir until smooth and completely blended. Transfer the mixture to a large bowl or container, cover tightly and cool to room temperature. Refrigerate the mixture until it is the consistency of thick pudding, 2 to 3 hours. If the chocolate becomes too firm, it will need to soften before using.

9 In a large mixing bowl, using an electric mixer beat the ganache on low speed. Add the orange liqueur (if using) and vanilla, and beat until the mixture holds soft peaks. Do not overbeat the chocolate or it will become grainy.

10 To assemble the pastry, run a sharp knife around the edges of the baking pan to loosen the cake. Cover the cake with wax paper or parchment paper. Place the bottom of another jelly roll pan over the paper and invert the cake. Peel the parchment paper off the back of the cake and cut it in half across the width..

11 Spread the beaten ganache over the bottom half of the cake evenly using a flexible-blade spatula. Carefully place the second half of the cake on top, making sure all the edges are even. Press gently on the top. Line a jelly roll pan with wax paper and place a cooling rack in the middle of the pan. Set the assembled cake on the cooling rack. Chill the cake while preparing the glaze.

12 For the glaze, melt the chocolate in the top of a double boiler over hot water or in a microwave oven on low power for 30-second bursts. Stir often with a rubber spatula. In a separate small saucepan, scald the cream. Remove the top pan of the double boiler and wipe the bottom and sides very dry. Pour the cream into the chocolate and stir until smooth and completely blended.

13 Remove the cake on its pan from the refrigerator. Pour the glaze over the top of the cake. Quickly use a metal flexible-blade spatula to smooth and spread it so that it covers the top. The glaze will begin to set up after a few seconds and will hold spatula marks. Chill the cake until the glaze is completely set, about an hour. Use a serrated knife to trim the ends of the cake, then cut into 2-inch squares using a sharp knife dipped in hot water and dried.

Tip: Don't beat the ganache for longer than 1 minute with an electric mixer, or it will become grainy and curdled.

Per serving: Calories 345 (From Fat 223); Fat 25g (Saturated 15g); Cholesterol 90mg; Sodium 27mg; Carbohydrate 27g (Dietary Fiber 3g); Protein 5g.

The best way to cut through chocolate-glazed desserts is to use a knife that has been dipped in hot water and dried.

Double-Chocolate Bûche de Nöel

This dessert is a classic French Christmas cake made in the shape of a Yule log.

Preparation time: 1 hour and 45 minutes

Baking time: 18 to 20 minutes

Yield: 14 to 16 servings

Cake:

1 tablespoon butter, softened, for the pan
1 tablespoon flour, for the pan
4 eggs
⅔ cup sugar
¾ cup flour

2 tablespoons unsweetened Dutch-processed cocoa powder
¾ teaspoon baking powder
3 tablespoons cornstarch
2 tablespoons butter, melted

Sugar syrup:

¼ cup sugar

½ cup water

Chocolate buttercream:

8 ounces bittersweet or semisweet chocolate, finely chopped
3 eggs
3 yolks

2 cups sugar
¾ cup water
½ teaspoon cream of tartar
2¾ cups (5½ sticks) butter, softened

Garnish:

3 ounces marzipan
Green paste food coloring

Confectioners' sugar in a sifter
Red paste food coloring

1 Preheat the oven to 375 degrees. Line a 12-x-17-x-1-inch jelly roll pan with parchment paper. Use the tablespoon of butter to grease the parchment paper, then dust with the tablespoon of flour and shake off the excess.

2 In a large mixing bowl, using an electric mixer, whip the eggs and sugar together until very pale colored and the mixture holds a slowly dissolving ribbon as beater is lifted.

3 Sift together the flour, cocoa powder, baking powder, and cornstarch. Fold these ingredients into the egg and sugar mixture in 3 stages, blending well. Fold in the melted butter. Transfer the batter to the prepared pan, spreading it smoothly and evenly into the corners. Bake for 18 to 20 minutes, until the top of the cake springs back when touched.

4 While the cake is baking, lay a kitchen towel on a flat surface and place a piece of parchment paper over the towel. Remove the jelly roll pan from the oven. Immediately use a small sharp knife to release the edges of the cake from the pan. Carefully lift the cake from the pan by the parchment paper and turn it upside down onto the parchment paper and towel. Carefully peel the parchment paper off of the back of the cake and discard. Roll the cake lengthwise tightly in the towel and parchment paper and leave to cool completely. The cake can be prepared up to a day in advance and stored at room temperature tightly wrapped in plastic wrap.

5 For the sugar syrup, combine the sugar and water together in a small saucepan and bring to a boil over medium heat. Remove the pan from the heat and cool.

6 For the buttercream, melt the chocolate in the top of a double boiler over hot water or in a microwave on low power for short bursts. Stir often with a rubber spatula. Combine the eggs and egg yolks in a large mixing bowl. Using an electric mixer, beat them until they're very pale colored and hold a slowly dissolving ribbon when the beater is lifted, about 8 minutes. At the same time, combine the sugar, water, and cream of tartar in a 2-quart heavy-duty saucepan. Cook the mixture, without stirring, until it reaches 242 degrees on a candy thermometer. Wash down the sides of the pan with a damp pastry brush twice as the mixture is cooking to prevent the formation of sugar crystals.

7 Turn the mixer speed to low; pour the sugar syrup into the eggs in a slow stream. Turn the mixer speed to high; beat until the bowl is cool to the touch, about 8 minutes. Beat in the butter in 4 or 5 stages. Continue to beat until the buttercream is fluffy and well blended, about 3 minutes. (It may look curdled, but it will smooth out.) Remove the top pan of the double boiler; wipe the bottom and sides very dry. Pour the chocolate into the buttercream; blend together thoroughly. The buttercream can be prepared in advance and kept in a tightly covered container in the refrigerator for 3 to 4 days or in the freezer for up to 4 months. To rebeat the buttercream, place chunks of it in a large mixing bowl and place the bowl in a saucepan with 1 inch of warm water. When buttercream begins to melt around the bottom, remove the bowl from the water and wipe very dry. Use an electric mixer to beat the buttercream until fluffy, about 2 minutes.

8 Unroll the cake and remove the towel. Brush the sugar syrup over the inside of the cake. Spread about 1 cup of the buttercream evenly over the cake, leaving a 1-inch border at the long end farthest away from you. Carefully re-roll the cake using the parchment paper as a guide. To make a tight roll, pull about a third of the parchment paper over the top of the cake. Position a ruler against the cake and parchment and push it against the cake while pulling the parchment from the bottom edge toward you.

9 Cut a diagonal slice about 2 inches thick from each end of the cake and set aside briefly. Fit a 14-inch pastry bag with a large closed star tip; fill partway with the remaining buttercream. Working from one long end to the other and from the bottom to the top, pipe buttercream in rows on the log. Place diagonal cut ends on top of the log near each end to simulate sawed-off branches. Use buttercream to build up around them so they look like part of the log. Dust the log lightly with confectioners' sugar. Divide the marzipan into two portions: one 2 ounces and the other 1 ounce. Color the larger portion with green. Dip a toothpick into the green paste food coloring, and dab the coloring into the marzipan. Dust the work surface with confectioners' sugar and knead the marzipan until the color is evenly distributed. Roll out the marzipan on the flat work surface using more confectioners' sugar as needed. Cut out holly-leaf shapes.

10 To color the remaining portion of marzipan red, dip a toothpick into the red paste food coloring, and dab the coloring into the marzipan. Dust work surface with confectioners' sugar and knead the marzipan until the color is evenly distributed. Roll out the marzipan on the flat work surface using more confectioners' sugar as needed. Pinch off pieces of the marzipan; roll into small balls to be holly berries. Decoratively arrange the marzipan holly leaves and berries on top of the log and around the branches. Store the cake tented with foil in the refrigerator for up to 3 days. Serve slices of cake at room temperature.

Per serving: Calories 618 (From Fat 386); Fat 43g (Saturated 25g); Cholesterol 225mg; Sodium 54mg; Carbohydrate 56g (Dietary Fiber 2g); Protein 6g.

Queen of Sheba Cake

This dense, moist cake is a French classic that has become well known. Ground almonds give this cake a lot of texture and delicious flavor. After the cake is baked, it is coated with a layer of whipped ganache that provides a smooth surface for the poured chocolate glaze. I've made this cake for a few weddings when the bride and groom wanted a truly special cake — and what bride and groom don't? Whatever the occasion, your guests will love it! Be sure to use a 2-inch tall cake pan, which is available at cookware shops, the cookware section of department stores, and through online and mail-order sources. Cardboard cake rounds are also available through the same sources, as well as at many craft stores.

Preparation time: *1½ hours*

Baking time: *35 minutes*

Yield: *12 to 14 servings*

Cake:

1 tablespoon butter, for the pan

2 teaspoons flour, for the pan

5 ounces bittersweet chocolate, finely chopped

1 ounce unsweetened chocolate, finely chopped

¾ cup (1½ sticks) butter, softened

1 cup sugar

⅛ teaspoon almond extract

4 eggs, separated

⅔ cup finely ground almonds

1 egg white

¼ teaspoon cream of tartar

¾ cup flour

Ganache coating:

6 ounces bittersweet chocolate, finely chopped

½ cup heavy cream

¾ cup (1½ sticks) butter, softened

Glaze and garnish:

8 ounces bittersweet chocolate, finely chopped

¾ cup heavy cream

½ cup sliced almonds, toasted

1 Preheat the oven to 350 degrees. Cut a round of parchment paper to fit the bottom of a 9-x-2-inch cake pan. Use the tablespoon of butter to grease the inside of the cake pan and one side of the parchment paper round. Dust the inside of the pan with flour, shake out the excess, and place the parchment paper round in the pan, butter side up.

2 Melt the chocolates in the top of a double boiler over hot water or in a microwave oven on low power for short bursts. Stir often with a rubber spatula.

3 In a large mixing bowl, using an electric mixer beat the butter until fluffy. Add the sugar and cream together. Add the almond extract and blend well. One at a time add the egg yolks, beating well after each addition. Stop and scrape down the sides of the bowl occasionally with a rubber spatula.

4 Remove the top pan of the double boiler and wipe the bottom and sides very dry. Pour the melted chocolate into the butter-sugar mixture and blend well. Add the ground almonds and blend thoroughly.

5 In a large mixing bowl, using an electric mixer, whip the egg whites and cream of tartar until they are glossy and hold firm peaks. Alternately fold the egg whites and flour into the chocolate mixture. The batter will be very thick.

6 Transfer the batter to the prepared cake pan and spread evenly using a rubber spatula. Bake the cake for 35 minutes, until the top is slightly cracked and a tester inserted into the center has moist crumbs clinging to it.

7 Remove the cake from the oven and cool on a rack for 20 minutes. Place a 9-inch cardboard cake round over the top of the cake pan and invert. Peel the parchment paper off the back of the cake. Leave the cake on the cardboard with the top down. Finish cooling the cake on the rack.

8 For the ganache coating, melt the chocolate in the top of a double boiler over hot water or in a microwave oven on low power for short bursts. Stir often with a rubber spatula. In a small saucepan, scald the cream over medium heat. Remove the top pan of the double boiler, wipe the bottom and sides very dry, and pour the cream into the chocolate. Stir together until smooth and well blended. Transfer the mixture to another bowl or container and cover tightly. Cool to room temperature, then chill until the mixture is the consistency of thick pudding, about 2 hours.

9 In a large mixing bowl, using an electric mixer, beat the butter until very fluffy. Add the chocolate ganache in 3 stages and beat until the mixture holds soft peaks. Be careful not to overbeat the ganache, or it will become grainy and curdle.

10 Use a flexible-blade spatula to cover the top and sides of the cake smoothly with the ganache coating. Dip the spatula in hot water and dry, then sweep over the top of the cake to make the coating very smooth. Chill the cake in the freezer for 30 minutes while preparing the glaze.

11 For the glaze, melt the chocolate in the top of a double boiler over hot water or in a microwave oven on low power for short bursts. Stir often with a rubber spatula. In a small saucepan, scald the cream over medium heat. Remove the top pan of the double boiler, wipe the bottom and sides very dry, and pour the cream into the chocolate. Stir together until smooth and well blended. Stir for about 8 minutes to cool the glaze.

12 Line a jelly roll pan with parchment or wax paper and place a cooling rack on top of the paper. Remove the cake from the freezer and center on the rack. To pour the glaze, work quickly starting from the center of the cake and working toward the outer edge. Use a flexible-blade spatula to push the glaze over the edges, if necessary, but don't do more than two strokes with the spatula or the marks will show in the glaze. Let the glaze set for 10 to 15 minutes.

13 Press the sliced, toasted almonds into the sides of the cake up to the top edge. Create a decorative design of sliced almonds around the top rim of the cake. To remove the cake from the rack use the flexible-blade spatula to wedge underneath it and balance it from underneath with your hand. Gently move the cake to a serving plate. Store the cake tented with aluminum foil in the refrigerator, but serve at room temperature.

Per serving: Calories 686 (From Fat 476); Fat 53g (Saturated 27g); Cholesterol 147mg; Sodium 40mg; Carbohydrate 47g (Dietary Fiber 5g); Protein 10g.

You need to work very quickly when glazing the top of a cake with chocolate because the glaze sets rapidly. After the glaze is poured, use a flexible-blade spatula to push it over the edges, using no more than two strokes, or the glaze will show the spatula marks.

Chocolate Marquise

This is a very dense mousse. It has intense chocolate flavor, so a little goes a long way. I like to serve it with Raspberry Sauce, which adds a nice tartness to balance the chocolate. But it's also very good with whipped cream. Because the dessert needs time to set, it's best made several hours to a day in advance.

Tools: *8½-x-5½ inch glass loaf pan*

Preparation time: *30 minutes*

Yield: *10 servings*

1 tablespoon butter, softened, for the pan	4 egg yolks
10 ounces bittersweet or semisweet chocolate, finely chopped	1 tablespoon instant espresso powder dissolved in 1 tablespoon water
¾ cup (1½ sticks) butter, softened	2 teaspoons pure vanilla extract
½ cup sugar	1 cup heavy whipping cream
2 tablespoons unsweetened Dutch-processed cocoa powder, sifted	

Garnish:

Raspberry Sauce (see the recipe in Chapter 15)	2 teaspoons confectioners' sugar
½ cup heavy whipping cream	1 teaspoon pure vanilla extract

1 Butter the sides and bottom of the glass loaf pan. Line the pan with aluminum foil, fitting it smoothly into the corners and against the sides.

2 Melt the chopped chocolate in the top of a double boiler over hot water or in a microwave oven using low power for 30-second bursts. Stir often with a rubber spatula.

3 In a large mixing bowl, using an electric mixer, cream the butter with half of the sugar. Add the cocoa powder and blend well. Stop occasionally and scrape down the sides of the bowl with a rubber spatula.

4 In a large mixing bowl, using an electric mixer, whip the egg yolks with the remaining ¼ cup sugar until pale colored and the mixture holds a slowly dissolving ribbon as the beater is lifted. Fold this mixture into the butter mixture in Step 2 until well blended.

5 Remove the top pan of the double boiler and wipe the bottom and sides very dry. Fold the chocolate into the mixture in Step 3. Add the espresso and vanilla and blend well.

6 In a large mixing bowl, using an electric mixer, whip the cream on medium until it holds soft peaks. Fold the whipped cream into the above mixture in 4 stages, blending well. Transfer the mixture to the lined loaf pan. Use a rubber spatula to spread it smoothly and evenly into the corners and to smooth the top. Cover tightly with plastic wrap and chill until firm, 2 to 3 hours. The marquise can be held in the refrigerator up to 4 days.

7 To unmold the marquise, hold a hot cloth against the sides of the pan for about a minute. Place a serving plate over the top of the loaf pan and invert. Gently peel the aluminum foil off the marquise. Run a flexible-blade spatula under hot water and dry. Use this to smooth and even the sides, if necessary.

8 For the garnish, whip the cream in a mixing bowl using an electric mixer until frothy. Add the confectioners' sugar and vanilla and continue to whip until the cream holds soft peaks.

9 Serve slices of the marquise in a pool of Raspberry Sauce and top with a dollop of whipped cream.

Per serving: Calories 509 (From Fat 360); Fat 40g (Saturated 24g); Cholesterol 176mg; Sodium 20mg; Carbohydrate 35g (Dietary Fiber 4g); Protein 4g.

Chocolate-Filled Mini Cream Puffs with Warm Chocolate Sauce

These mini cream puffs also go by the name of *Profiteroles* (pro-FEET-air-rolls). They're a classic dessert, but don't think they're stuffy. On the contrary, these little two bite-size gems are fun to eat. Whether you choose to fill them with ice cream or chocolate whipped cream, they are always a hit.

Preparation time: *20 minutes*

Baking time: *22 minutes*

Yield: *6 servings*

Cream puffs:

½ cup water

4 tablespoons (½ stick) butter, cut into small pieces

1 tablespoon sugar

⅛ teaspoon salt

½ cup flour

2 eggs

Egg wash:

1 egg yolk

1 teaspoon milk

Filling:

2 cups Chocolate Silk Ice Cream (see the recipe in Chapter 14) or 1 recipe Chocolate Whipped Cream (see the recipe in Chapter 15)

Sauce:

2 recipes Warm Chocolate Sauce (see the recipe in Chapter 15) or 1 recipe Hot Fudge Sauce (see the recipe in Chapter 15)

1 Preheat the oven to 400 degrees. Line two baking sheets with parchment paper.

2 In a 1-quart heavy-duty saucepan, combine the water, butter, sugar, and salt and bring to a boil over medium heat. Add the flour and stir vigorously with a wooden spoon until smooth and completely mixed. The mixture will be very thick.

3 Remove the pan from the heat and beat with the wooden spoon, just until the steam stops rising from the mixture. Transfer the mixture to a medium mixing bowl. Add one of the eggs and using an electric mixer beat well. The batter will start to break apart, but keep beating until it is smooth. Add the second egg and beat until the mixture is smooth.

4 Fit a 12– or 14-inch pastry bag with a large plain round pastry tip with a ½-inch (#5) opening. Fill the pastry bag partway with the batter. Holding the pastry bag about an inch above the parchment paper–lined baking sheet, pipe out mounds about 1 inch in diameter, leaving an inch of space between them.

5 For the egg wash, beat the egg yolk and milk together in a small bowl. Using a small pastry brush, brush the top of each mound with the egg wash. Bake 22 to 24 minutes, until puffed and deep golden colored. Remove the baking sheets and cool completely on racks. If not filling the same day, the puffs can be frozen in a plastic bag for up to 4 months.

6 Use a sharp serrated knife to split the puffs in half horizontally, leaving a small hinge on one side.

7 For the filling, if using the ice cream, soften it slightly, then place in a large mixing bowl. Using an electric mixer beat the ice cream until it holds soft peaks. Fit a 12– or 14-inch pastry bag with a large plain round pastry tip with a ½-inch opening. Using a serrated knife, cut each puff in half horizontally. Pipe or spoon the ice cream or whipped cream (if using) into the bottom of each puff until it mounds slightly over the top. Cover each puff with its top half.

8 To serve, stack 5 filled puffs in a serving bowl in a pyramid shape. Drizzle 3 to 4 table-spoons of Warm Chocolate Sauce or Hot Fudge Sauce over them. Serve immediately.

Per serving: *Calories 900 (From Fat 564); Fat 63g (Saturated 38g); Cholesterol 316mg; Sodium 132mg; Carbohydrate 77g (Dietary Fiber 4g); Protein 10g.*

Chocolate Meringue Desserts to Swoon Over

These chocolate desserts both have a component of meringue: a crisp layer that's made with whipped egg whites and ground nuts. This layer provides an ethereal quality to these desserts that almost makes them seem to float. Or maybe it's that they are so light that you feel like you're floating. Whichever it is, these are delicious. Your guests will practically swoon over how good they are, but they'll stay alert for the next bite.

Chocolate Marjolaine

This is a classic cake made famous by the legendary French chef, Ferdinand Point, at his restaurant La Pyramide, in Vienne, France. Four layers of a nut meringue cake is sandwiched with three flavors of buttercream — chocolate, hazelnut, and vanilla — then covered and decorated with chocolate buttercream and ground hazelnuts. This is a sophisticated and complicated dessert that is not for the beginner, but it's well worth the effort. Make this several hours or a day before serving so the meringue has time to soften and the flavors to marry.

Preparation time: *1 hour and 45 minutes*

Baking time: *30 minutes*

Yield: *14 to 16 servings*

Cake:

1 tablespoon butter, softened, for the pan

1 tablespoon flour, for the pan

1 cup hazelnuts, toasted and skinned

1 cup sliced, slivered, or whole almonds, toasted

2 tablespoons flour

1¼ cups sugar

7 egg whites

½ teaspoon cream of tartar

Buttercream:

2 eggs

2 egg yolks

1 cup plus 2 tablespoons sugar

½ cup water

¼ teaspoon cream of tartar

1¾ cups (3½ sticks) butter, softened

2 teaspoons pure vanilla extract

¼ cup toasted and finely ground hazelnuts

8 ounces bittersweet or semisweet chocolate, finely chopped

Assembly:

¾ cup toasted and finely ground hazelnuts

16 whole, skinned hazelnuts

1 Preheat the oven to 325 degrees. Line a 12-x-17-x-1-inch jelly roll pan with a sheet of parchment paper. Use the tablespoon of butter to generously grease the parchment paper, then dust with the flour and shake off the excess.

2 In the work bowl of a food processor fitted with a steel blade, combine the hazelnuts, almonds, flour, and ¾ cup of the sugar. Pulse until the mixture is very finely ground.

3 In a large mixing bowl, using an electric mixer, whip the egg whites with the cream of tartar until frothy. Slowly add the remaining ½ cup sugar and whip until the egg whites are glossy and hold firm peaks. Fold in the ground nut mixture from Step 2 in 4 stages, blending well after each addition.

4 Transfer the mixture to the prepared jelly roll pan and spread it out evenly using an offset spatula. Bake the cake for 30 to 35 minutes, until it is light golden colored and springs back when touched on top.

5 Remove the pan from the oven and place on a rack to cool completely. Use a sharp knife to release the sides of the cake from the pan. Cover the top with a sheet of parchment or wax paper. Place another jelly roll pan over the paper and invert the cake. Carefully peel the parchment paper off the back of the cake. Use a serrated knife to trim the edges and cut the cake into 4 equal strips across the width, so they each measure 4 by 12 inches.

6 For the buttercream, combine the eggs and egg yolks in a large mixing bowl. Using an electric mixer, beat them until they are very pale colored and hold a slowly dissolving ribbon when the beater is lifted, about 8 minutes. At the same time, combine the sugar, water, and cream of tartar in a 2-quart heavy-duty saucepan. Cook the mixture, without stirring, until it reaches 242 degrees on a candy thermometer. Wash down sides of pan with a damp pastry brush twice as the mixture is cooking to prevent sugar crystals.

7 Turn the mixer speed to low and pour the sugar syrup into the eggs in a slow stream. Turn the mixer speed to high and beat until the bowl is cool to the touch, about 8 minutes. Beat in the butter in 4 or 5 stages, then continue to beat until the buttercream is fluffy and well blended, about 3 minutes. It may look curdled, but keep beating and it will smooth out. The buttercream can be prepared in advance and kept in a tightly covered container in the refrigerator for 3 to 4 days or in the freezer for up to 4 months. To rebeat the buttercream, place chunks of it in a large mixing bowl and place the bowl in a saucepan with an inch of warm water. When the buttercream begins to melt around the bottom, remove the bowl from the water and wipe it very dry. Use an electric mixer to beat the buttercream until it is fluffy, about 2 minutes.

8 Place ¾ cup of the buttercream in a small bowl and mix with the vanilla. Place another ¾ cup of the buttercream in another small bowl and mix with the ground hazelnuts. Melt the chocolate in the top of a double boiler over hot water or in a microwave oven on low power for short bursts. Remove the top pan of the double boiler and wipe the bottom and sides very dry. Stir the chocolate to cool for 5 minutes, then mix the melted chocolate with the remaining buttercream.

9 Cut a piece of cardboard to fit the cake strips, 4 by 12 inches. Place one strip of the cake on the cardboard and spread evenly with the hazelnut buttercream. Place another strip of the cake on top of hazelnut buttercream and spread evenly with three-fourths of the chocolate buttercream. Place a third strip of cake on top of chocolate buttercream and spread evenly with the vanilla buttercream. Place the last strip of cake on top and press gently with your fingertips. Transfer the cake to a baking sheet and chill for 15 minutes.

10 Reserve ¾ cup of the chocolate buttercream for the final decoration. Use the remaining chocolate buttercream to fill in the sides and cover the top of the cake with a flexible-blade spatula. Dip the metal spatula in hot water and dry, then use it to smooth the buttercream. Place a large piece of wax paper on a flat work surface and place cake on this. Press the ground hazelnuts into sides and ends of cake up to top edge.

11 Fit a 12– or 14-inch pastry bag with a large star tip and pipe a design of shells along the top border. Place the whole hazelnuts decoratively along the shell border. Refrigerate the cake until 30 minutes before serving. Store the cake, covered with wax paper and plastic wrap in the refrigerator for up to 3 days. Slice the cake thinly to serve.

Per serving: Calories 402 (From Fat 206); Fat 23g (Saturated 5g); Cholesterol 56mg; Sodium 36mg; Carbohydrate 44g (Dietary Fiber 4g); Protein 8g.

Chocolate Hazelnut Dacquoise

This is a truly spectacular dessert. Rich and creamy bittersweet chocolate ganache is the filling between crisp layers of chocolate and hazelnut meringue. It's the perfect dessert to make in stages because the meringues take a couple of hours to dry in the oven and the ganache filling needs to cool and thicken before use.

Preparation time: *1½ hours*

Baking time: *2 hours*

Yield: *12 servings*

Meringues:

5 egg whites (¾ cup) at room temperature

½ teaspoon cream of tartar

¾ cup sugar

1 tablespoon cornstarch

3 tablespoons unsweetened Dutch-processed cocoa powder

1 cup toasted, skinned, and finely ground hazelnuts

3 tablespoons sugar

Bittersweet chocolate ganache:

1 pound bittersweet chocolate, finely chopped

2 cups heavy cream

1 tablespoon pure vanilla extract

Assembly:

¾ cup shaved bittersweet chocolate

Confectioners' sugar

1 Line 3 baking sheets with aluminum foil with the shiny side up. Using a 9-inch cardboard cake circle as a guide, trace a circle onto each sheet of foil with a pencil and place the foil (pencil side down) onto the baking sheets.

2 Place the egg whites and cream of tartar in a large mixing bowl. Using an electric mixer, whip the egg whites until frothy. Slowly add ½ cup of the sugar and continue beating until the whites hold firm, but not stiff, peaks. Sprinkle on the remaining ¼ cup sugar and mix quickly.

3 Into a medium bowl, sift together the cornstarch and cocoa powder. Combine with the ground hazelnuts and sugar, and toss to blend well. Fold into the whipped egg whites in 3 stages. Preheat the oven to 200 degrees.

4 Fit a pastry bag with a pastry tip with a ½-inch round opening. Fill the bag partway with the meringue mixture. Using the traced circles from Step 1 as a guide, pipe concentric circles onto the foil very close together, or spread the meringue mixture to fill the lines of the guide, about ¼-inch high.

5 Place the baking sheets in the oven and let bake for 2 hours. Turn off the oven and leave the meringues to set until the oven is cool. Remove the pans from the oven and carefully peel the foil off the back of the meringues. Store the meringues at room temperature wrapped in foil for up to 1 week. If it is humid, the meringues may soften, but they can be dried in a 200-degree oven for 45 minutes.

6 For the ganache, melt the chopped chocolate in the top of a double boiler over hot water. Stir often with a rubber spatula. In a separate small saucepan, scald the cream. Remove the top pan of the double boiler and wipe the bottom and sides very dry. Pour the hot cream into the chocolate and stir together until smooth. Add the vanilla and blend well. Transfer the ganache to a bowl or other container, cover tightly and refrigerate until thick, but not stiff, about 2 hours.

7 Place the ganache in a large mixing bowl. Using an electric mixer, beat the ganache on medium speed for 1 minute, until it becomes fluffy. Do not overbeat or the ganache will curdle.

8 To assemble, use a sharp small knife to carefully trim the edges of the meringues so they are even. Place one meringue layer on a 9-inch round cake cardboard or on a plate. Use a flexible-blade spatula to spread evenly to the edges one-fourth of the ganache. Place a second meringue layer on top, positioning evenly. Spread this layer evenly with another quarter of the ganache. Turn the third meringue layer upside down and position it evenly over the ganache. Spread the top with a third quarter of ganache and use the rest to fill in the sides smoothly and evenly.

9 Spread the shaved chocolate on a large sheet of wax paper. Use a flexible-blade spatula to gently lift the pastry up, and place one of your hands underneath it. With the other hand, gently press the shaved chocolate into the ganache on the side so it adheres. Any excess shaved chocolate will fall off. Carefully place the cake down on a flat surface onto wax paper. Lightly dust the top with confectioners' sugar.

10 Place the pastry on a serving plate and refrigerate for at least 2 hours, but let stand at room temperature for 30 minutes before serving. To cut the pastry use a sharp serrated knife dipped in warm water and dried.

Per serving: Calories 555 (From Fat 342); Fat 38g (Saturated 20g); Cholesterol 57mg; Sodium 41mg; Carbohydrate 48g (Dietary Fiber 5g); Protein 8g.

Because the oven temperature is so low, meringues are technically said to *dry* rather than bake.

Part VI
The Part of Tens

"...and here's where the chocolate bars are crushed the old fashioned way to make our premium reserve chocolate milk."

In this part . . .

This part is packed full of all kinds of helpful suggestions and neat tips for giving your chocolate away. Also in this part you'll find the best sources I know of for finding the right ingredients and equipment. You may want to stock up a little for a rainy day — oh heck, for *every* day (after all, it's *chocolate!*).

Chapter 18

Ten Tips for Giving Away Your Chocolate

*W*hen you're giving a gift, you obviously hope the recipient will like it. When it's chocolate you're giving, you don't have to worry about that. Chocolate is the ideal gift. You don't have to concern yourself with choosing the right size, style, or color. Chocolate is always appropriate and always appreciated.

Knowing Your Recipient

Obviously, you want to give people the type of chocolate that they most like. Some people like all chocolates equally. If this is the case, it's hard to go wrong. But there are those who like some chocolates better than others.

Not only do you want to consider the type of chocolate, but the type of dessert you give. Here again, most people have preferences about their favorite type of dessert. It's hard to go wrong with chocolate cake if you're not sure of someone's favorite. I've never seen anyone turn it down.

Make your best effort to find out what type of chocolate your recipient likes. If it's a gift, you may be able to check with a relative or friend beforehand. If you're not sure, you can always make a few different chocolate desserts or candies and give a little bit of each.

Some people are allergic to nuts, in particular peanuts. Be sure to find out if this is the case before giving someone chocolate made with this ingredient. Also, tell people what the chocolate dessert contains, in case they're allergic to one of the ingredients.

Knowing What's the Right Amount

When it comes to giving chocolate, giving more is better than giving less. This way the recipients can share it with others, if they choose. For chocolate candies, a dozen pieces makes a nice gift. For cookies, you may want to give more than a dozen — they always seem to disappear quickly. For muffins and scones, a half dozen is a good amount. And for loaf cakes, regular cakes, pies, and tarts, give the whole thing.

Giving Chocolate for Special Occasions

Many different occasions are perfect for giving chocolate. The first one that comes to mind is a birthday. For this occasion, a chocolate cake with candles on top is perfect. A scoop of chocolate ice cream on the side is a great way to add extra flair. However, don't rule out a chocolate pie or tart for a birthday, anniversary, or other special occasion. For casual occasions I like to give cookies, candies, scones, muffins, or loaf cakes. Unlike many chocolate desserts, all of these can be eaten without plates and utensils.

Considering the Holiday

For Thanksgiving, Christmas, and Hanukkah I like to make a variety of cookies and chocolate truffles in several flavors to give as gifts. I sometimes mold solid chocolate into appropriate holiday shapes and then wrap them in colorful foil. For Valentine's Day, nothing is better than molded chocolate hearts wrapped in red foil. And for Easter, solid chocolate bunnies are the best! Other special days, such as Mother's Day, Father's Day, Secretaries Day, and so on are perfect for giving chocolate. Here again, cookies and candies, muffins, scones, and loaf cakes always make great chocolate gifts.

Paying Attention to Containers

I like to look for interesting and unusual containers for chocolate treasures. Tins are great for cookies and some candies. Food-safe cellophane bags are also a nice way to wrap cookies and candies. Of course, boxes, are appropriate whether you're giving candy, cake, pie, or cookies. I also like to use colorful paper plates wrapped in clear cellophane to give chocolate gifts. On occasion I've given a gift of chocolate on a serving plate, which is also part of the gift. There are many types of containers for holding chocolate. When you start to focus on them, you'll find all sorts of things you never realized existed. Have fun! And, remember, it's chocolate, so whoever the recipients are, they'll love it.

Getting All Wrapped Up in Wrappings

Think about color when wrapping gifts of chocolate and use color appropriate to the occasion and season. I like to use gold and silver, but occasionally I use red if it's for Valentine's Day or Christmas. A nice plate wrapped in clear cellophane and tied with festive ribbons is a beautiful way to present a gift of chocolate. Keep several colors of ribbon available. Also, have on hand rolls of clear cellophane with gold stars or other gold and silver designs. These are appropriate for most occasions and seasons, so you're always prepared to wrap a spontaneous gift of chocolate.

Check to make sure that the cellophane or other wrapping you use for chocolate doesn't have any scent, because that will taint the chocolate.

Sending Chocolate Home with Your Guests

Whenever I have guests at my home they never leave empty-handed. I always make sure they take home some of the chocolate dessert I've served. No one has ever turned down my offer of chocolate to take home. It makes me feel good to give them something they've enjoyed and I know they look forward to being able to enjoy the dessert again. It's a win-win situation. Keep a good supply of nice paper plates on hand so you'll always ready to send chocolate home with your guests.

Taking Chocolate on the Road

When you're invited to a gathering and need to bring a chocolate dessert, choose a recipe that's appropriate for the occasion, season, and location. If it's a summer beach party, chocolate ice cream may be the perfect dessert, but you'll need a good cooler for transporting and storing it until it's time to dish it up. Delicate chocolate desserts usually don't travel very well.

If you're taking a chocolate cake, pie, or tart, be sure to place it in a box and set the box on a flat surface in the car, so it won't slide around or (horrors!) fall off the seat. If you're transporting cookies, bring them on a baking sheet covered with foil and arrange the platter when you arrive at your destination. The same is true for candies. Don't stack the cookies or candies more than two layers deep or they may get crushed. Pack cookies, brownies, loaf cakes, and candies with similar flavors together. If the flavors are too different, they'll wind up tasting like each other. If you're transporting a cold dessert, pack it in a cooler with a freezer pack that won't melt into liquid and spoil the dessert.

Sending Chocolate through the Mail

Chocolate candies, some cookies, muffins, scone, and loaf cakes travel well, if wrapped appropriately. Most other chocolate desserts are too delicate to be mailed. Sturdy containers that won't be crushed or broken are the best bet for sending chocolate through the mail. I like to use tins for this purpose. Place layers of waxed paper between each layer of candies or cookies and fill any extra space in the container with crumpled waxed paper. This keeps the chocolates from moving around and bumping into each other. Then pack the tin in another container and surround it with crushed paper or bubble wrap. Send the container either overnight or by priority mail so it will arrive quickly. Also, include a note for the recipient as to what's in the container and how it should be stored. You don't want someone to place a gift under the Christmas tree, as an example, and let it sit there for a week or so before opening it, especially if it needs to be refrigerated.

Organizing a Chocolate Potluck Party

Having a chocolate potluck party is a really fun way to get together with a group of friends and family and share your chocolate. Pick a date and a location and either send invitations or call and invite everyone. Request what each guest brings or leave it up to each person to decide what to bring. Have plenty of tables and counter space for displaying all the chocolate desserts. Provide plates, forks, spoons, and napkins. Provide drinks to accompany the dessert. Why not ask each guest to also bring something appropriate to drink? Then sit back and enjoy the party. You can never have too much chocolate on hand.

Chapter 19

Ten Sources for Ingredients and Equipment

● ●

In This Chapter

▶ Finding what you need for making great chocolate desserts

▶ Discovering new sources for supplies

● ●

The reliable sources listed in this chapter can supply you with all the equipment and ingredients you need. Sometimes browsing through a catalog or Web site gets me inspired to go into the kitchen and make a delicious chocolate dessert. Maybe it'll do the same for you!

Beryl's Cake Decorating and Pastry Supplies

Beryl's offers cake and baking pans, chocolate and sugar thermometers, chocolate molds and dipping tools, pastry bags and tips, parchment paper, extracts and dried fruit. A catalog is available upon request.

P.O. Box 1584
North Springfield, VA 22151
Phone: 800-488-2749 (toll-free) or 703-256-6951
Fax: 703-750-3779
Web site: www.beryls.com
E-mail: beryl@erols.com

Chocosphere.com

This Web site has a large selection of chocolate and cocoa powder from around the world, including Callebaut Michel Cluziel, Côte d'Or, El Rey, Green & Black's organic, Scharffen Berger, Schokinag, and Valrhona. Please note that the address listed is only for mailed inquiries; there is no in-person shopping.

5200 S.E. Harney Drive
Portland, OR 97206
Phone: 877-992-4626 (toll-free) or 503-292-2772
Fax: 877-912-4626 (toll-free)
Web site: www.chocosphere.com
E-mail: chocolate3ocosphere.com

ChocoVision

This is the manufacturer and supplier of the Revolation series of chocolate tempering machines.

P.O. Box 5201
Poughkeepsie, NY12602
Phone: 800-324-6252 (toll-free) or 845-473-4970
Fax: 845-473-8004
Web-site: www.chocovision.com
E-mail: sales3ocovision.com

The King Arthur Flour Baker's Catalogue

This source has loads of baking equipment and ingredients, including Callebaut, Scharffen Berger, and Merckens chocolate; chocolate chips; several types of cocoa powder; extracts and other flavorings; flour; nuts; specialty sugars; measuring spoons and cups; scales; baking pans; timers; thermometers; candy and chocolate thermometers; chocolate tempering machines; chocolate chippers; and dipping tools. A catalog is available upon request.

P.O. Box 876
Norwich, VT 05055-0876
Phone: 800-827-6836 (toll-free)
Fax: 800-343-3002 (toll-free)
Web site: www.kingarthurflour.com
E-mail: arlene.osgood@kingarthurflour.com

New York Cake and Baking Distributor

This source carries a very large variety of equipment including baking pans, thermometers, rolling pins, marble boards, dredgers, parchment paper, cake decorating turntables, scales, timers, metal and rubber spatulas, chocolate molds, dipping tools, pastry bags and tips, pastry brushes, and mixing bowls. They also carry some ingredients including Callebaut, Van Leer, and Valrhona chocolate and cocoa powder. A catalog is available upon request.

56 West 22nd Street
New York, NY 10010
Phone: 800-942-2539 (toll-free) or 212-675-2253
Fax: 212-657-7099

Parrish's Cake Decorating Supplies, Inc.

This company makes excellent quality baking pans, chocolate molds, pastry bags and tips, cake-decorating turntables, and other cake-decorating equipment. A catalog is available upon request.

225 West 146th Street
Gardena, CA 90248
Phone: 310-324-2253
Fax: 310-324-8277
Web site: www.parrishsmagicline.com
E-mail: CustomerService@parrishsmagicline.com

Sur La Table

With several retail locations around the country, this is a well-known source for a large variety of baking and dessert-making equipment, including baking pans and cookie sheets, pastry bags and tips, knives, electric mixers, rubber spatulas, measuring tools, chocolate molds, and dipping tools. They also carry a variety of chocolate including Scharffen Berger and E. Guittard, as well as vanilla extract. A catalog is available upon request.

1765 Sixth Avenue South
Seattle, WA 93134-1608
Phone: 800-243-0852 (toll-free)
Fax: 206-682-1026
Web site: www.surlatable.com
E-mail: customerservice@surlatable.com

Sweet Celebrations

Here you'll find a large selection of cake and baking pans, cake-decorating and candy-making equipment, specialty sugar, and domestic and imported chocolate, including Callebaut, Lindt, Merckens, Peter's, Nestle's, and Valrhona. A catalog is available upon request.

P.O. Box 39426
Edina, MN 55439-0426
Phone: 800-328-6722 (toll-free) or 612-943-1508
Web site: maidofscandinavia.com
E-mail: sweetcel@maidsofscandinavia.com

Williams-Sonoma

This is a well known source with several retail locations around the country for a large selection of dessert-making equipment and baking pans, baking and pastry tools, measuring tools, electric mixers, knives, nonstick baking pan liners, Scharffen Berger and Valrhona chocolate and cocoa, Pernigotti cocoa, vanilla extracts, and more. A catalog is available upon request.

P. O. Box 7456
San Francisco, CA 94120-7456
Phone: 877-812-6235 (toll-free) or 415-421-4242
Web site: www.williams-sonoma.com

Wilton Enterprises, Inc.

This source has a large selection of cake and baking pans, pastry bags and tips, cake-decorating tools, cookie cutters, chocolate molds, and dipping tools. Their products are available in many stores that sell baking and candy-making equipment.

2240 West 75th Street
Woodridge, IL 60517
Phone: 800-794-5866 (toll-free) or 630-963-1818
Fax: 888-824-9520 (toll-free) or 630-963-7196
Web site: www.wilton.com

Appendix

Metric Conversion Guide

* *

*N**ote:* The recipes in this cookbook were not developed or tested using metric measures. There may be some variation in quality when converting to metric units.

Common Abbreviations

Abbreviation(s)	What It Stands For
C, c	cup
g	gram
kg	kilogram
L, l	liter
lb	pound
mL, ml	milliliter
oz	ounce
pt	pint
t, tsp	teaspoon
T, TB, Tbl, Tbsp	tablespoon

Volume

U.S Units	Canadian Metric	Australian Metric
¼ teaspoon	1 mL	1 ml
½ teaspoon	2 mL	2 ml
1 teaspoon	5 mL	5 ml

(continued)

Volume *(continued)*

U.S Units	Canadian Metric	Australian Metric
1 tablespoon	15 mL	20 ml
¼ cup	50 mL	60 ml
⅓ cup	75 mL	80 ml
½ cup	125 mL	125 ml
⅔ cup	150 mL	170 ml
¾ cup	175 mL	190 ml
1 cup	250 mL	250 ml
1 quart	1 liter	1 liter
1½ quarts	1.5 liters	1.5 liters
2 quarts	2 liters	2 liters
2½ quarts	2.5 liters	2.5 liters
3 quarts	3 liters	3 liters
4 quarts	4 liters	4 liters

Weight

U.S. Units	Canadian Metric	Australian Metric
1 ounce	30 grams	30 grams
2 ounces	55 grams	60 grams
3 ounces	85 grams	90 grams
4 ounces (¼ pound)	115 grams	125 grams
8 ounces (½ pound)	225 grams	225 grams
16 ounces (1 pound)	455 grams	500 grams
1 pound	455 grams	½ kilogram

Measurements

Inches	Centimeters
½	1.5
1	2.5
2	5.0
3	7.5
4	10.0
5	12.5
6	15.0
7	17.5
8	20.5
9	23.0
10	25.5
11	28.0
12	30.5
13	33.0

Temperature (Degrees)

Fahrenheit	Celsius
32	0
212	100
250	120
275	140
300	150
325	160
350	180

(continued)

Temperature (Degrees) *(continued)*

Fahrenheit	Celsius
375	190
400	200
425	220
450	230
475	240
500	260

Index

• Q •

• R •

Notes

Notes

Notes

FOR DUMMIES®

A world of resources to help you grow

TRAVEL

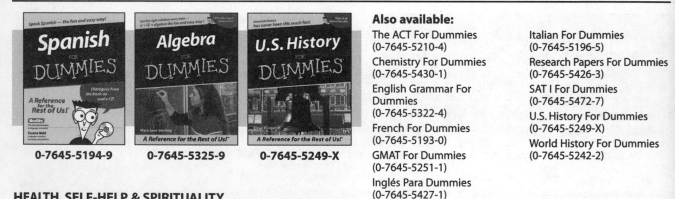

0-7645-5453-0

0-7645-5438-7

0-7645-5444-1

EDUCATION & TEST PREPARATION

0-7645-5194-9

0-7645-5325-9

0-7645-5249-X

HEALTH, SELF-HELP & SPIRITUALITY

0-7645-5154-X

0-7645-5302-X

0-7645-5418-2

Available wherever books are sold. Go to www.dummies.com or call 1-877-762-2974 to order direct

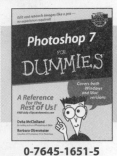